THE THEATER OF MARIA IRENE FORNES

PAJ BOOKS

Bonnie Marranca & Gautam Dasgupta

Series Editors

EDITED BY MARC ROBINSON

THE THEATER OF

MARIA IRENE FORNES

A PAJ BOOK   *The Johns Hopkins University Press, Baltimore and London*

© 1999 The Johns Hopkins University Press

The collection, preface, introduction, and "*The Summer in Gossensass:*
Fornes and Criticism" © 1999 Marc Robinson

The Johns Hopkins University Press
2715 North Charles Street
Baltimore, Maryland 21218-4363
www.press.jhu.edu

Library of Congress Cataloging-in-Publication Data
The theater of Maria Irene Fornes / edited by Marc Robinson.
p.   cm. — (PAJ books)
Includes bibliographical references and index.
ISBN 0-8018-6153-5 (alk. paper). — ISBN 0-8018-6154-3 (pbk. : alk. paper)
1. Fornes, Maria Irene—Criticism and interpretation.   2. Theater—New York
(State)—New York—Production and direction—History—20th century.
3. Feminism and theater—New York (State)—New York—History—20th century.
4. Women in the theater—New York (State)—New York—History—20th century.
I. Robinson, Marc, 1962–   . II. Series.
PS3556.O7344Z89   1999
812'.54—dc21   99-21138
                                                                    CIP

A catalog record for this book is available from the British Library.

Pages 277–78 are an extension of the copyright page.
Title page illustration: © 1998 by Susan Johann

CONTENTS

III FORNES ON FORNES

Photo gallery appears following page 108

PREFACE

MARIA IRENE FORNES'S critics are just beginning to keep pace with their prolific subject. The number of dissertations about her grows steadily; two monographs have recently appeared; the journals now regularly feature essays in many of the fashionable critical languages; and at least one symposium has been held in her honor. Set alongside the bibliography of Fornes's near contemporaries—Sam Shepard, for instance, or Lanford Wilson—this activity is still modest. But unlike them, Fornes seems to provoke the kind of polemics and critical soul-searching that in themselves become subjects for analysis, thereby sustaining whole cycles of essay and book publication. Some of her critics are already assigning themselves to camps, from which they wage various battles of interpretation. Fornes's own allegiances are subject to debate, as scholars try to define her relationship to absurdism, realism, feminism, Hispanic (and Hispanic-American) theater, and numerous other traditions. Fornes herself has not been shy about joining the argument, correcting one interviewer who said she was part of Off Broadway—"I'm a part of *Off-Off* Broadway"—and suggesting elsewhere that the only tradition she belongs to consists of *Ubu*, *Woyzeck*, Beckett, Genet, and Ionesco.

The fact that *any* serious criticism about Fornes exists at all is remarkable when you consider how underappreciated her theater remains, more than thirty-five years after she wrote *Tango Palace*. The list of Fornes plays that have never been given second or third professional productions is staggering: *The Office, Aurora, Cap-a-Pie, Evelyn Brown (A Diary), Eyes on the Harem, A Visit,* and *Oscar and Bertha,* among many others. Her plays that *have* become part of the repertory entered through the back door: As several critics in this anthology point out, Fornes is the reigning playwright of the ninety-nine-seat house— the intrepid Theater for the New City and INTAR in New York, for instance; in other cities, theaters with such names as the Blind Parrot (Chicago) and the Kitchen Dog (Dallas), the Unsafe (Rock Island, Ill.) and the Stark Raving (Portland, Oreg.). As a result, few of Fornes's critics have been able to see more than a handful of her works. And none has been able to read her in depth: Only twenty of her thirty-nine (and counting) plays have been published.

This situation has skewed the scholarly literature. Most of her critics address only her best-known works (*Fefu and Her Friends, Mud,* and *The Conduct of Life*); the plays flanking them—from the 1960s and the 1990s—as well as the unpublished plays of the 1970s and early 1980s still await rigorous discussion. Without it, the story of Fornes's stylistic development is distorted, as is the image of Fornes herself. With any luck, this anthology will renew interest in the forgotten plays and, just as important, encourage a closer look at the plays we thought we knew.

No editor is without bias, but in the hope of sparking the liveliest possible rethinking of Fornes I have tried to be as ecumenical as possible. Here, scholarship shares space with journalism; reviews follow production case-histories; a director's reminiscence segues into a critic's analysis—sometimes in the same essay. Within those genres, the styles of address are just as various. Different kinds of analysis speak to one another as much as to Fornes, urging readers comfortable with one approach to reexamine the same texts and productions on other levels.

Seven essays appear here for the first time, along with some of the best published criticism of Fornes, much of which has slipped from view since its first appearance. After my introduction, Ross Wetzsteon presents an overview of Fornes's life and art, beginning with her emigration to New York just after World War II and her early work as a painter and designer. Written on the occasion of her 1986 musical *Lovers and Keepers,* the profile also introduces and describes the relationship among the three main areas of Fornes's career—writing, directing, and teaching—each pursuit guiding the development of the others. The next two essays, by Phillip Lopate and Susan Sontag, erect frames of reference for two periods of Fornes's theater: Critical habit, not altogether useless, defines them as pre– and post–*Fefu and Her Friends.* The focus narrows in the following five essays, as critics address individual plays in detail. W. B. Worthen examines (among other topics) the political implications of performance styles in *Tango Palace, Fefu and Her Friends, The Danube,* and *The Conduct of Life.* The three parts of Bonnie Marranca's piece were occasioned by three separate plays: *Mud, Abingdon Square,* and *Enter* THE NIGHT. Herbert Blau, Fornes's first director, revisits his 1963 production of *Tango Palace* and locates the beginnings of her lifelong preoccupation with the "rot" and "loathsome mess" (Leopold's words) of human experience. Elinor Fuchs also begins in the dirt—in this case, the underside of the stone that so fascinates Fefu. Fuchs's essay unfolds against the history of feminist scholarship on Fornes, and also is that now all-too-rare phenomenon in criticism: a close reading. After my own piece on Fornes's 1998 play, *The Summer in Gossensass*, Tony Kushner closes this section with a tribute to the writer he claims as one of his main influences; he also opens a debate about the best way to teach playwriting.

The second part of the anthology represents four different perspectives on Forness's work in performance—those of the director, the actor, the designer, and finally the reviewer. Richard Gilman staged a well-regarded production of *The Successful Life of 3* with The Open Theater in 1965: What he discovered about the play in rehearsal forms the basis for his piece published here. Forness's own directing is chronicled in Susan Letzler Cole's rehearsal logs of *Abingdon Square* and *Uncle Vanya*. Robert Coe interviews five actors to learn how they have met the demands of Forness's writing and directing. The actors' styles—precise, spare, bold—are often matched by a production's decor, as Scott Cummings demonstrates in a consideration of several designers' use of space.

The perspective shifts from inside to outside in the series of reviews that rounds out this section. The sampling is by no means representative. With one or two exceptions, I have focused on lesser-known plays, some of which (like the intricately choreographed *Evelyn Brown*) are difficult to appreciate fully without a sense of what they could look like in production. Two of the earliest pieces about Fornes appear in this section—by Michael Smith ("he was our critic," Fornes once said) and Robert Pasolli, both regular contributors to *The Village Voice* in the 1960s. Reading these reviews now, three decades after their original publication, can be especially inspiring to the contemporary critic who, with no loss of affection, may now take Forness's styles and subjects for granted. In Smith's and Pasolli's prose, we see reviewers working by trial and error to devise a language versatile enough to do justice to the strange new theater confronting them.

Forness's own attempts to describe her work comprise the final section of the anthology. With the possible exceptions of Richard Foreman and the late Charles Ludlam, no contemporary American playwright has matched her energy for public self-questioning. She is a willing exegete of her own work, a generous interview subject, and a merry scourge of those critics who misinterpret her. All these sides of her expository self are on display here, providing much valuable information about the origins of particular plays, the rituals of her typical workday, and her ever-evolving philosophies of acting, teaching, and writing. Like so many of her characters, Fornes can't—won't—separate doing from thinking, the making of her art from the evaluation of her art—a union which this anthology, in its own mix of critical and creative perspectives, tries to preserve.

ACKNOWLEDGMENTS

WHEN IRENE FORNES called to say she had a great idea—"How about making it a pop-up book, showing the sets of my plays!"—it was only the most startling instance of her enthusiasm for this anthology. Ever since she first learned of my plans, she has been generous about opening her files, loaning unpublished scripts, describing works-in-progress, and entertaining my many questions and improvised theories. This book could not have been completed without her support.

At the Johns Hopkins University Press, Douglas Armato, Linda Tripp, and Maria denBoer have been careful and solicitous editors, whose commitment has sustained mine. Bonnie Marranca of PAJ Books first recognized the need for a Fornes anthology. Along the way, she has offered much wise advice. Thank you, also, to a number of other people who have helped in diverse, essential ways: Elizabeth Bennett, Robert Castro, Susan Letzler Cole, Jan Foery, Wynn Handman, Martha Hostetter, James Leverett, Gloria Loomis, Gerald Rabkin, Don Shewey, Christina Sibul, Alexis Soloski, Elise Thoron, and Dawn Williams. My wife, April Bernard, once again made time for many sensitive readings of my own prose.

Finally, I owe a special debt to Ross Wetzsteon, whose death in 1998 has left a terrible hole in the New York theater landscape. As critic, editor, and Obie-award chairman, Ross was an unflagging, discerning supporter of Fornes, nowhere more so than in his 1986 profile reprinted here. I'm sure I was only one of many new–to–New York theatergoers that year who decided to track down all of Fornes's plays because of what Ross wrote about them.

THE THEATER OF MARIA IRENE FORNES

INTRODUCTION

A BOOK, a pitcher of water, and a glass sit on a bedside table. On the bed itself lies a nightgown, dark against the field of a turned-down sheet. Later, the floor will be scattered with photographs, and the woman who dropped them will pause for a moment, look down, and in her shock (the photographs are pornographic) seem to consider the arrangement before bending quickly to retrieve them. A rocking chair sits in the middle of the room, as if its owner hasn't decided where it goes, or perhaps wants to call attention to it—a prize relic put on display. A letter, a watch, the book on the table: all attract characters worried about their uses and meanings. When a woman stares at an envelope without opening it, or picks up a book but doesn't read it, turning the object carefully to examine it from all sides, she behaves as if she had never seen any of their kind before, so delicate is her touch and so intimate is her engagement. Each object's stillness demands her own; and when she finally moves to read by the light of a window or an open door, the architecture frames her, and she becomes an object as well.

These compositions are all from Maria Irene Fornes's own 1997 production of her short play *Springtime*, originally part of the 1989 tetralogy *What of the Night?* It is among Fornes's sparest works—only ten pages long when first published, and devoid of the antic spirit and harrowing violence that characterize most of her other plays. Not that *Springtime* lacks humor or violence altogether, but under Fornes's disciplined direction neither is able to pervade the play. A playful moment erupts and subsides quickly, completely, as if Fornes had opened and shut a valve. The one explicitly brutal scene—a rape—is staged with such fastidious attention to detail that it seems distant and clinical: There is nothing ferocious about the encounter. Instead, Fornes slows it down, arranging the actors' bodies against one another as if they were mannequins. The strongest charge occurs when the woman turns her head away and stares at the wall. Even at the peak of fear and aggression, the actors submit to the same organizing intelligence that placed the objects on the nightstand beside them.

Fornes's commitment to control and clarity is matched by the characters themselves. Her protagonists, two women named Rainbow and Greta, are trying to stitch together a relationship strong enough to resist numerous intrusions: The rape is only the most disturbing in a series that includes Greta's mysterious illness and Rainbow's betrayal. (Hoping to raise money for Greta's care, Rainbow poses nude for a sleazy photographer.) Against these sordid realities, the women set more comforting truths—the sturdiness of the monastic room they share; the brilliant sunlight and fresh air they let in through the windows and door; the simple, strong construction of their furniture; and the corresponding simplicity of their conversation—only necessary words and declarative statements, questions and answers exchanged with care. Everything we see and hear expresses a concern for order—a concern the women reinforce with their actions. The play opens with Rainbow sweeping the floor; she later spends an entire scene making the bed. Greta seems visibly to arrange the effects of her illness into something lyrical—a tableau of pain. When she stumbles upon the photographs of Rainbow's body arranged in artful poses, they seem a calculated insult to the purer compositions she herself has been making.

The love story may be poignant, and its violation unsettling, but Fornes also dramatizes an aspect of psychology that subsumes these events (and the emotions connected with them) and that, if properly managed in performance, won't seem sentimental: *Springtime* is about being civilized, or trying to be so, as the pressures of daily life cause her characters to doubt that they'll ever be able to balance their reason against their passion. This theme links plays from all periods of Fornes's life in the theater—a career that, as many have pointed out, consists of many stylistic experiments. That very unpredictability may be why Fornes's idea of being civilized lacks the pomposity that one sometimes hears in the term. For Fornes, being civilized is never effortless, and never other than a personal achievement. At least it begins as personal, and her most worldly characters remain aware of the awkwardness preceding grace. In this theater, the pressure to be civilized is answered first on an elementary level, with everyday tasks. A character asks herself where she should stand; how much furniture should fill a room, and when she should use it; if she should move closer to her companion, or if discretion requires keeping her distance. Only when the landscape is set—and her proper place in it has been determined—is it possible for a Fornes character to resolve larger matters of conduct. But even then, civilized behavior never becomes so mannered that it obscures its origins in observation. Her best plays (and even a relatively minor one like *Springtime*) teach lessons in attention, lessons similar to those that a painter of still lifes hopes his or her own audience will heed. With such art, we are asked not just to admire the virtuosity or thoroughness of the artist's realism, or to covet the pretty things in his or her composition, but also to respond to a moral essay about the dignity of things (and, in Fornes's case, of people and their actions) seen and valued alone, apart from any possible utilitarian or symbolic purposes.

Fornes began her professional life as a painter and textile designer, and (as several critics have suggested) a visual artist's sensitivity to pattern and composition informs her theater. Elinor Fuchs proposes a link to Frida Kahlo; Paul Berman suggests, in passing, Phillip Pearlstein; Erika Munk thinks of Vermeer; Fornes herself compares her realist side to Edward Hopper.[1] My own contributions to this ever expanding genealogy are Zurbarán (1598–1664) and Juan Sánchez Cotán (1561–1627). Two famous paintings—Zurbarán's *Lemons, Oranges, and a Cup of Water* and Cotán's *Quince, Cabbage, Melon, and Cucumber*—capture the discipline at the heart of Fornes's theater. Both titles suggest the paintings' virtues: modesty, lucidity, directness, the patience needed to take stock. Cotán's still life is the best of his so-called kitchen pictures, in which he depicts food stored in the dark stone spaces, called *catareros*, that once served as makeshift refrigerators. The first two perishables listed in *Quince, Cabbage, Melon, and Cucumber* hang from strings like Christmas ornaments, or parts of a mobile; next to them, on the ledge beneath, sits the melon, with one slice in its shadow; finally, on the right, the cucumber punctuates the sentence like an exclamation mark.

Zurbarán's painting obeys the same linear structure: a silver plate of four lemons on the left; a basket of oranges crowned with leaves and orange blossoms in the center; another plate with a white cup and a flower lying beside it on the right. The envelope-shaped canvas directs the sequence: Zurbarán seems to depict each part of his trio independently, refuses to stress connections. As a result, we develop the same patience, and ponder his objects one at a time. Only after they have been seen for themselves, in order, do the objects then reveal their relationship. The basket of oranges, taller than the things flanking it, forms the top of a triangle; and now the whole composition reinforces the solidity that each item has alone. Perhaps this tight, evenly weighted structure is what allows us to linger over these objects longer than we might in busier, denser still lifes. The tranquil atmosphere helps: Warm afternoon light falls from the left, sharpening contours and heightening the mystery of these familiar objects, but otherwise Zurbarán eliminates anything that might identify a time or place. He banishes from the background any distracting suggestion of a room; his only concession to practicality is a table for displaying the objects— but this, like the background, is a dark, flat rectangle, more color-field than realistic thing. Cotán is just as minimalist: His objects are suspended against empty black space; the sill and frame of the *cantarero* window look more like an echo of the picture frame. Cast upon darkness, Cotán's and Zurbarán's objects summon up no enchanted world; they tell no story. Mute, yet also forthright, stubborn about their presence, their sheer gravity, they resist our efforts to turn them into metaphors, participants in an allegory, or props of a mythology. All they ask is to be acknowledged.

Cotán's reference to the picture frame stresses the point. By reminding us that we're looking at an artist's arrangement of objects—not a natural scene happened upon by chance—he makes the act of looking itself his true subject. The fruits and vegetables have been summoned less for their own virtues (although Cotán does persuade us of the elegance of things we once thought workaday, or ignored altogether) than for their uses in an exercise in vision. As we complete the exercise, we will (Cotán hopes) lose the habit of judging, and even classifying, the things that we see. Almost without thinking, we will find ourselves emulating the painting's poise and restraint. In the absence of narrative, theatrical imagery, or emotional upheaval, a world of hitherto unspoiled and unvalued beauty beckons us. On leaving it, we look at our own environment and ultimately ourselves with a refreshed and newly curious eye. Norman Bryson describes this change in his book on still-life painting, *Looking at the Overlooked* (a phrase that could also be the title of a book on Fornes):

Against the vices of fallen vision, Cotán administers his antidote: hyperreality. . . . Mere realism would not bite deep enough into vision to dislodge the habitual vanities and blindnesses which lurk there. . . . The enemy is a mode of seeing which thinks it knows in advance what is worth looking at and what is not. Against that, the image presents the constant surprise of things seen for the first time. Sight is taken back to a vernal stage before it learned how to scotomize the visual field, how to screen out the unimportant and not *see*, but scan.[2]

Maria Irene Fornes widens this commitment, matching the painter's scrutiny of objects with the dramatist's scrutiny of people, and in doing so battles many of the same "enemies" that Bryson identifies. The spectators who think that they know in advance *who* is worth looking at are often surprised by the people at the center of Fornes's theater, as are those spectators accustomed to scanning the stage for messages or parables. Fornes also knows how "habitual vanities" can cause a spectator to see only those aspects of a character that match established patterns of behavior, recognizable from one's own experience. Hoping to overcome these limits, Fornes insists that her audiences practice the same kind of close seeing that Bryson describes: fanatic about detail, unsatisfied with one's first impressions, undistracted, careful not to imagine events deliberately left undramatized and words left unspoken, yet also ready to be surprised. Fornes would add that this is a skill that must be constantly sharpened: Our urge to explain must be deferred, yet our engagement with her characters and their world must be ongoing, if it is to be worth anything at all. In her plays, the stage composition never rests, never settles into mere decor, but instead remains tentative, as if the fact of attention—first the writer's (to her characters), then the characters' (to one another and their environment), and finally our own (to the play)—works like an electric current to keep this dramatic world thriving. (This quality, incidentally, also makes Zurbarán's and Cotán's still lifes so much richer than the merely decorative versions of the genre. The two painters candidly depict their anxieties: We are asked to imagine them trying to establish geometrically precise relationships among things—the blossom perched on the edge of the saucer, the melon paired with a melon slice—then pushing to the margins what they don't want us to see, erasing the background, controlling our access, nervous lest the composition come unbalanced. This drama becomes visible beneath each painting's surface gloss the longer one looks at it: There is nothing "still" about these still lifes.)

Fornes's similar anxiety, evident in many of her plays, deepens her idea of being civilized. She addresses herself first of all. As she tries to do justice to the dramatic world she imagines, she is always opening the aperture of her scenes one more notch, or zooming in closer, demanding of her characters and her audience that they, too, amend their earlier conclusions about what they've seen. The individual who can keep up with her, taking strength from this exercise of perpetual revision, capable of both the intense scrutiny of a single object and adventurous exploration of a broad landscape, has mastered (to borrow Fornes's title) the conduct of life. Both challenges are invoked in a passage from another Fornes play, *Abingdon Square*. Juster and his son Michael are playing chess:

> JUSTER: Play Michael, make up your mind.
> MICHAEL: I don't know what move to make.
> JUSTER: *(to Marion)* What should Mike do? Should he scrutinize the board and imagine each move and its consequences, or should he just play and see what happens? I imagine both are good ways of learning.[3]

Plays from every stage of Fornes's career are structured by the tension between the two styles. Characters are consumed by curiosity, and then by the shame it causes them. They seek virtue and welcome abjection simultaneously. Their commitment to unvarnished reality and truth makes them no less prone to romanticism. Their desire for freedom doesn't cancel their need for security. The pleasure they take in being outlandish or vulgar coincides with their self-protective attention to their dignity. They value both spiritual and secular revelations. Because they are so susceptible to ideals, and serious about their promise, they remember to be skeptical of them. They seize and savor each moment, yet are anxious to move on, lest equally spectacular moments fade before they can experience them.

> You have, perhaps, made me feel something
> But the moment has passed.
> And what is done cannot be undone.
> Once a moment passes, it never comes again.[4]

The lyric is from *Promenade*, Fornes's 1965 musical with Al Carmines, and it suggests the other spirit animating her theater, the flanerie celebrated in her title, seemingly at odds with the patience demanded of her more selective still-life writing. Only seemingly: In fact, the two attitudes coexist naturally, and often within the same play. Both derive from fascination, and a sense of obligation toward the things that trigger fascination. Her characters want to register fully the beauty (or ugliness, or ambiguity) of particular things, but not to the exclusion of the phenomena surrounding them, each meriting the same rigorous appreciation. Fornes's characters are careful not to become pedants, but they *are* obsessive, almost hypnotized in their engagement with the world. Yet even this description, like so many when it comes to Fornes, needs to be qualified further. The seriousness of her characters isn't leaden, or self-righteous. They concentrate while also exulting in the fact of concentration. For them, being interested is buoyant, is life itself. After each encounter with a person, an idea, or even a thing, they are propelled outward, back into the world, their capacity for enthusiasm replenished. To conduct themselves any other way—to allow their enthusiasms to pull them so far inward that they lose their awareness of context and history—would be to diminish and thus betray the phenomena that got them interested in the first place.

An artist from another nontheatrical discipline helps one see this aspect of Fornes's art. In their commitment to no commitment—or, more precisely, to many equally sincere, and total, commitments—Fornes's characters resemble the promenading speakers in the poetry of James Schuyler. Each object in their path promises revelation—and even a kind of reprieve, if only from the rough justice of time passing too quickly—if they pause to see it clearly and register their impressions fully. Schuyler won't generalize about a city street, for instance—or a building on that street, or a shop window in that building. Each consists of an infinite number of pieces visible only to those with a zeal for inventory and an interest in detecting relationships. Schuyler learns to see the whole by acknowledging the integrity of each part. Landscapes, to him, are always collages.

As in collage, Schuyler's poetic world has no background. He summons each image to the front of the poem, where he and his readers can consider it until another, equally deserving image approaches. The work is not journalism, nor journal-keeping. Despite the revolving-eye quality of some poems, they are never disinterested; and despite their autobiographical richness, they are never wholly private. Each poem expresses the speaker's overwhelming sense of responsibility to his world, as well as his healthy self-interest. (Only in the moments of observation does he seem able to verify his presence: He sees, therefore he exists.) The two attitudes keep one another in check. With each line of verse, rich in sensuous detail, he secures an object's presence in the world, but also, and more important, he brings it into his own world, his own history— the history of his writing. This is the explicit subject of "The Morning of the

Poem," forty-nine pages (in one edition) about everything that happened or occurred to Schuyler, crucial as well as trivial, during the hours of writing. Here,
the poem recovers its own landscape, and its life in time, that would otherwise
have been lost, had Schuyler wrenched each of his observations out of context
to use them in less autobiographical poems. The things he passes on the avenues or sees from his windows need his eye if they are to evolve from detritus
into resonant imagery; just as the writer needs the things, or rather the opportunity to name and think about them, in order to feel more fully human, a
citizen instead of a mere occupant of his world—to become an active partici-
pant in the social contract because he has become an active chronicler of its
various applications. In other words, he becomes civilized by writing.

> A gray hush
> in which the boxy trucks roll up Second Avenue
> into the sky. They're just
> going over the hill.
> The green leaves of the tulips on my desk
> like grass light on flesh,
> and a green-copper steeple
> and streaks of cloud beginning to glow.
> I can't get over
> how it all works in together
> . . .
> It's getting grayer and gold and chilly.
> Two dog-size lions face each other
> at the corners of a roof.
> It's the yellow dust inside the tulips.
> It's the shape of a tulip.
> It's the water in the drinking glass the tulips are in.
> It's a day like any other.[5]

Schuyler's readers learn a flexible, rolling kind of awareness that will serve
them well in Fornes's audience. To Schuyler, one's movement through experiences is as important as the experiences themselves. To capture in verse the
quality of an object or person, you must preserve something of the surprise
and suddenness of meeting them for the first time, and then the melancholy of
losing them to the flow of the day. Their beauty reveals itself as part of a day's
music, rather than as isolated sound. So it is with Fornes. Her best plays resist

thumbnail description; their admirers often have to resort to scene-by-scene, and character-by-character, explanation to make their case. A succession of short episodes in one play; in another, a meandering dialogue, designed less to argue a point than simply to test the possibilities (and indulge the pleasures) of conversation; in many more plays, the non sequiturs, interruptions, bizarre incidents, scenes that begin in the middle of a crisis and end abruptly—all of these formal devices prevent us from generalizing too much and analyzing too efficiently. As we add perception to perception, correcting and deepening our first impressions, we find ourselves unconsciously emulating Fornes's characters: They, too, spend much of their time rearranging their perceptions and memories. As each piece falls into place, they try to guess at the design of their lives, rather than merely dwelling uncritically in them. For Fornes, this uncertain effort is the very essence of morality.

The obligations of a moral life also have Fornes's characters forever trying to synchronize their consciousness with their experience, as the following passage from her play *Oscar and Bertha* (1991) suggests. Bertha's subject is desire, and it comes through even in the rhythm of her sentences, the accumulation of partial definitions (no simile is vivid enough for something so alive), and the insistent movement of the whole paragraph. Bertha is describing what happens when another woman, Eve, speaks to men:

> Something sexual. Like being hit in the head with a big stone or a blunt instrument. Or being burnt with a high voltage electric charge which is powerful like electricity but it doesn't hurt. Or feeling the ground sink under your feet—. When she's not touched, she feels a longing that weakens her. But when she's touched she burns with desire powerful like a rocket taking off the ground. And tearing her entrails. Either way it's strong.[6]

Set against such a compulsive series of descriptions, how misleading it is when Fornes's more facile critics themselves discuss the theme of desire, as if it were a stable emotion in her work, susceptible to shorthand analysis. The word "desire" is too general for a writer as observant as Fornes—as are, alas, most words: The continuous emendation in speeches such as these betrays her understanding that an emotion's complexity is rarely served by the language describing it. (Like all eloquent writers, Fornes distrusts eloquence. It suggests a self-mastery and detachment that her characters don't in fact enjoy.) But Fornes isn't discouraged by such a truth. It seems to galvanize her, prompting her to seek an ever more precise vocabulary. She knows that, ultimately, her search will fail—

even the most lucid dialogue will only approximate a state of mind. No matter: Writing that begins in skepticism results in drama more faithful to the equally restless lives of her characters.

Like Bertha running through her sequence of similes, Fornes seems to gather all the synonyms of an emotion, and remark upon their differences from one another, before she assigns one to a character. "Desire" is almost infinitely divisible. Interest, curiosity, affection, longing, love, lust: Its variants are each crucially different (in some cases the differences are imperceptible to all but Fornes herself) and demand a specific style of speech and movement. Moreover, for her an emotion is never abstract, but rather a series of occasions when a particular individual experiences it, coloring it with his or her own temperament, watching it change over time. In other words, an emotion has a history, which Fornes consults in order to dramatize a character's condition as accurately as possible. If we are to understand desire, then (or hatred, or fear), Fornes expects us to speak of its hours, even its minutes, each impossible to compare exactly to any other minute in the life of that emotion. Fornes isn't being coy by refusing to let us speak of Marion "in love," or Nena "afraid," or Mae "hopeful." (We may try, but listen to how flat such descriptions sound.) Such labeling is anathema to a writer whose desire to rescue the unseen and the undervalued aspects of life has taught her never to confuse actual experience with its subsequent interpretation or ideology.

A late play by Gertrude Stein teaches the same lesson. In *Listen to Me* (1938), characters discussing public and private forms of loss—the imminent world war and the longing of "Sweet William for his Lillian"—reject elaborate analyses in favor of "words of one syllable." They challenge themselves to speak both simply and comprehensively. The two goals don't have to be contradictory: Knowledge, they insist, is rarely served by superfluous or coded description. Adjectives and adverbs meant to vivify a noun only obscure it. The Acts themselves explain: The Fourth Act says, "The air is there which is where it is. Kindly notice that is all one syllable and therefore useful. It makes no feeling, it has a promise, it is a delight, it needs no encouragement, it is full."[7] The play is not just about writing, however: For Stein, the form of a sentence, and not just its subject, reveals the soul of the person speaking. The respect a character shows language indicates the respect he or she is capable of showing the world. Exaggeration, vagueness, clichés, pretension, even grammatical sloppiness all warn of a deeper, and more dangerous, indifference. There is a one-syllable version of character, too—shorn of all the affectations that pass for personality and the sociological labels that confer identity. In all her plays, Stein summons these naked, unsupported characters—individuals, not types—and sets them apart from those whom they resemble or recall, hoping "to find out what is moving inside them that makes them them."[8]

Fornes also perceives the world in syllables—syllables of behavior, thought, and feeling, which her plays enunciate in order to secure a character's presence onstage. Her pronunciations are often unconventional: In her version of an emotion or an action, the emphases are perverse, the rhythms are willfully awkward. She is willing to sacrifice the sense of the whole if it means we'll finally "hear" parts slurred over in everyday "speech." She manages to be candid and coy at the same time—graphic about areas of experience we never thought deserved such scrutiny: ironing in *Mud*, getting dressed in *What of the Night?*, a modest marriage ceremony in *A Vietnamese Wedding*. Although she says (in Allen Frame's interview, excerpted here) that she dramatizes only the high points in a character's particular ordeal, her idea of an essential scene (as these examples suggest) lacks the confessional fluency or confrontational tension one might expect, just as her endings avoid bathos or uncomplicated joy.

In *Springtime*, one of Greta's quirkier observations points to where Fornes's own interests lie: "A person in love," Greta says, "holds his breath a little after inhaling or while they inhale. They inhale, stop a moment, and inhale a little more."[9] It's typical of Fornes that she finds the most reliable indication of an overpowering emotion in the way a character breathes, rather than in anything he or she says. Even when her characters do have "big" speeches, Fornes often hears an equally interesting disclosure in the small talk that follows—the half-sentences, irrelevant words grasped as if they were life buoys, keeping the embarrassed speaker from sinking into a more embarrassing silence. Finally, to Fornes's eye, the unselfconscious gestures made by a character pausing between two more emphatic actions best express what he or she is really thinking. In Fornes's *A Visit* (1981), Rachel describes a spatial equivalent of the kind of event or speech to which Fornes redirects our attention. She has her arms and one leg around a elderly character named Popo:

Between the living-room and dining-room
is a space which hardly exists,
the threshold of a door,
an invisible space
which holds
the spirit of a house.
In this threshold I thee hold.[10]

When Fornes treats familiar subjects, as in the following passage from the same play, such panoramic seeing is particularly valuable. Rachel straddles another man, Michael; they begin having sex; passion peaks. But Rachel is drawn, and draws us, to the margins: "Years afterward [she says], when I am a woman, the sunlight falling on the wall through the skylight over the staircase will bring back this moment to me, the moment when the world first began to open itself before me and puzzle me."[11] The best critics of Fornes remember this light and these thresholds as they try to explain the more obviously significant events that happened nearby. They also respect the puzzlement, and the fascination with the invisible, that Rachel describes, balancing their obligation to explain the play against their desire to linger in, and preserve, its unsettled, transitory atmosphere.

The characters themselves can't help lingering in such an uncertain world. They seem to exist in perpetual anticipation—of exactly what, not even they know. A number of them await judgment—for the sin of being female, according to Julia in her hallucinatory monologue in *Fefu and Her Friends*; for the sin of faith, according to Joan in *The Trial of Joan of Arc*; and for the sin of sexual desire, according to Jack in *Enter THE NIGHT*. In *The Conduct of Life*, Nena counts the minutes until Orlando's next assault. Leopold does the same as he waits for Isidore in *Tango Palace*. Still other characters look for some sign to guide their next move or warn them of imminent danger. *Sarita* opens with Sarita asking her friend Yeye to tell her fortune and reassure her that Julio loves her. After the chess-playing scene in *Abingdon Square*, Marion walks six paces in silence, then stands still, listening, until she finally says "six steps and the sky did not fall." The absurd version of the same state is in *The Successful Life of 3*, which opens with 3 taking off one of his shoes and letting it fall to the floor. The character named He watches this and freezes: He says he's waiting for the other shoe to drop.

Most of Fornes's characters, comic or tragic, expect at some distant moment to be able to see the pattern of their past thoughts and actions, to understand the consequences of their choices and the reasons for their fears. Lacking such understanding, and the self-mastery it brings, they feel doomed to permanent immaturity—to be nothing more than a collection of random responses to the world that never add up to a complete individual with a consistent point of view. This is the source of Fefu's energy (a kind of manic intimacy), Mae's resolve, and Marion's pain. Marion could be speaking for all three women when she says, "I feel sometimes that I am drowning in vagueness—that I have no character."[12] But she, along with the others, are no closer to lives of pure instinct. Self-consciousness always keeps them from submitting completely to passion or pursuing an ambition so single-mindedly that they don't worry about all the goals they *aren't* pursuing.

Fornes keeps many of her characters fluctuating, unable to commit to an action or arrive at a conclusion, yet equally incapable of indifference. They spend the bulk of their energies on rituals of self-doubt, advancing one step toward a resolution, an ideal, or a desired companion in one scene, then retreating two steps in the next. The plays as a whole reflect the temperament of the characters: One minute the mood is relaxed, the tempo leisurely; the next minute it constricts, as a character finally gives in to her terror, or another at last focuses her curiosity and propels herself toward its object. This unpredictability affects the language as well, redoubling the anxiety Fornes already feels in her search for "words of one syllable." Conversation in her plays, as we've seen, is sometimes deliberate, sometimes fervent; either way, speakers are eager to win their listeners' undivided attention. But they also worry about being misunderstood. The listening characters are under similar pressure: They hope to catch everything, but also worry that if they listen too closely, or get too involved in what they're hearing, they won't have the presence of mind to prepare a satisfactory reply. The overall tone of a typical Fornes play is bright and engaged, but also cautious, as if the characters are disturbed by something they can't (or won't) name, or provoked by an invisible force, not necessarily unpleasant. Their behavior has the edginess of people excited by an adventure they have yet to begin, but also fearful of what they might discover—about themselves as much as about their ostensible destination. Throughout their talk, they strive for the kind of relaxation available only to those who enjoy total control.

Such tension is sharpest in Fornes's stillnesses and silences. Indeed, Fornes worries over the tone and duration of silences the way a musician does: These spaces are as busy with choices, regrets, and retreats as more obviously active passages. Like Harold Pinter, Franz Xaver Kroetz, and Suzan-Lori Parks, she assigns distinct emotional meanings to different kinds of silence. Ellipses following a line of dialogue, she has explained, imply hesitation, as if the speaker is pondering a further speech, or hopes to hear a reply. In either case, the character is gauging the effect his or her words have made before moving on. On another level of silence is the dash, usually preceded by a period. Unlike ellipses, which suggest that the hesitant speaker is still engaged with the listener, the period and dash mark a break: The speaker moves into a private space, sealed in fantasy, perhaps, or memory. The most significant silences (Fornes says) are indicated by stage directions. "Pause" has the same weight as a line of dialogue; it is an event unto itself, or a window onto mental activity that runs parallel to the dialogue.[13]

Sometimes Fornes gives over whole scenes to silence, and here the tranquillity, so visible, is most vulnerable to disruption. You sense that a character's momentary inattention to her deportment, the clarity of her thinking, or the ties binding her to another character could cause the stage to rupture; Fornes's own writerly self-mastery could even dissolve as well. That being the case, the beautiful stage compositions, Fornes's signature tableaux, should never seem settled, nor should their inhabitants seem smug. When Rainbow sits by a window, looking at her garden, or when Marion waits by her own window, letting the afternoon pass, they may appear contented, rooted in their landscapes, possessed of the peace of mind that eluded them in earlier, agitated conversations. But in fact here the deepest anxiety reveals itself; here the characters are most active. Suspended, during these moments, in a seemingly timeless zone, they conduct ruthless acts of self-scrutiny. They look at themselves as if at an intruder, or a long lost and much changed relative, or a dreaded messenger. The favorite window view, or the objects they ponder, exist to help them feel at ease as they look at themselves. In *Evelyn Brown*, Evelyn's many tasks—making bread, setting the table, sweeping the floor—serve the same function. Like a metronome, the rhythm of chores structures otherwise chaotic thought.

In each act of self-examination, a Fornes character seems to ask herself if there is a core, or bottommost level, to the self—something visible and truly her own only when all influence has been resisted. Some of her most besieged characters fear that there isn't—that their every thought has been anticipated, preprinted on index cards as in *Tango Palace,* or that they'll never acquire a personal style or power of choice, as in *The Danube,* where Hungarian/English language lessons have leached the personality out of their sentences, and puppets eventually replace their bodies. But many other Fornes characters delight in their unreliability. They reinvent themselves as often as their imagination allows. Molly slides in and out of a Marlene Dietrich impersonation in *Molly's Dream.* Marion leads a secret life in her diary. In *Enter* THE NIGHT, Tressa and Jack dress up as characters from *Broken Blossoms* and *Lost Horizon.* In *The Summer in Gossensass,* real actresses (Elizabeth Robins and Marion Lea) lose themselves in their roles in *Hedda Gabler.* Even when Fornes's characters aren't explicitly playing parts, they are responsive to their passing fancies, ready to adjust their temperaments and rewrite their itineraries according to the emotional weather of the moment. The ease with which She in *The Successful Life of 3* accommodates a sexual overture is typical: "Thank you," she says agreeably, when He says "I'd like to bounce on you." In *Fefu and Her Friends*, the women allow a water fight to override their obligations to plan their club's fund-raiser. The fragmentation of *Fefu's* second act is in keeping with this openness to chance: There are four different, equally valid paths through the play. A chorus in *Promenade* sums up the dramatic structure of many Fornes plays: "Why not? Why not? Why not?," the characters sing, and then answer their own question: "Why not!"

In such a world, drama derives from confident digression—the only way that characters can cover all the territory open to their imaginations. At every turn, they reconsider their assumptions, regauge the intensity of their original wishes, and discard ideas about themselves no longer appropriate to this new environment. They enjoy the illusion that they are answerable only to their curiosity; and able, with their capacity for attention, to remap the world according to their own enthusiasms. Ever the flaneurs, they treat even their thoughts and feelings as aspects of an undiscovered country awaiting their curiosity. They travel down avenues of inquiry that seem to stretch into infinity. They feel in and of the world, almost synchronized with its spinning, as they work through a problem, piece together a plan, or describe how an emotion affects them. The phenomena that they arrest with their curiosity, and then threaten to disable with their obsessions, they in fact create anew, returning them to the world invigorated from being thought about so thoroughly. The characters are just as invigorated: They have the persistence of the most principled artists, who feel they know their subject truthfully only when they're in the midst of trying to represent it—when they have only a sheet of paper filled with scratches and scribbles, none yet cohering as form. Even as they near completion, they can't feel they've done their subject justice. The minute they stand back from the finished work, they are compelled to try again, for only in acts of renunciation and revision do they feel most themselves.

Fornes could teach her characters the art of revision by her own example. Her actual work on a text—at the desk, in rehearsal—is only one aspect of a multifaceted revising temperament, one that seeks a forum for its corrections and amplifications everywhere it turns. Fornes thinks of this seeking and these forums literally: Visible behind the plots of her plays is the narrative of her journey toward their completion. The texts themselves are tributes to travel without a map, or more precisely, to the adjustments of vision and thought that come from such voluntary displacement. So many of Fornes's plays, she has told us, began on the street, when she was unconcerned about her destination. She decided on the setting for *Mud* when she saw two old wooden chairs at a California flea market. Venturing deeper into the same market, she came across an ironing board and a set of farm tools: Now she knew who her characters were. The characters of *Fefu and Her Friends* came to her when she wandered into a Manhattan thrift store and saw a rack of dresses from the 1930s—six of them for six women. Later, when she was touring a loft being considered as a theater for the production, and passed through its "backstage"—a kitchen, an office, a storeroom— she decided to rework some half-finished scenes, setting them in each room, and to stage the play environmentally, for an audience as mobile as she had just been. (In another story of the play's origins, Fornes says she may have been influenced by her participation in an early Claes Oldenburg happening that took place in a Manhattan railroad flat.) *Evelyn Brown* started taking shape in a New Hampshire antique store, where her friend Dan Wagoner showed her the title character's 1909 diary. The genesis of *The Danube* is perhaps the best known instance of her flanerie: She discovered the set of language lessons in a sidewalk peddler's used-record bin. Listening to them at home, she dreamed her way back to the world about to crumble around her three beleaguered characters.

Each encounter with an artifact blurs Fornes's view of the here-and-now and muffles its insistence on its own reality. Just as a chair in a flea market is no longer in its original world—a Midwest living room, say, in the 1940s—Fornes, as she looks at it, is no longer in hers. They are both in an intermediate place, where she is free to assign new meanings and devise new uses for the object. These acts of revision are repeated in the strange new spaces she prowls. The rooms in the loft that eventually housed *Fefu*—or the fields of Padua Hills, in California, where she has developed many of her plays—are no longer just rooms or fields when she walks through them; but neither are they yet theatrical stages, with meanings hemmed in by a plot, or the uses to which an actor puts the spaces in performance. They are full of possibility; they can be redesigned at any moment.

Of course, in her willingness to respond to found material and chance encounters Fornes hardly differs from most artists. What *is* different is her reluctance to emerge from this experimental state. The promise (or threat) of constant transformation—of a world in which everything seems temporary, one fragile version among many—is preserved in performance. The stage of *Mud* balances atop a mound of dirt, literalizing her characters' feelings of abandonment and spiritual squalor in the face of their mutually destructive triangle. They seem about to sink into the mud, taking the stage with them, or to dread the return of some river, certain to overrun their island and carry them off to points unknown. In *The Danube,* blasts of steam rise from beneath the floorboards after each scene, underscoring the unreliability of the characters' prewar world: How long before the volcano erupts? The starkest image of this precariousness is in *Enter THE NIGHT.* The stage, according to Fornes's notes, is dominated by a dark pit—"as large as the space permits." One imagines the actors inching their way around it to avoid falling. In fact, the hole merely links two stories of a character's home—Tressa walks up a staircase from under the stage as the play opens—but the feeling of expanding blackness, of a world teetering on the edge of oblivion, never leaves a play that confronts more specific threats: terminal illness, self-hatred, disintegrating love.

Fornes's interest in precariousness is evident in the very language of her plays as well, for she favors a diction that, in its simplicity, calls attention to structure. We see the joints and beams holding up her characters' sentiments. As we admire a sentence's craftsmanship we also see, and learn to value, what little saves her characters from incoherence, a void as awful as Tressa's pit. But Fornes calls attention to the building and maintenance of a language in other, larger ways, as well. Time and again, with an eagerness unusual in a writer with such a strong voice, she relinquishes her authority over her plays, opening them to numerous alien texts and observing the effects of the encounter. (Perhaps only a writer whose style is so distinctive could be so welcoming.) Susan Sontag traces this interest in found texts back to Fornes's first play, *The Widow,* compiled from a cousin's letters. The interest has deepened over time. The last act of *Fefu and Her Friends* is dominated by a long speech from Emma Sheridan Fry's 1917 *Educational Dramatics. Abingdon Square* contains passages from Dante and the garden writer E. A. Bowles, recited by characters experiencing traumas too painful, or emotions too intimate, to be spoken of without shame in their own language. *The Summer in Gossensass* incorporates so much writing by and about Ibsen—scenes from *Hedda Gabler,* letters and diaries, reviews and historical background—that the two playwrights seem to jostle for space.

In some of Fornes's other plays, the found writing succeeds in crowding out her own. These works are in fact collages, assembled around a character for whom texts are one of several kinds of material (and reading and writing only two of many possible activities) with which he or she builds a hospitable, habitable world. In these plays, Fornes treats passages of prose as she elsewhere

treats objects and furniture—making arrangements, handling them with cura-
torial care. *Evelyn Brown* is drawn entirely from the New Hampshire diary.
The overheated quality of *A Visit* comes from Victorian pulp novelists, quoted
throughout the play. *The Annunciation*, produced at Judson Church in 1967,
combines texts from Rilke and the Gospels of John and Luke. *The Trial of Joan
of Arc in a Matter of Faith*, produced in 1986, relies on the transcripts of Joan's
testimony during her interrogation by the bishop of Beauvais. In these last
two plays, Fornes's language, which often approaches devotional intensity (as
Bonnie Marranca demonstrates), literally becomes a form of prayer. Actors resemble apostles in their handling of an inherited text, honoring the passion that
accompanied its creation with the exactness of their reiteration. The sensuality
of all this work is not lost on Fornes. She has said that one reason she quotes
other writers so often is that she likes the feeling of typing their words. Here, her
vision of the shapeliness of language is fulfilled: She literally caresses the text.

Even when Fornes adapts other writing in the conventional way, she suggests
a private drama going on behind the plot. Her versions of *Blood Wedding, Uncle
Vanya, Hedda Gabler,* and *Life Is a Dream* read (and may play) like the transcript
of a heated debate rather than an homage, the adapter contesting the original's history of translation and critical reception in every line. Canonical works
whose texture we've long taken for granted after a lifetime of productions, and
whose cadences we've grown accustomed to in school-taught versions, she renders newly strange, even awkward, and sometimes outrageous—too direct to
be "Chekhovian"; too morally neutral to please the Ibsenites; lacking the mys-
ticism we expected from Lorca and the high-flown rhetoric we thought we
wanted from Calderón. The disorientation is deliberate, and links these works,
usually ignored by her critics, to her own plays more metaphorically concerned
with translation. (Most of her protagonists struggle to turn private thought
into public language.) The odd new versions of the classics also preserve an
image of the questioning common to all her work. But now it's Fornes rather
than her characters who voices the doubts and presses for clarification: She is
certain that translators before her had unnecessarily embroidered the original,
and so obscured its uncomfortable truths. For her, an adaptation is a rejection,
an argument, and a rescue all at once.

The adaptations and collages are only the most explicit expressions of
Fornes's belief that writing is never as solitary as its romantics would have it
seem. Theater writing, of course, *has* to be collaborative, but Fornes is committed to exploring a more particular, and hence more intense, relationship.

Her dialogues with Ibsen, Dante, or Emma Sheridan Fry are refinements of an interest in the nature of community-forming that she pursues elsewhere in *The Summer in Gossensass* (in which she stages scenes of rehearsal), *Abingdon Square* (the scene of Marion, Michael, and Juster reading together in silence), and *Fefu and Her Friends* (the run-through of the fund-raiser in Act 3). They are also abstracted versions of the very real companionship among artists that Fornes deems essential to vital writing and, on a more fundamental level, to clear and comprehensive vision. As Ross Wetzsteon reports, Fornes began her writing career sitting across a kitchen table from her onetime roommate, Susan Sontag: The two women kept each other company as they worked on stories. This scene is recreated every time Fornes offers one of her famous workshops, in which she writes alongside her students. At Padua Hills, where Fornes developed *Mud*, she worked another variation on this theme. Every morning she gathered her cast and dictated new scenes that she had drafted only the night before. In this concrete application of a theater commonplace, the actors shared responsibility for writing the play.

In each place—at the kitchen table, in the classroom or rehearsal hall, and also at the thrift store or flea market—writing is an image of engagement. The artist is out in public instead of secluded in her imagination; she filters a community's competing sounds, cuts a path through its crowd of images, learns to recognize herself by the choices she makes and the sensations she responds to—by everything we call "taste." The work of writing is indistinguishable from the work of living itself—a union Fornes stresses each time she shows a woman on the verge of a crucial life change (Sarita is one) pausing to write a letter describing it.

Fornes's vision of writing as companionship is best captured in *Evelyn Brown*, where two actors play Evelyn, each reading from her diary: One writer demands another—as witness, respondent, collaborator. This kind of doubling is continued in Fornes's own life. Fornes faces Fornes as she returns to plays from all stages of her career and rewrites them, sometimes several times, usually when asked to publish them in a new anthology or direct a new production. (For Fornes, as Susan Letzler Cole points out, rehearsal is writing conducted by other means.) This is the most explicit instance of her theater's preoccupation with revision. All writers revise, of course, but it's hard to imagine Fornes's compulsiveness, and understand how her theater manages to maintain its extraordinary poise with such turmoil going on just beneath the surface. Few artists are as openly doubtful of their own achievements. Yet doubt is Fornes's element: A habit of rewriting is only fitting for a playwright who believes that *nothing* ever reaches its final form—whether it's a vintage dress, a servant's diary, a loft, an audience arrangement, a much-translated classic play, or a character's identity. She chases her plays in line after line, production after production, and, eventually, in edition after edition. Critics who have been trained to be mindful of other writers' inconsistent editions and who adapt easily to the inherent changeability of performance have to be even more flexible when writing about Fornes, for whom every play, even her oldest, remains provisional, a compromise with an imagination certain there is more she could be saying. It's the rare draft that she is content to let stand, definitive at last.

The history of *Abingdon Square* is typical: It was revised after its New York premiere in 1987; again for publication in *American Theatre* magazine; again for a Buffalo production in 1988 (directed, as in New York, by Fornes herself); and still once more when Fornes translated it into Spanish and directed it in San Diego. Similar stories can be told about many of her plays. In Robert Coe's interviews with five of Fornes's actors (published here), Sheila Dabney tells of the playwright merrily arriving backstage on the opening night of *The Trial of Joan of Arc* with twenty-two new pages of dialogue. Dabney's description of how the actors coped (they carried their new scripts onstage and, as they read from them, tossed each page to the floor) is the perfect image for the impermanence of all Fornes texts. No page can be trusted longer than the time it takes to read it; it would be futile to try to recover a script once it has been performed.

The most disconcerting of Fornes's revisions affects *Fefu and Her Friends*. In 1996, Fornes created a one-set version of the play, eliminating the need for mobile spectators. She has said that she made the change for practical reasons, to allow theaters to produce it for larger audiences. (The four scenes of the original second act require intimate playing spaces.) But those who know of Fornes's aversion to theory might reasonably suspect a more devious motive: The new *Fefu* upsets nearly twenty years of criticism about the political and philosophical significance of her original, nonlinear structure. It is as if Fornes feared that her innovation—so exciting in its day—was turning duller and more conventional each time a critic told her what it meant.

In Fornes's ideal world, revision would go on forever: Her understanding of her characters deepens with every new approach. Her irritation with those who insist that the process *can't* be endless—who want a play to settle down so their interpretations can get a foothold—pervades her latest full-length work. *The Summer in Gossensass* is about writing, translation, rehearsal, performance, and, finally, criticism. At every stage of this sequence, Fornes seems to argue, your questioning of a text should be so aggressive that none of your preconceptions can survive and none of your subsequent thoughts can harden into dogma. In her possessive relationship with her theater, Fornes disputes Auden's famous aphorism (via Valéry) about poems never being finished, only abandoned. Why must they ever be abandoned, she asks, as long as the artist is around to tend to them?

Eventually, we may begin to think of each of Fornes's plays as a series rather than a single work, or as a current that eddies into pools of text (manuscripts, editions) and production. Perhaps a better image is of something animate, or organic, growing in time. Fornes does seem to cultivate a play instead of simply write it, and in the process she provides lessons in being cultivated. Her constant theme—how to be civilized—deepens as it is reflected in her way of working. Writing as a vocation, rather than as simply a task: When the commonplace is taken to heart, as Fornes does, then our way of reading changes. We are reading the writer as much as her writing. To a degree never admitted by those critics dogmatic about the intentional fallacy, the story of creating does matter. It affirms the example set by many of her characters. As in so many other instances, the convicts of *Promenade* speak for them all: "Dig!" they sing, as the play begins. "Dig! Dig!"

PART I

THE PLAYS

IRENE FORNES

The Elements of Style

SPRING 1961. A warm Saturday night. The Cafe Figaro. Irene and Susan have come down to the Village from the apartment they share on West End Avenue to hang out over a couple of cups of coffee, to see if anyone'll invite them to a party.

Irene immediately notices that Susan's restless, distracted. "What's wrong?" Susan's feeling a little depressed, nothing to worry about.

"But why? What's bothering you?"

Well, she wants to write a novel, but she hasn't been able to get started.

"I didn't know you wanted to write a novel," Irene says. They've been living together for several months, Irene painting, Susan teaching philosophy at Columbia, but this'd never come up before.

"Well, what are you waiting for?"

The usual things—she has to get settled first.

"How silly. If you want to write, why not just sit down and write?"

Susan laughs. Sure.

"You think I'm kidding. We're going to finish our coffee, go back to the apartment, and you're going to write."

Originally published in *The Village Voice*, April 29, 1986.

At that moment—"just like the devil," Irene thinks, tempting them from their path—a friend stops by, tells them about a party. Why don't they come?

We'd love to, Susan says. "No," Irene says firmly, "we have to go home to write."

"Just to show you how easy it is," Irene says when they get back to their apartment, "I'll write something too." She's never written anything before, but she wants to help Susan get started. She almost feels like she's babysitting.

They sit on opposite sides of a large table in the kitchen. Susan knows exactly what she wants to do—she begins work on her first novel. Irene doesn't know what to write about, so on an impulse she takes down a cookbook, opens it at random, and decides to write a short story by making herself use the first word of every sentence.

Susan Sontag would have become a writer in any case—it just took that Saturday night at the Figaro to get her started—but Maria Irene Fornes still wonders if she would have become a playwright if she and Susan had gone off to that party. "I had all this creative energy that I had to use. I never really loved painting. Still, I might never have even thought of writing if I hadn't pretended I was going to show Susan how easy it was."

Within a few years, Sontag had become one of the most visible members of the intellectual establishment, but while Fornes has written more than two dozen plays since that night at the Figaro, her career has taken a virtually invisible trajectory. Rarely reviewed in the weeklies, stupidly reviewed in the dailies, utterly unknown to the electronic media, unproduced by most of the country's major cultural centers, and rarely anthologized, she has nevertheless established herself, to a loyal and ardent following of Off-Off-Broadway theatergoers, as one of the half-dozen most gifted playwrights in the American theater. As Lanford Wilson puts it: "She's one of the very, very best—it's a shame she's always been performed in such obscurity. Her work has no precedents, it isn't derived from *anything*. She's the most original of us all."

Irene Fornes is not only one of the few writers from the Golden Age of Off-Off-Broadway to have sustained a life in the theater, she is the *only* one who has radically altered both her form and subject matter. Fornes, in fact, is in the midst of a creative period unrivaled in our theater—three Obie-winning plays in 1984, one in 1985 (plus two other new plays), three new plays again this season (including *Lovers and Keepers,* a chamber musical with music by Tito Puente, playing at INTAR, and a short play in *Orchards,* the evening of Chekhov adaptations at the Lucille Lortel Theater), plus a commission from Peter Sellars's American National Theater for next season, a collection just published by *Performing Arts Journal*, and a book on writing, *The Anatomy of Inspiration*.[1]

But the very experiments in form and content that have made her career so compelling, the very changes in style that have kept her work so alive, are precisely the reasons she's received so little recognition. There's no Fornes "signature" to capture the attention of either the casual theatergoer or the middlebrow critic (the kind of critic who always catches up one or two plays too late, who is finally able to acknowledge that Sam Shepard is a major playwright only when he writes the most self-imitative play of his career). She has never given a larger audience a chance to "catch on," for by the time theatergoers begin to get a fix on her work, she's already moved on.

As Sontag points out, she isn't even consistently avant-garde. How could the same playwright have written both the antic incongruities of *Tango Palace* (1963) and the implacable logic of *The Danube* (1984), surely the most devastating antinuclear play in our theater? How could the same playwright have conceived both the lethal brutalities of *The Conduct of Life* (1985) and the affirming tenderness of *A Vietnamese Wedding* (1967), one of the most transcendent works of the imagination responding to the war in Southeast Asia? Even her admirers are sometimes discomfited by Fornes's different voices—a recent *Voice* review of her spare, monastic *Joan of Arc* was grounded in nostalgia for the quirky, whimsical tones of her best-known work, *Promenade* (1965).

Rich and famous? It's about the last thing one would associate with Fornes, but she could have had it by writing another *Promenade*, a third, a fourth. Repetition would have made more comprehensible her discontinuities of language, character, space, and time; repeated exposure would have made accessible her matter-of-fact surrealism. She could have gradually created, as both Beckett and Shepard did, her own audience, and with her deft gaiety, her bittersweet gentleness, she might even have become one of our most commercial playwrights.

Yet the same playwright *did* write both *Tango Palace* and *The Danube*, both *The Conduct of Life* and *A Vietnamese Wedding*, both *Joan of Arc* and *Promenade*. For despite that ever-changing style, that continuing formal exploration, the crucial elements in Fornes's vision have remained unalterable. From the first, her writing has involved a process of distillation, stripping away the behavioral and psychological conventions that pass for realism, and seeking instead a kind of hyperrealism (whether it appears in the guise of exuberant fantasy or severe documentation). And from the first, her plays have been formally shaped by an intuitive search not merely for a new theatrical vocabulary but for a new theatrical grammar. There is, then, a Fornes signature after all—emotional complexity conveyed through ruthless simplicity, moral concern conveyed through a wholly dramatic imagination.

Spring 1986. A warm Wednesday morning. The INTAR Hispanic Playwrights Lab on West 53rd Street. Irene Fornes and six young playwrights sit in a circle at small wooden tables. They've "centered" themselves with a half-hour of yoga and Tai Chi exercises; now they're doing writing exercises. "Close your eyes," Fornes instructs. "Visualize two people in conflict." After a minute's silence, she picks up a paperback she'd found in the street that morning, skims through several pages, finds a sentence at random. "Use this sentence," she says. "'It's all just as you left it.'" Everyone begins to write, including Fornes—she's written almost every word of her last half-dozen plays in the workshop. After half an hour, she speaks again. "Now it's a week later," she says, and reads another random sentence from the paperback: "'I haven't the faintest idea what you want me to do.'" It's just like opening that cookbook back in 1961, using the first word of each sentence to get started. After another half-hour, Fornes interrupts for the last time. "A month later. 'My head was smashed open and I was unconscious for weeks.'" After two hours, Fornes asks them to read what they've written. Some have followed the exercise, others have ignored it, but there's no discussion. When they've finished reading, they simply break until tomorrow.

"The purpose isn't just to get one play out of them, but to help them become writers," Fornes says over a quick lunch before rushing off to rehearse *Lovers and Keepers*. "If they just respond to what the teacher says, instead of opening themselves up to their own images, the workshop won't do them any good. My philosophy of writing is, don't make it happen, let it happen. Mind and will come at a later time—when they have piles of pages."

Listening to Fornes is often a disorienting experience—she seems somehow both sober and playful, offhand and to the point, leaving that impression of naive sophistication so enchanting in her earlier plays (a lyric from *Promenade*: "It is true I told you I would love you / And I never did. / But remember, I'm forgetful . . .").

"Ideas are not productive," Fornes goes on. It's the kind of statement anyone else would put in italics, but there's always a tentative tone to even her most decisive remarks. "There's a difference, in all writers, between what they think they're interested in and what they're really interested in. You have to open yourself up to the world beneath your ideas. You don't tell the characters what to say or do, you listen to what they're telling *you*. They shouldn't speak for my benefit but from their own needs. It's their voices, not mine, that speak the mind of the play. Any conceptual thinking, any premeditation on my part, is just manipulation. That's the purpose of those sentences—to force the students to leap from their ideas into their imaginations. It's like jumper cables, giving them a sudden, unpredictable flow of energy."

Harvey Fierstein says that Fornes once told him the best way to break though writer's block was to masturbate. "Well, you do whatever needs to be done," she says with a shrug. "I guess masturbation is like those writer's exercises in a way—getting centered, so you can let your inner creativity express itself, listen to it instead of giving it orders. When you give it orders from your conscious mind, you're going to write plays just like everybody else's."

It's hard to imagine a play more unlike everybody else's than *The Danube*. Fornes was walking past a thrift shop on West Fourth Street, saw some 78 rpm records in a bin, liked the way they looked even before she knew what they were. She's always buying odds and ends—who knows, maybe they'll come in handy as props—so she bought one for a dollar. Turns out it was a language record, the simplest sentences, first in Hungarian, then in English. "There was such tenderness in those little scenes," she recalls—introducing people, ordering in restaurants, discussing the weather—"that when Theater for the New City asked me to do an antinuclear piece, I thought of how sorrowful I felt for the bygone era of that record, and how sorrowful it would be to lose the simple pleasures of our own era." The dialogue of *The Danube* consists almost entirely of commonplace interactions in basic sentences, Hungarian on tape, English translation by the actors, but gathers unutterable poignancy as the characters begin to deteriorate before our eyes. The play forces us to face what we're making of our world, not through stylistic flair or nuanced characterization or polemical narrative, but solely through a strikingly theatrical formal concept.

On a more mundane level, this is the kind of distillation of dramatic essence director Bob Falls encountered when he called Fornes, a couple of months ago, to ask her how many characters there'd be in her contribution to the Chekhov evening. "I don't want to pressure you," he said. "I just need to have some idea how many actors I'll need." "Oh, there aren't any actors," Fornes answered graciously. "They're potatoes."

"I'd like to get in touch with why we're together." One of the actresses in *Lovers and Keepers* wants some motivational guidance. The wife and husband seem constantly on the verge of splitting but they never do, and the actress finds it difficult to understand. "You're supposed to show how much you love each other in the manner in which you fight," Fornes explains, but that doesn't help much, so they psychologize for five or ten minutes. Turns out there're two ways you can scream—to vent your feelings or as a rupture in a relationship—and to the actress screaming always indicates a rupture. "My mother's deaf," Fornes says, understanding the problem at last, "and sometimes I have to scream at her. '*Do you want some milk?*' Can you think of it as just a vocal thing?" This time the actress gets it right—but Fornes's heart doesn't seem to be in psychologizing, she seems to use it only to *depsychologize* the scene, she's much more comfortable explaining to the actress how she wants her to sit down; that's the kind of grounding she focuses on.

Fornes's trademark as a director—she's been staging her plays since 1968— is a gestural and intonational formality, an emphasis on declamatory line readings in particular, that rejects the cumulative effect of naturalistic detail in favor of the spontaneous impact of revelatory image, that rejects emoting, behavioral verisimilitude, and demonstration of meaning in favor of crystallization, painterly blocking, and layers of irony. The contrast, in many of Fornes's plays, between the surface and the subtext helps account for their disorienting paradoxes: the simpler her work, the more mysterious its meanings; the more violent the action, the more tender its feelings.

"What I ask actors to do is never the obvious thing," Fornes says, "so I feel I have to explain to them why they're doing it. The old man in my new play, for instance—the actor kept doing this feely-touchy thing with his wife, and when I asked him not to do that, he wanted to know why, doesn't he love her? In real life, I told him, people as close as those two characters know when the other person needs that kind of support. The thing you have to focus on, I told him, is that these two people are so deeply in touch that they have no need to *manifest* their feelings for one another." So the brief scene plays, like most Fornes scenes, with a seemingly flat, almost detached surface, leaving us wondering why we're so touched—unaware that the subliminal hyperrealism of the staging has affected us far more deeply than the overt demonstrations of feeling we're used to in the theater.

"So many directors, so many actors," Fornes goes on, "add so much that's fake just to make it *seem* more real. So much behavior, so many gestures, belong exclusively to 'realistic' theater. People don't think they're realistic because they've seen them in real life, they think they're realistic because they've seen them so often on the stage. So when actors finally do behave on stage the way people actually behave in real life, everyone says, 'Oh, what an unusual style!'"

In directing (and of course she's talking about her writing as well), she tries to "eliminate everything superfluous, like an actor scratches his face and everyone says, 'How realistic!' I don't like to play those games with theatrical language and behavior. I don't even like to mimic the gestures and tones of voice of social behavior, which may be 'accurate,' but which are really just a mask concealing a deeper reality. All that's extraneous. All that's irrelevant. Get rid of it."

And replace it with? "For one thing, in real life people think as they talk, but how often do you see that onstage? That process of *mind*. I prefer to have my actors reflect rather than emote. I like to capture that moment when thought becomes language."

But some critics feel she occasionally falls into a performance monotone. "I don't like scenes to build up or peter out. In fact, I don't even like to present the entire scene—most of my scenes actually start in the middle, almost at the climax. That way, both the writing and the acting go from one critical moment to the next."

Almost all her plays of the past decade, in fact, have been written in a series of brief scenes. She's more concerned with the emotional core of a situation than with its quotidian details, she focuses on the psychological pivot of a relationship rather than on its causes or consequences. The realism of her theater, then, is not to be found in the observation of the ordinary or the examination of the exemplary. She is creating a form of drama in which narrative and myth, character and archetype, become virtually synonymous.

Irene Fornes was born in Cuba in 1930. Her parents weren't exactly bohemians, and they weren't exactly gypsies—in fact, she says, they didn't know *what* they were until the film version of *You Can't Take It with You* came to Havana. But in any case her father didn't believe in school and allowed her to attend only the third through sixth grades. Even now, she rarely reads—she suffers from dyslexia—and prefers conversation. "It's a very Spanish thing. We don't do our thinking reading, we do our thinking talking." While this sometimes leads to a sense of intellectual loneliness—"In this country people almost never talk about what they're really thinking or how they really feel, they just give you their opinions"—it made playwriting a natural form of expression.

After arriving in New York with her widowed mother in 1945, she worked at a series of menial jobs—making battle service ribbons, fashioning dolls out of rope—and in her late teens began hanging out in the Village. (An acquaintance from those days recalls a party at which Fornes, "very vivacious and pretty in a zaftig, cuddly kind of way," showed she knew how to take care of herself. Some guy made a pass at her, and the next thing he knew he was screaming and holding up his hand, bleeding from her toothmarks.) Soon she began painting, studying with Hans Hofmann, then went to Europe for three years in the mid-1950s, then returned to New York to work as a textile designer, still floundering until that Saturday night in the Figaro.

The only play she'd ever read was *Hedda Gabler* (she still hasn't read Shakespeare) but she had seen *Waiting for Godot* in Paris, in the legendary Roger Blin production. "I didn't understand a single word of it," she says. "I didn't speak any French at all. But I understood the world in which it took place, I got the rhythm. And it turned my life upside down." Her first play, *Tango Palace,* was written in an obsessive nineteen-day outburst. "It came out of nowhere," she recalls, "almost like a dream. I only left the house to buy groceries. I didn't see a single person for three weeks. I even slept with my typewriter next to me."

Throughout the 1960s, Fornes continued to write her giddily insouciant, goofily debonair plays. Recalling their tone, and the period during which she shared an apartment with Sontag, one friend from those days says he can't read "Notes on Camp" without thinking of Fornes. "She was never an intellectual, she was never as articulate as Susan in that way, but I can't help thinking that a lot of that point of view originated with Irene." With her own innocently blasé take, however. Listen to this lyric from *Promenade:*

> To walk down the street
> With a mean look on my face,
> A cigarette in my right hand
> A toothpick in my left;
> To alternate between the cigarette
> And the toothpick
> Ah! That's life.

"That really happened to me," Fornes recalls. "One day I was walking down Fifth Avenue with a cigarette in one hand, a toothpick in the other, just thinking how wonderful it was to be able to sing when you wanted to, to eat bread when you're hungry. I grew up so poor in Cuba there weren't even any bread lines—there wasn't any *bread.* To be able to do all those wonderful things—

that's what that song means." (Perhaps it's not only the questioning wonder of the autodidact that's influenced her style, but also the necessity of writing in a second language. Anyone who's learned a language in a foreign country, instead of in a class, immediately learns how central the most mundane interactions actually are to our lives—where is, how much, that's called, I like, what do you want? Yes, to walk down the street, ah, that's life.)

And when you add irony to this simplicity, you have another great lyric from *Promenade*:

> I saw a man lying in the street,
> Asleep and drunk,
> He had not washed his face.
> He held his coat closed with a safety pin
> And I thought, and I thought
> Thank God, I'm better than he is.
> Yes, thank God, I'm better than he.

Notice how taking the straightforward innocence out of this lyric—substituting, say, as a more "sophisticated" writer might, "Thank God, I got into Dalton" —makes it "wittier," but at the expense of a psychological savviness, and savagery, worthy of Brecht.

From the late 1960s through the mid-1970s, Fornes virtually stopped writing. At the time, she recalls, she thought it was only because she was devoting so much of her time to the New York Theatre Strategy, an experimental theater organization, but looking back she acknowledges that that must have been a rationalization. Was it because Off-Off-Broadway itself was going through a period of lethargy, or because directors' theater had become the focus of its energy? She's still uncertain. All she knows is that "my work was becoming vague and disoriented. Maybe I just needed a long rest."

The breakthrough finally happened in 1975, when Fornes was working with a group of Spanish actors, making a play out of their reminiscences. "I was enjoying it," she remembers, "but at the same time I kept thinking, 'I could never write this way myself, it's too sentimental.' Then one night a friend came to visit, I showed her the script, and when she finished reading it she said, 'But this isn't sentimental at all!' Thinking about it, I had to admit she was right, that I'd only called it sentimental out of shyness and embarrassment. The feelings were so exposed! And it made me realize how I'd been hiding my feelings behind humor and charm and silliness. But I thought, why should anyone be embarrassed about exposing their feelings? People do it all the time, and no one ever pays any attention!

"It would have been so easy just to go on doing one thing nicely, doing what I knew I could do, what I liked, what everyone else liked. I didn't consciously set out to change my style, but when I started writing again, *Fefu* started coming out"—*Fefu and Her Friends*, one of the seminal plays of the 1970s, and a pivotal work for Fornes, the beginning of her switch from antic abstraction to a more three-dimensional realism.

A group of women gather at Fefu's home, and in a series of fragmented encounters (the second act, in fact, takes place in four different locations, with the audience breaking into four groups and seeing each scene in random sequence), reveal how they feel about themselves and one another—women not as wives or mothers, but women free to explore their own consciousness—yet women fatefully shadowed by the play's first line: "My husband married me to have a constant reminder of how loathsome women are."

"As I was writing," Fornes says, "I could sense how the characters breathed, how they sweated—this was all completely new to me. The characters were more fully rounded, yet the language was much simpler. This was less like a sketch or a line drawing, this was more like a full-scale portrait. But I still wasn't aware what was happening until I was writing a scene in which I had to have the characters introduce themselves to one another—and I suddenly realized that they had last names! They were real people, not just abstractions! They were *real* cardboard dolls! I mean before, my characters were cardboard dolls, they were just there to serve my purpose, but I realized that now I was pretending they were *real*. It was so *embarrassing*."

Since *Fefu*, in fact, she feels that she changes styles daily—"it's the only thing that keeps me alive!" Fornes is not given to hyperbole, not even in her most capriciously whimsical texts, so it's worth trying to figure out what she means by such a seemingly exaggerated claim. It's perhaps an oversimplification to say that while her style prior to *Fefu* was blithe, wicked, loonily logical, and anarchically coherent, for the past decade, it's been lucid, emotionally direct, and almost entirely denuded of verbal flair (on several occasions she's even used found texts). But at least this kind of stylistic overview makes clearer the extent to which she's moved from cartoon-like sketches to full-bodied canvases, and helps account for the disturbing rather than merely endearing effect of her recent plays.

It's as if her earlier style created a fanciful, depersonalized world a level above that of "real life," while her later style discovers an imaginary but densely populated world a level beneath. In going deeper, her plays are no longer singular visions but plural worlds—they are inhabited by people with last names—and of course to a writer of conscience, embarrassment soon gives way to obligation.

To such a writer, no longer imagining Life but imagining lives, a constantly changing style could become a moral commitment as well as an emotional necessity. It's her way of indicating she's eager to enter other lives rather than merely commenting upon them, and thus to honor their styles by forsaking her own. Style, in short, has become a matter less of aesthetics than of virtue. So while Fornes may be speaking figuratively in saying that changing styles is "the only thing that keeps me alive," she is not speaking hyperbolically in the slightest.

To point out that her style since *Fefu* has become more personal precisely as it has become more self-effacing is a paradox that can more easily be understood by examining a similar change in her subject matter. Most of her early plays took their direction from "the compass of joy" she invented in her first piece, *Tango Palace,* its needle pointing unfailingly toward optimism. The warm, effervescent personality of their author could be seen in the benign approach to even the most volatile situations, in the savoir faire with which naiveté triumphed in even the most lethal encounters—as if (and here, of course, one thinks of camp) striking an "attitude" was sufficient to control the dénouement.

"Say you're sorry and my wound will heal," speaks one of the characters in *Tango Palace,* and *Promenade* ends with the mother asking the two escaped convicts if they've found evil. "No," they respond blissfully. "Good night, then. Sleep well. You'll find it some other time." Even the melancholy irony of this ending became increasingly inadequate, however, and in her only out-and-out failure, an antiwar play called *The Red Burning Light* (1968), the disparity between the buffoonery of the characters and the destructive consequences of their behavior was too great to be bridged by even the most charming obliviousness.

It seems likely, in fact, that it was an increasing awareness of the inadequacy of puckish irony and music hall playfulness as a response to Vietnam and sexism (and to the darker implications of her own seemingly serendipitous scenarios) that led to her absence from the stage during the first half of the 1970s. Her work since *Fefu* has become considerably more somber, and has concentrated largely on political and sexual violence. "As I get older," Fornes says, "the world seems somehow more serious. There's still a part of me that believes life is a big, wonderful game, that our main purpose on earth is to enjoy, but it doesn't always turn out so nicely. I could never end a play now the way I ended *Promenade*."

But even as the plays have become more somber, the warm, effervescent personality of their author can still be seen—and this tonal consistency is why it's an oversimplification to say that her style has moved from throwaway fantasy to compassionate realism. Although her plays are now less likely to take the form of celebration than of mourning, they have always been both exquisite and visceral, both joyful and tender. If there was a rueful undertone to her *jeux d'esprits* of the early 1960s, there's a jubilant affection underlying her tragedies of the early 1980s. All four of her most recent Obie-winning plays have ended in death—three in sexually motivated murders. But, as she says, "The only character I've ever written who I didn't love at least in part was Orlando," the sadistic, fascistic army lieutenant in *Conduct of Life*.

When it's pointed out that guns and knives figure prominently in nearly every play she's written about sexual relationships in the past decade, but that in her new play, *Lovers and Keepers,* the couples at last struggle toward some sense of reconciliation, Fornes is momentarily stunned. "Really?" she says. "I didn't realize that. But that doesn't have anything to do with what I'm saying," she insists. "The ways plays end have only to do with the nature of the situation at the start. It's like the flight of an airplane, once it's taken off you can't reverse it."

But who sets up the situation in the first place? Fornes seems distressed—as if to focus on narrative analysis is to ignore emotional structure. "The way a play ends is not the statement of the play! Take Anna Karenina. I don't even remember if she dies at the end or not, what I remember is her unhappiness. In every one of my plays I'm concerned with kindness, selfishness, generosity. Sometimes the stress changes, but I'm not even very aware of that. My new play? The characters in the third play have the least of anyone in terms of everything but love—and there they have the most. I just think of these plays as very tender. I don't know what to say except that."

Play? Plays? Fornes uses the words interchangeably to describe *Lovers and Keepers*—three acts dealing with three different couples (the middle act still in sketch form only ten days from opening night). The first and third acts were initially conceived as separate one-act plays, but when they were produced last summer at Woodstock, one of the characters in the first play showed up ("it was a complete accident") in a wordless role in the third. "Afterwards, people kept referring to the play instead of to the plays," she muses with a kind of baffled serenity. "It was only after other people saw the connection that I saw it too."

One pattern Fornes *has* noticed, however, is the two men involved with one woman triangle in so many of her plays (*Mud,* in particular, seems a mirror image of *The Successful Life of 3*), but she doesn't have any idea where it comes from, doesn't seem to particularly *care*, and even the suggestion of psychoanalyzing her inspiration makes her clearly, and uncharacteristically, annoyed. "I could pretend I have psychological thoughts," she says, "like the two men are the father and the brother, or God and her lover" (or perhaps the cruel male as sexual, the kind male as asexual?), "but it's all nonsense, it's just applying concepts to life. In order to make it work, the person doing the analyzing has to push a little here, pull a little there, stretch some things, and lie about others. It ends up fitting the theory, but it doesn't fit the characters. I get so upset when people reduce my work to patterns like that.

"Psychological analysis always looks for the ugly. When psychological meaning is applied to my work, I always end up seeming brutal—I hate men, or I hate women. How dare they say that!" Feminist criticism—to Fornes, that's another approach that too often turns her plays into pronouncements. "Party members don't think I'm much of a feminist," she says, now more distressed than angry. "The only bad review *Fefu* got was in *Ms.* magazine. The reviewer thought I was portraying women as whining victims. I don't know how to respond when people think in party lines. Sometimes I think I should just deny that I wrote *Fefu* so I can be left alone by people like that."

It'd be tempting to suspect that Fornes is protesting too much, except that in spite of the sexual hostility so frequent in her recent plays there's just as much carnal tenderness, and in spite of the *Ms.* critique she's created numerous characters with a profoundly female consciousness. When we remember that "ideas are not productive"—or the pure Fornes line from *Promenade,* "God gave us understanding just to confuse us"—we can see that what she's really protesting is the reduction of her work to concepts. It's as if she's listened so attentively to the voices of her characters that they've become real to her, so she not only resents, she's baffled by, any attempt to deny their autonomy.

"I remember when one of my plays was published in a college textbook," she told me a year or so ago. "At the end, they had a series of questions for the students—you know, 'What does Fornes symbolize by this? What does Fornes mean by that?' I didn't have any idea what they were talking about. I had to send to the publisher for the teacher's manual so I could find out what the answers were."

There's one more pattern. Fornes's sets have doors in the craziest places—

two or three doors adjacent to one another in a single wall, or doors leading nowhere. What's going on? "That's the first time anyone's noticed that," Fornes says, trying to hide her embarrassment with a quick laugh. "When I was directing *Eyes on the Harem,* I had the set designer put in entrances and exits all over the place so I wouldn't have to worry about how to move the characters on and off stage. By now it's become an almost unconscious technique. I guess what it means is that if I ever get into a situation where I don't know what I'm going to do next, there'll always be an exit to help me get out."

So far, Fornes hasn't needed any help. How could she? As she wrote in *Promenade:*

I know everything.
Half of it I really know,
The rest I make up.

CUE THE GIANT MARASCHINO

MARIA IRENE FORNES is a playwright originally from Cuba who has written some of the most enjoyable works in the American theater. They have been produced by most of the major innovating troupes in the last ten years: The Actor's Workshop in San Francisco, the New Dramatists Workshop, The Open Theater, Caffe Cino, La MaMa, the Judson Church, and Firehouse Theatre in Minneapolis. As part of the original Judson Poets Group (Al Carmines, Rosalyn Drexler, Remy Charlip, etc.) Miss Fornes helped clear a way through the claustrophobic landscape of Broadway vapidity and Off-Broadway ponderous symbolism, by making theater that was fresh, adventurous, casual, fantastic, perceptive, and musical. Now these plays have been collected for the first time by an alert Winter House (as part of their fine series of drama books). *Promenade and Other Plays* should not only bring her work to the general public's attention but also give college repertory some of the new blood it desperately needs.

If the jacket critics unite in calling Maria Fornes's theater pieces "ebullient," "exuberant," "euphoric," "blithe," and the like, they are only at fault for overlooking the melancholy that suffuses her work. Like Buster Keaton's, here is

Originally published in *The Herald* (New York), January 23, 1972.

39

a world of sudden mutations, reversals, betrayals, and casual time warps. A character will exit and reemerge the next moment five years older, or a plump middle-aged woman in pink tights will burst out of a cake and sing about her irresistible attractions. But no matter how bizarrely the action shifts, the people quickly accustom themselves to windfalls and disappointments and sink back into a philosophical self-absorption that releases itself in song. What gives the metamorphoses a plausibility is their placid unfurling and the rationalizing reflexes of the characters in the midst of the dream. This is much the same strategy Kafka used, if put to gentler ends.

Miss Fornes never stops poking fun at the habit of operatic complaint. There is one delicious moment in *Molly's Dream* in which the music starts up and Molly says: "No, I'm not breaking into song. The moment is too sad." But generally when her people sing it is precisely because their restless chagrin forces them to break with the social farce of interaction and speak about their most egoistic, solitary feelings. Since the characters are types (The Jailer, The Mother) stripped to their emblematic wishes, joys, and laments, their songs have a naive simplicity at once universal and ironic. Consider the Servant who has "just discovered what life is all about."

To walk down the street
With a mean look in my face
A cigarette in my right hand
A toothpick in my left;
To alternate between the cigarette
And the toothpick,
Ah! That's life.

Yes, I have learned from life.
Every day I've learned some more.
Every blow has been of use.
Every joy has been a lesson.
Yes, I have learned from life.
What surprises me
Is that life
Has not learned from me.

It is as if a child had remained alive inside the body of the adult to record with astonishment the fact that things were not supposed to turn out this way.

The plays, for all their enchanting movement, focus again and again on the process of disappointment and hardening. Miss Fornes's favorite way of showing this is through the faulty distribution of love (traced in a stage direction from *Promenade* with geometric wryness): "*R takes a step toward I. I takes a step toward T. T takes a step toward U.,*" and so on, and everyone joins in a paean to Unrequited Love, the beautiful masochism of suspended romantic yearning.

Attractions come and go "like vapor." Someone is always flirting and being ignored, and when these elaborate coquettries score, the flirt loses interest. In the Fornesian world of evanescent and mysterious sex appeal, timing is crucial. Miss O in *Promenade* turns to two convicts: "Let's you and me embrace." The men, not knowing which one she means, bow to each other, offer the way to each other, and so on. They finally reach her with open arms, but Miss O sings:

The moment has passed.
You have, perhaps, made me feel something,
But the moment has passed.
And what is done cannot be undone.
Once a moment passes, it never comes again.

I once had a man who loved me well.
His mouth was smaller than his eye.
But I loved him just the same.
Yes, I loved him just the same.

He said he would kill for me.
and I said, "like, for instance, whom?"
And he said, "like for instance, you,
Like for instance you."

The most intense play in the collection, *Molly's Dream,* is set in that twilight of lost women, saloons, and dashing men lifted from Dietrich and Garbo films. The pop camp overtones somehow sharpen rather than cheapen the dramatic confrontation, in which Molly the waitress circles around Jim the handsome customer, whose sex appeal is so enormous that five women literally hang on him wherever he goes. Though neither protagonist gets what he or she wants in the end, they conclude magnanimously that they have to go through many stages; if they had met some other time . . . or perhaps they will meet again.

The author's characters don't usually respond so maturely. Most draw the strength to continue from a triumphant discovery of their advantage over someone else. In Fornes's malicious tour de force, *Dr. Kheal*, the good professor manages to gloat over a "weird-looking spider, with legs ten times longer than its body, who moved in the most senseless and insane manner. I said, 'Spider, you are spastic and I am a superior beast.'" The lording of rich over poor also gets celebrated, in the bittersweet manner of Brecht's plays. No matter what romantic entanglements occupy the stage, the backdrop of inhumanity and class struggle is never far away. Two of these plays deal specifically with the politics of the Vietnam War. *The Red Burning Light*, an agitprop cartoon about the American Way taking over a tropical country, has the zany bad taste to be Son of *Ubu Roi* but none of Fornes's customary sympathy. Somehow I like much better her serene event, *A Vietnamese Wedding*—performed, incredibly enough, for Angry Arts Week—which invites the audience to become participants in an exotic wedding ceremony. I can think of no antiwar theatrical statement so effective and generous to its audience. It has the quality of a fairy tale come true.

One should speak of course of influences. Fornes's work is like a cross between Brecht and *Midsummer Night's Dream*, with von Sternberg and Gertrude Stein standing in the wings. But many other playwrights have worked with these same sources and regularly fallen into preciosity or grossness. Both traps are oddly not a problem for this author. What makes Maria Fornes's fantasies so solid is her maternal tenderness for the feelings of everyone, and her sense of normality beneath all the world's mutations. These plays are delicate not by virtue of turning away from the cruelties and selfishness in people, but by demonstrating them with a lightness that approaches wisdom.

A PREFACE TO THE PLAYS
OF MARIA IRENE FORNES

Mud, The Danube, The Conduct of Life, Sarita—four plays, recent work by the prolific Maria Irene Fornes, who for many years has been conducting with exemplary tenacity and scrupulousness a unique career in the American theater.

Born in Havana, Fornes arrived in this country with her family when she was fifteen; in her twenties she spent several years in France (she was painting then), and began writing plays after she had returned to New York, when she was around thirty. Although the language in which she became a writer was English, not Spanish—and Fornes's early work is inconceivable without the reinforcement of the lively local New York milieu (particularly the Judson Poets Theatre) in which she surfaced in the early 1960s—she is unmistakably a writer of bicultural inspiration: one very American way of being a writer. Her imagination seems to me to have, among other sources, a profoundly Cuban one. I am reminded of the witty, sensual phantasmagorias of Cuban writers such as Lydia Cabrera, Calvert Casey, Virgilio Piñera.

Of course, writers, these or any other, were not the conscious influences on Fornes or any of the best "downtown" theater of the 1960s. Art Nouveau

Originally published in *Plays* by Maria Irene Fornes (New York: PAJ Publications, 1986).

and Hollywood Deco had more to do with, say, the Theatre of the Ridiculous, than any plausible literary antecedents (Tzara, Firbank, etc.). This is also true of Fornes, an autodidact whose principal influences were neither theater nor literature but certain styles of painting and the movies. But unlike similarly influenced New York dramatists, her work did not eventually become parasitic on literature (or opera, or movies). It was never a revolt against theater, or a theater recycling fantasies encoded in other genres.

Her two earliest plays prefigure the dual register, one *volkisch,* the other place-less-international, of all the subsequent work. *The Widow,* a poignant chronicle of a simple life, is set in Cuba, while *Tango Palace,* with its volleys of sophisti-cated exchanges, takes place in a purely theatrical space: a cave, an altar. Fornes has a complex relation to the strategy of naiveté. She is chary of the folkloris-tic, rightly so. But she is strongly drawn to the preliterary: to the authority of documents, of found materials such as letters of her great-grandfather's cousin that inspired *The Widow,* the diary of a domestic servant in turn-of-the-century New Hampshire that was transformed into *Evelyn Brown,* Emma's lecture in *Fefu and Her Friends.*

For a while she favored the musical play, in a style reminiscent of the popu-list parables in musical-*commedia* form preserved in films from the 1930s like René Clair's *A Nous la Liberté.* It was a genre that proclaimed its innocence and specialized in rueful gaiety. Sharing with the main tradition of modernist drama an aversion to the reductively psychological and to sociological explanations, Fornes chose a theater of types (such personages as the defective sage and the woman enslaved by sexual dependence reappear in a number of plays) and a theater of miracles: the talking mirror in *The Office,* the fatal gun wound at the end of *Fefu and Her Friends.* Lately, Fornes seems to be eschewing this effect: the quotidian as something to be violated—by lyricism, by disaster. Characters can still break into song, as they did in the dazzling bittersweet plays of the mid-1960s, like *Promenade* and *Molly's Dream* and *The Successful Life of 3.* But the plays are less insistingly charming. Reality is less capricious. More genu-inely lethal—as in *Eyes on the Harem, Sarita.*

Character is revealed through catechism. People requiring or giving instruc-tion is a standard situation in Fornes's plays. The desire to be initiated, to be taught, is depicted as an essential, and essentially pathetic, longing. (Fornes's elaborate sympathy for the labor of thought is the endearing observation of someone who is almost entirely self-taught.) And there are many dispensers of wisdom in Fornes's plays, apart from those—*Tango Palace, Dr. Kheal*—specifically devoted to the comedy and the pathos of instruction. But Fornes is neither literary nor antiliterary. These are not cerebral exercises or puzzles but the real questions, about . . . the conduct of life. There is much wit but no nonsense. No banalities. And no non sequiturs.

While some plays are set in never-never land, some have local flavors—like the American 1930s of *Fefu and Her Friends*. Evoking a specific setting, especially when it is Hispanic (this being understood as an underprivileged reality), or depicting the lives of the oppressed and humiliated, especially when the subject is that emblem of oppression, the woman servant, such plays as *Evelyn Brown* and *The Conduct of Life* may seem more "realistic"—given the condescending assumptions of the ideology of realism. (Oppressed women, particularly domestic servants and prostitutes, have long been the signature subject of what is sometimes called realism, sometimes naturalism.) But I am not convinced that Fornes's recent work is any less a theater of fantasy than it was, or more now a species of dramatic realism. Her work is both a theater about utterance (i.e., a metatheater) and a theater about the disfavored—both Handke *and* Kroetz, as it were.

It was always a theater of heartbreak. But at the beginning the mood was often throwaway, playful. Now it's darker, more passionate: Consider the twenty-year trajectory that goes from *The Successful Life of 3* to *Mud*, about the unsuccessful life of three. She writes increasingly from a woman's point of view. Women are doing women's things—performing unrewarded labor (in *Evelyn Brown*), getting raped (in *The Conduct of Life*)—and also, as in *Fefu and Her Friends,* incarnating the human condition as such. Fornes has a near faultless ear for the ruses of egotism and cruelty. Unlike most contemporary dramatists, for whom psychological brutality is the principal, inexhaustible subject, Fornes is never in complicity with the brutality she depicts. She has an increasingly expressive relation to dread, to grief, and to passion—in *Sarita*, for example, which is about sexual passion and the incompatibilities of desire. Dread is not just a subjective state but is attached to history: the psychology of torturers (*The Conduct of Life*), nuclear war (*The Danube*).

Fornes's work has always been intelligent, often funny, never vulgar or cynical; both delicate and visceral. Now it is something more. (The turning point, I think, was the splendid *Fefu and Her Friends*—with its much larger palette of sympathies, for both Julia's incurable despair and Emma's irrepressible jubilation.) The plays have always been about wisdom: what it means to be wise. They are getting wiser.

It is perhaps not appropriate here to do more than allude to her great distinction and subtlety as a director of her own plays, and as an inspiring and original teacher (working mainly with young Hispanic-American playwrights). But it seems impossible not to connect the truthfulness in Fornes's plays, their alertness of depicting, their unfacile compassionateness, with a certain character, a certain virtue. In the words of a Northern Sung landscape painter, Kuo Hsi, if the artist "can develop a natural, sincere, gentle, and honest heart, then he will immediately be able to comprehend the aspect of tears and smiles and of objects, pointed or oblique, bent or inclined, and they will be so clear in his mind that he will be able to put them down spontaneously with his paint brush."

Hers seems to be an admirable temperament, unaffectedly independent, high-minded, ardent. And one of the few agreeable spectacles that our culture affords is to watch the steady ripening of this beautiful talent.

THE ECONOMY OF TENDERNESS

THE REAL LIFE OF MARIA IRENE FORNES

EVER SINCE *Fefu and Her Friends* Maria Irene Fornes has been writing the finest realistic plays in this country. In fact, one could say that *Fefu* and the plays that followed it, such as *The Danube* and now *Mud,* have paved the way for a new language of dramatic realism, and a way of directing it. What Fornes, as writer and director of her work, has done is to strip away the self-conscious objectivity, narrative weight, and behaviorism of the genre to concentrate on the unique subjectivity of characters for whom talking is gestural, a way of being. There is no attempt to tell the whole story of a life, only to distill its essence. Fornes brings a much needed intimacy to drama, and her economy of approach suggests another vision of theatricality, more stylized for its lack of exhibition-

The first section of this essay was originally published in *Performing Arts Journal* 22, vol. 8, no. 1 (1984). The second section was originally published under the title "The State of Grace: Maria Irene Fornes at Sixty-Two" in *Performing Arts Journal* 41, vol. 14, no. 2 (1992). Both pieces appear here in slightly different form. The third section is an expanded version of a portion of the Introduction to *Plays for the End of the Century,* ed. Bonnie Marranca (Baltimore: Johns Hopkins University Press, 1996).

ism. In this new theatricality, presence, that is, the act of being, is of greatest importance. The theatrical idea of presence is an aspect of the idea of *social being* expressed by character. The approach is that of a documentary starkness profoundly linked to existential phenomenology.

Fornes's work goes to the core of character. Instead of the usual situation in which a character uses dialogue or action to explain what he or she is doing and why, her characters exist in the world by their very act of trying to understand it. In other words, it is the characters themselves who appear to be thinking, not the author having thought.

Mud, which has as its center the act of a woman coming to thought, clarifies this process. Here is a poor rural trio, Fornes's first lower depths characters, which consists of Mae, Lloyd, and Henry, who lead lives devoid of any sense of play or abandonment; their lives are entirely functional. Each of them exists in varying relations to language—Mae through her desire to read and acquire knowledge realizes that knowledge is the beginning of will and power and personal freedom; Henry, who becomes crippled in an accident during the course of the play, must learn again how to speak; Lloyd, barely past the level of survival beyond base instincts, has no language of communication beyond an informational one. *Mud* is the encounter of the characters in seventeen scenes that are separated by slow blackouts of "eight seconds," the story of struggles for power in which Henry usurps Lloyd's place in Mae's bed, and Lloyd kills Mae when she eventually walks out on Henry and him and their destitute existence. The violence committed in this play is the violence of the inarticulate.

Through the plays of Bond, Kroetz, Fassbinder, Wenzel, Vinaver, plays that outline the contemporary vision of tragedy, a new and different realism stripped bare came into drama in the 1970s in Europe. But this refinement of realism, to the extent that it could be called a movement, never happened here, largely because of the heavy input of psychology and speech in American theater, the scant interest in stylized gesture and emotion, the lack of attention to the nuances of language as a political condition. (Though one could point to such plays as Tavel's *Boy on the Straight-Back Chair,* Shepard's *Action,* Mamet's *Edmond,* Shank's *Sunset/Sunrise* as steps toward an American rethinking of realism, they are only isolated phenomena.) What Fornes has done in her approach to realism over the years, and *Mud* is the most austere example of this style to be produced in the theater on this side of the Atlantic, is to lift the burden of psychology, declamation, moralism, and sentimentality from the concept of character. She has freed characters from explaining themselves in a way that attempts to suggest interpretations of their actions, and put them in scenes that create a single emotive moment, as precise in what it does not articulate as in what does get said.

She rejects ordinary realism's clichés of thought patterns, how its characters project themselves in society; she rejects its melodramatic self-righteousness. Though her work is purposely presented in a flat space that emphasizes its frontality, and the actors speak in a noninflected manner, it is not the detached cool of hyper- or super- or photorealism, but more emotive, filled with content. Gestures, emptied of their excesses, are free to be more resonant. *The Danube* resounds with the unspeakable horror of nuclear death precisely because it is not named.

Mud's scenes seem, radically, to be a comment on what does not occur in performance, as if all the action had happened offstage. Fornes's realism subtracts information whereas the conventional kind does little more than add it to a scene. She turns realism upside down by attacking its materialism and in its place emphasizing the interior lives of her characters, not their exterior selves. Hers is not a drama infatuated with things, but the qualities that make a life. Even when Henry buys Mae lipstick and a mirror in which to see herself, the moment is not for her a cosmetic action but a recognition of a self in the act of knowing, an objectification of the self.

There is no waste in her productions. Fornes has always had a commonsense approach to drama that situates itself in the utter simplicity of her dialogue. She writes sentences, not paragraphs. Her language is a model of direct address, it has the modesty of a writer for whom English is a learned language. She is unique in the way she writes about sexuality, in a tender way that accents sexual feelings, not sex as an event. It is a bitterly sad moment when Henry, his body twisted, his speech thick with pain, begs Mae to make love to him: "I feel the same desires. I feel the same needs. I have not changed." Emotion is unhidden in her plays. Just as language is not wasted, so the actors don't waste movements. Each scene is a strong pictorial unit. Sometimes a scene is only an image, or a few lines of dialogue. Here realism is quotational, theater in close-up, freeze frame, theater made by a miniaturist: In *The Danube* an acted scene is replayed in front of the stage by puppets, creating a fierce honorableness in its comment on human action. It is not aggressive in its desire to create a world on a stage invested with moral imperatives, it is interested only in tableaux from a few lives in a particular place and time. Each scene presents a glimpse of imagery that is socially meaningful.

The pictorial aspect of this realism signifies an important change in theatrical attitudes toward space. Whereas traditional realism concerned itself with a confined physicality determined by "setting," the new realism is more open cosmologically, its characters iconic. That is one of the reasons why this emotive, aggressive realism is rooted in expressionist style. (Expressionism keeps realism from becoming melodrama.) Contemporary painting also turned to expressionism, after a period of superrealism, in order to generate an approach to emotion, narration, and content. If styles change according to new perceptions of human form and its socialization, then painting and theater, arts that must continually revise their opinions of figuration, should follow similar directions in any given period. Today, the exaggerated theatricality in everyday life has brought painting and theater closer together.

The new realism would be confined by mere setting, which is only informational. It needs to be situated in the wider poetic notion of "space" that has ontological references. In the ecology of theater, setting is a closed system of motion while space is more aligned to the idea of landscape that influences theater, not only in writing but in design, as a result of now regarding the stage as "performance space." The very idea of space itself indicates how much the belief that all the world's a stage has been literalized. The concept of theatrical space alludes to the global repercussions of human action, if only metaphorically. (It is not coincidental that the concept of "performance space" developed in the same period, the 1960s, as the exploration of outer space.)

In recent years Fornes has become such a self-assured director that the movement in her productions seems nearly effortless, totally inhibiting actorly artificiality. She doesn't force her actors' bodies on us in an attempt for them to dominate space. She leaves spaces on the stage unused. She makes the actors appreciate stillness as a theatrical idea, they are considerate toward other theatrical lives. And Fornes acknowledges the audience by giving them their own space and time in the productions. In *Mud* the short scenes and blackouts emphasize this attitude toward reception. They leave room for the audience to enter for contemplative moments. The authorial voice does not demand power over the theatrical experience. It is not territorial. There is room for subjectivity, as a corrective to evasive objectification, on the part of all those involved in the making and witnessing of the event. *Fefu and Her Friends* is the play that most literally invites the audience into the playing space—there are five of them to be exact—and in order to achieve this effect Fornes creates a style of acting that seems, simply, a way of talking, it is so real.

Fornes has found her own stage language, a method of discourse that unites play, actor, and space in an organic whole that is always showing how it thinks, even as it allows for fragments of thought, unruly contradictions. One of the characteristics of Fornes's plays is that they offer characters *in the process of thought*. Her characters often question received ideas, conventions, the idea of emotion, even how one engages in thought. "What would be the use of knowing things if they don't serve you, if they don't help you shape your life?" asks Henry. All thought must be useful to characters and find meaning through life itself, to allow life its fullest expression. Mae, who is studying reading and arithmetic, rejoices in the process of acquiring knowledge, even if, as she admits, her poor memory keeps her from retaining all that she is learning. *Mud* is imbued with a feminism of the most subtle order, an understanding based on the ruling idea that a free woman is one who has autonomy of thought. Mae's decision to leave home and seek a better life coincides with her new knowledge of her self and a sense that there is a world outside of the self.

On one level, Fornes's plays equate the pleasure of thinking with the measure of being. That so many of her plays—*Dr. Kheal, Tango Palace, Evelyn Brown*—besides those already mentioned here, to one degree or another deal with the acquisition of language, alludes to what must surely be one of her consistent interests: the relationship of language to thought and action. The dramatic language is finely honed to exclude excessive qualifiers, adjectives, clauses. Sentences are simple, they exist to communicate, to question. There is a purity to this language of understatement that does not assume anything, and whose dramatic potential rests in the search for meaning in human endeavor. That is why the human voice, as an embodiment of social values, has so significant a place in this kind of writing.

Fornes's work has a warm delicacy and grace that distinguish it from most of what is written today. Apart from her plays there is little loveliness in the theater. And yet I must stop to include Joseph Chaikin and Meredith Monk in this special group of artists, for they also reflect this "loveliness" of presence. Loveliness?—a humanism that guilelessly breathes great dignity into the human beings they imagine into life, and so propose to reality. Working for more than twenty years in Off Broadway's unheralded spaces, Fornes is an exemplary artist who through her writing and teaching has created a life in the theater away from the crass hype that attends so many lesser beings. How has she managed that rare accomplishment in this country's theater—a career? What is admirable about Fornes is that she is one of the last of the real bohemians among the writers who came to prominence in the 1960s. She never falsely tuned her voice to the times. She has simply been busy writing, working. If there were a dozen writers in our theater with Fornes's wisdom and graciousness it would be enough for a country, and yet even one of her is, sometimes, all that is necessary to feel the worth of the enormous effort it takes to live a life in the American theater.

STATE OF GRACE: MARIA IRENE FORNES AT SIXTY-TWO

Early in *Abingdon Square* a young woman says to an inquisitive friend, "You have to know how to enter another person's life." In many ways that rule of etiquette has shaped the theater of Maria Irene Fornes, whose profound theme has always been the conduct of life.

This is particularly true of *Abingdon Square,* in which she creates a universe more Catholic than any of the other worlds of her plays. The teenage Marion marries a loving older man, has an affair with another man, a child with a third, descends into a personal hell, and in the end nurses her husband after his stroke out of a sense of compassion and remembered love. At a time when so much writing about women (and men) celebrates the joys of sexual freedom, Fornes is writing about sin, penance, forgiveness, the power of love. She does not deny her characters the choice and excitement of self-discovery in transgression—in this case, adultery—but concerns herself instead with the repercussions of such liberating acts. *Abingdon Square,* then, is a counterreformation for our ideological age, in which responsibility for one's actions is regarded as a hindrance to personal fulfillment. Fornes's abiding humanism is in stark contrast to contemporary drama's moral relativism and contingency ploys.

Fornes is an unabashed moralist, which is why her thinking is so suited to the epic style she has been developing as a writer and director in recent years, at least since *Fefu and Her Friends.* Epic dramaturgy is rooted in the medieval morality play, which produced a synthesis of theatrical and spiritual style. If Brecht used this form to proselytize for his secular religion of communism, and the expressionists for the rebirth of modern man, Fornes makes it her own to represent the spiritual lives of women—the kinds of choices they make and why.

In her recent production of *Abingdon Square* at the San Diego Repertory Theatre she has brought all of these strands together in a staging of more clarity and evocativeness than the original production of the play in 1987, at the American Place Theatre in New York. The play itself has been considerably revised since a workshop at the Seattle Repertory Theatre in 1984 and Forness's own 1988 staging at the Studio Arena Theatre in Buffalo. In San Diego it was performed on alternate nights in English and in Spanish.

Stylistically, *Abingdon Square* is a journey play, but more important, another kind of *Lehrstück*, or learning play. Enlightenment must be spiritual, not merely the absorption of received ideas. Knowledge is understood in the Platonic sense, as absolute beauty, virtue. Forness's moral tale is strengthened by its distance from contemporary life and values and its elaboration over a ten-year period in the World War I era. It exudes a willful circumspection and sense of refinement.

In such a universe a person must know his or her worth. Marion looks to Dante for instruction. She keeps a diary to chronicle "things that are imagined." Learning—the book, the diary, the act of writing—holds a special place in the work of Fornes, for knowledge struggled over is a form of empowerment, a way of mastering one's life, a guide to value, the cultivation of worldliness. A manuscript must be of the illuminated kind, revelatory. (Kroetz develops this same theme in *Through the Leaves,* also using the epic form.) One of Forness's preoccupations in her work is the evolution of a higher, transcendent knowledge from sexual knowledge. The body is a body of knowledge.

Fornes takes a very ascetic approach to life. It is important to live in a state of grace and to save your soul, for there is a sense of heroism in the admission of shame. Her asceticism accepts the dualism of body and soul. Nothing must be extraneous, merely decorative, self-destructive. The good life is measured in terms of accountability, purity of heart, transformation through work and study. Chekhov had that code of ethics; his thought moved along the same bourgeois lines of self-improvement. The comedy of characters who fail to achieve this gracefulness, therefore, is never one of mockery or the grotesque. It is that of manners—humors—as when the dour husband Juster reads a long, suggestive passage about pollination from an E. A. Bowles garden book in a brief scene after Marion and a cousin gossip with "sinful" delight about a menage à trois they've heard of. How do the three of them make love? Forness's laughter sometimes comes in threes instead of the usual comic pairs. One of her early plays she called *The Successful Life of 3.*

More than any of her other works, *Abingdon Square* develops rhetorically through a prayerlike formality. Sentences are simple, short, unequivocating. Very few contractions are used. There is genuine communication, not diversionary chitchat. Characters tend to understand themselves and reflect on their behavior, traits reinforced by the liberal use of the pronoun "I" in strong, declarative sentences. At times the language is confessional, transcendent. In this way, the quality of voice is given primacy in the writing: It is the link to God. There is a certain sacredness attributed to the word because it expresses self-knowledge, which in Fornes's hierarchy of values is esteemed as a gift. The upper-class Marion shares this intuition, as well as the innate qualities of goodness and charity, with her earlier embodiment, the dirt-poor Mae of *Mud*.

Fornes's lessons evolve in a precisely defined horizontal space that emphasizes stations of a life. The lack of depth in the stage privileges the portrait, the still life of tableau, as an object of contemplation, accenting the iconic nature of the scenes. There are thirty-one of them, usually brief, some only visual, others in monologue, separated from one another by a blackout. The sense of miniaturization also enhances the dimension of scale, making the events onstage at times more dramatic. Every element of the staging moves toward a meditative rhythm, space to breathe between scenes, darkness and stillness to welcome thought. The stage space and the auditorium forge a single architectural unit.

The (didactic) pictorial frame, reflecting Fornes's early life as a painter, is well suited to the epic construction of the play. Doorways, windows, walls, glass panes serve to emphasize the sense of the frame. In one important scene—a frame within a frame—part of the center back wall gives way to reveal an alcove wherein Marion is practicing the mortification of the flesh, as it were, shaking, arms stretched heavenward, in a trancelike recitation of "Purgatorio" from *The Divine Comedy*. A concerned old aunt finds her and in the final moment of the scene lays her body over the conscience-stricken Marion, evoking the Pietà-like resonance of religious painting. Fornes's space is theological.

If this drama is positioned between heaven and hell, light and dark are its poetic counterparts. Before her marriage to the much older Juster, Marion rejoices, "In this house light comes through the windows as if it delights in entering. I feel the same." Toward the end of the play, when both husband and wife are at the brink of madness, Juster will say, "Paper would burn if it were held up to her glance. When I reached the door I saw her back reflected in the glass. She was so still that there was no life in her." The issue of enlightenment, which is so central to the work, is played out in the chiaroscuro effects of the staging. One can feel the sensuous interplay of light and emotion in the visual style that characterizes Fornes's directorial intelligence.

Besides emphasizing the pictorial, the San Diego staging, for all its quietude, was more operatic than the original. The highly emotional, taut quality of the writing, its subject matter of love, and the stylization of movements shaped the melodic line of the production. Scenes were played in many different musical moods, at times hymnlike, on occasion ragtime, then nocturne, or adagio. Richard Strauss's *Four Last Songs*, a touch of Vivaldi, or an aria from Purcell's *Dido and Aeneas* used between some of the scenes heightened their musical quality, transforming the work's epic nature by provoking at times a wonderful, humorous tension between melodrama and expressionism. The human, high drama was then subtly contrasted to the indifferent life of plants on the stage and of trees growing in the garden, glimpsed through the parlor doors leading outside, and through which Marion and her lover initially reveled in their illicit affair, now turned from farce to tragedy. If more and more directors here and abroad are becoming attracted to opera and music theater, this is a rare instance of the operatic informing dramaturgy in ways that point to new possibilities of rhythmic experimentation within the epic vocabulary. Melodrama is a natural inclination in the highly emotional space of passion and its repression that defines opera because it addresses, to a great degree, heroism. In fact, the triumph of passion over negotiation (the subject of contemporary life) is perhaps what is making artists and audiences turn now in increasing numbers to opera. The beauty of the soul *in extremis* is desperately needed on our stages ridden with role models instead of heroes, opinion in place of knowledge.

So is the imperative to create a greater place for artists with mature vision. It is one of the scandals of the American theater, obsessed as it is with "development," whether of the playwright or funding sources or subscribers (and the parallels between the real estate industry and the theater are notoriously striking in their attitude toward preservation), that at the age of sixty-two, after three decades of a richly committed life in the theater, Fornes is still working on the margins. Most of the theaters she works in, like the San Diego Repertory Theatre, which offered a home to this remarkable production, survive on the edge of bankruptcy. When *Abingdon Square* was produced recently in London it went from the fringe to the National Theatre.

At her age, and with such a long record of distinguished achievement entirely within the medium of theater, a fully elaborated directorial style, and a grand reputation as a teacher, Fornes should be given all that the American theater has to offer in terms of resources—choice of actors, technicians, designers, access to larger audiences, longer runs. Imagine what other artists might learn from Fornes. Imagine how her own work might grow under new artistic conditions. Yet, her work has never appeared on the main stage of any of the major theaters that pride themselves on providing an alternative to the commercial exigencies of Broadway—the Vivian Beaumont, the Guthrie, the Mark Taper Forum, Arena Stage, the American Repertory Theatre, the Public Theater, among countless others. At the center of theater's exclusionary practice and arrested development is the absence of the mature dramatic voice.

For too long the American theater system has ruthlessly infantilized artists and audiences by coddling "new" playwrights and directors, falsely setting up generation gaps where instead we should be able to see theater artists develop in relation to one another, generation to generation. An art form must carry on an internal dialogue with its own history, and the successive histories of artists and audiences, to honor cultural memory in any meaningful way. The American theater obscures the profound relationship between art and society at every turn. No space is created for American writers as they mature.

The American theater has never found a way to integrate its avant-garde artists into the larger world of theater as Europe did, by giving them a place in their major institutions after they've proved their worth, nor even the way that the film, literary, and art establishments/industries have done here. In theater the avant-garde spirit is made perpetual outcast. This dilemma increases as artists age, because they cannot constantly, to recall Lillian Hellman's good phrase, cut their conscience to fit each year's fashion, slavishly following the new hype of funding sources, theater publicists and boards, trendy "isms." Are you now or have you ever been an (avant-garde art) ist? The real twist in the theater scene is not that it pandered to the masses but that it pandered to the funding sources and their shifting "priorities." Both conservatives and progressives, the right and the left/liberal, have corrupted the funding process by politicizing culture at the most base level. Art has become a branch of journalism or the social sciences, and critical discourse mere publicity. Only the true artists of the theater can resist the grant hustle, the hype. They risk marginalization, obscurity, censure, unemployment. But then, being an artist is not a rights issue.

Fornes was in San Diego with her one-hundred-year-old mother Carmen, her frequent companion during theatrical engagements in this country and abroad. I hope that Fornes herself lives to be one hundred, still moving from place to place, bringing her work to the world without any trace of bitterness, simply considering herself lucky to be working in our economy of planned obsolescence of people and things, and that she may be fortunate in old age to have her own fellow travelers, if, that is, the light of our most courageous theater artists has not been snuffed out by the shades of official culture already appearing on the horizon of the twenty-first century.

ACTS OF KINDNESS

If spiritual sorrow is a quality of her moral universe, the physical reality of the body is at the center of its drama. In most of the plays Maria Irene Fornes has written in the past two decades illness and pain are everyday certitudes. Think of Julia with her open wound in *Fefu and Her Friends*, *Mud*'s hapless Henry and Lloyd, the mysteriously ill characters from *The Danube*, and the husband who suffers a stroke in *Abingdon Square*. Perhaps all along and all the while she has filigreed her work in delicate shades and with the economy of tenderness, Fornes, for whom a character's acquisition of knowledge is so insistent an ideal, has been imagining a language of pain. Her dramatic bodies act as epistemological sites, transformed by sexual experience, emotional expression, intellectual pursuit, or, symbolizing goodness, spiritual imbalance, evil. The individual body is never disconnected from the world but is a measure of its social biology.

More than any of her plays *Enter THE NIGHT* most completely attends to the perception of illness: AIDS, it is. But this play rejects the familiar comforts of social drama, even departing from convention and propriety in one piercing, long speech to expose the psychological process through which contemporary theater turns plays about illnesses into a genre, prophesying a future in which theater's subject matter is dictated by the illnesses most suffered by audience members, and funded willingly by pharmaceutical laboratories. Fornes's own drama is never cast with victims.

The disarming trio of the play, the nurse Tressa, her married friend Paula (she has heart trouble) who owns a farm, and Jack, a stage manager whose lover has died of AIDS, in the uninhibited bonds of a long friendship, dramatize different kinds of love and fantasy. Their unexpected cross-dressing and crossing of cultures elaborate the mysteries of spirit and flesh, race and gender, performance and fashion in scenes that are alternately innocent or psychosexually provocative, but surprisingly touching.

If the quoting of film dialogue and talk of actors and acting is a long-standing feature of Fornes's oeuvre, dating to the early plays *The Successful Life of 3* and *Molly's Dream*, in *Enter THE NIGHT* the performance situations are more emotionally charged, even allegorical in part. Fornes uses two films to highlight its themes: D. W. Griffith's 1920 silent *Broken Blossoms* and Frank Capra's *Lost Horizon* from 1937. The second act of the play opens with a cross-dressed enactment of the scene from *Broken Blossoms* in which the male character Huang (the Richard Barthelmess role, now played by Tressa), who has come to the aid of the young girl (Lillian Gish's role, now played by Jack) cruelly beaten by her father, with great care wraps her in an embroidered gown, crowns her with flowers, makes up her face, and places her softly in the bed in his room. Though they are never shown in the play itself, Griffith's actual film titles explain that Huang has left China to bring the message of the Buddha to the "barbarous Anglo-Saxons." He is the only civilizing force in the girl's wretched life.

The Oriental robe, slippers, box jacket, and pants that Tressa wears in this scene and earlier in the play have a strange attraction for her. The clothes make her feel like an Asian man: in her body, in her voice, in her face, in her feet. When she dresses like a Western man it is only for fun, whereas the Asian man in her clothes existential calm in the becoming suit of androgyny. Paula admires Tressa as a "lovely" man. Jack is soothed by seeing her dressed like this, and grows nervous if she wears women's clothes when they are together. But why? When for the first time Paula comes upon Jack and Tressa, cross-gendered, performing the last few minutes of their "act," which she recognizes immediately as a scene from *Broken Blossoms,* she is given a glimpse of their very private erotic world. The two who had made love one night long ago now caress each other in the silent signs of art, their ritualized behavior evolved into another form of lovemaking.

Tressa's cross-dressing is not mere play, but a state of mind inscribed in the most fervent gestures. Neither is it a subversive act: It is private, not social. It has no consciousness of a society beyond itself. Her performance, which comforts Jack and poeticizes her own passion for him, is more a reflection of Fornes's linkage of spirituality and sexuality, an ontological rather than a sociological condition. Elsewhere, in the more playful setting of *Fefu and Her Friends,* where the character Emma speaks of the "divine registry" of sexual performance and a heaven peopled with "divine lovers," the key to the kingdom is unequivocal: "If your faith is not entirely in it, if you just perform as an obligation and you don't feel the most profound devotion, if your spirit, your heart, and your flesh is not religiously delivered to it, you are condemned." Sexual feeling is a kind of spiritual energy, an exquisite radiance.

Fornes's characters, who always seem to be acting out scenes, reading, reciting, and listening to music—in general, demonstrating her love of the variousness of performance styles and rhetorical forms—know how to talk to each other and to share deeply felt emotions, often shocking in their combination of private revelation and guilessness. Heartbreak and humor generate the syncopated rhythms of the plays, making them seem remarkably light for all their soulful temper. The characters don't judge or psychologize: Among friends, there is only acceptance. In dramatic worlds that value human discourse and the knowledge gained from reading, conversation quickly develops into an exchange of questions and answers, books sometimes becoming metatexts, at other times, conversation flowing like the genre of philosophical dialogue. What is important is that one understands the arts of conversation and seduction, for the measure of a person's worth is the choice of words, the quality of voice, the generosity of spirit, the will to an erotic sublime. And when performance acts are used to explore hidden mind fields, there are subtle lessons between the lines on passion and intimacy, on faith, hope, and charity, on the significance of theatrical gesture as the tragicomic reality of human behavior. Fornes transforms drama into spiritual anthropology.

If *Broken Blossoms* amplifies the dramatic narrative at the level of the personal, *Lost Horizon* carries it to a cultural plane. Fornes, whose own writing at times has the simple ardor and openheartedness of a medieval nun, and not less an inclination toward instruction to compel the human drama, has intuited a metaphysical language in the manuals of piety that inspire these films, bestowing on them the pure yearning of folk art, or, considered in another perspective, the structure of myth. Her work is imbued with strong religious feeling, in its concern for the condition of the human soul and the moral issues attached to any contemplation of righteousness or redemption. When Jack, who is somewhat of a male version of *Fefu's* Julia, experiences a dark night of the soul in his nightmarish depiction of gang sex that can also be thought of as a mortification of the flesh, with much the same largesse that Chekhov would give the gift of consolation in the form of a beautiful image to one of his own grieving characters, in the closing scene of the play, Fornes has the women, now grouped with Jack in a Pietà image, recite with him moving passages from *Lost Horizon*. The three friends, in their sympathy of love and shared cultural memory, for their vision of the future marvelous turn to Shangri-La, a mythical abode in the mountains of Tibet that is the home of the High Lama, a more than two-hundred-year-old Catholic priest who founded this world of quietude and perfection, where neither sickness nor stress nor death rules. There is no irony, but rather a prepolitical innocence, in Fornes's use of the film as pure escapist fantasy.

While the world outside spirals toward disaster in its orgy of destruction

(Capra made the film as the Nazis prepared to tear apart European culture), the High Lama has been preserving its books, music, and other riches of the mind, so they can be rediscovered one day as a heritage of humankind, the "fragrance of history." His sermon on the mountain, only a fragment of which is quoted in the play, tells of a coming era when the meek shall inherit the earth and humanity weather its great storm. The filmic narrative is never revealed in the play, and neither is the film shown, but at its closing, as the High Lama's actual voice from the film is heard rhapsodizing on his dream of regeneration and tranquillity, the live voices join with his, their chorus echoing as if in prayer.

The three souls are brought together in a devout expression of healing and mercy. This is the true meaning of grace, always circulating in the world of Fornes, in the Augustinian sense it has come down through the ages. Or perhaps it is the glorious recompense of moral gravity sustained by charm. In her melody of virtue, the act of kindness has the most exquisite tone, reaffirming the transcendent power of art to bring spiritual renewal with the surrender to metaphor.

Isidore, I beg you.
Can't you see
You're breaking my heart?
'Cause while I'm so earnest,
You're still playing games.
—*Tango Palace*

STILL PLAYING GAMES

Ideology & Performance in the Theater of Maria Irene Fornes

A CLOWN tosses off witty repartee while tossing away the cards on which his lines are written; a love scene is played first by actors and then by puppets they manipulate; the audience sits in a semicircle around a woman desperately negotiating with invisible tormentors: The plays of Maria Irene Fornes precisely address the process of theater, how the authority of the word, the presence of the performer, and the complicity of the silent spectator articulate dramatic play. Throughout her career Fornes has pursued an eclectic, reflective theatricality. *A Vietnamese Wedding* (1967), for instance, "is not a play" but a kind of theater ceremony: "Rehearsals should serve the sole purpose of getting the readers acquainted with the text and the actions of the piece. The four people conducting the piece are hosts to the members of the audience who will enact the wedding." [1] In *Dr. Kheal* (1968) a manic professor addresses the audience in a form of speech torture; the stage realism of *Molly's Dream* (1968) rapidly modulates into the deliquescent atmosphere of dreams. *The Successful Life of 3* (1965) freezes the behavioral routines of a romantic triangle in a series of static tableaux, inter-

Originally published in *Feminine Focus: The New Women Playwrights*, ed. Enoch Brater (New York: Oxford University Press, 1989).

rupting the actors' stage presence in a way that anticipates "deconstructive" theater experiments of the 1970s and 1980s.[2] And the "Dada zaniness" of *Promenade* (1965; score by Al Carmines)—a musical parable of two Chaplinesque prisoners who dig their way to freedom—brilliantly counterpoints Brecht, Blitzstein, Bernstein, and Beckett, viewed "through Lewis Carroll's looking-glass."[3]

Despite their variety, Fornes's experiments share a common impulse: to explore the operation of the mise-en-scène on the process of dramatic action. Rather than naturalizing theatrical performance by assimilating the various "enunciators" of the stage—acting, music, set design, audience disposition— to a privileged gestural style encoded in the dramatic text (the strategy of stage realism, for instance), Fornes's plays suspend the identification between the drama and its staging.[4] The rhetoric of Fornes's major plays—*Fefu and Her Friends* (1977), *The Danube* (1983), and *The Conduct of Life* (1985)—is sparked by this ideological dislocation. At first glance, though, to consider Fornes's drama as "ideological" may seem capricious, for Fornes claims that except for *Tango Palace* her plays "are not Idea Plays. My plays do not present a thesis, or at least, let us say, they do not present a formulated thesis."[5] But to constrain theatrical ideology to the "thesis play," as though ideology were a fixed body of meanings to be "illustrated" or "realized" by an "Idea Play" or an "ideological drama," is to confine ideology in the theater too narrowly to the plane of the text.[6] For like dramatic action, theatrical action—performance—occupies an ideological field. Performance claims a provisional "identity" between a given actor and dramatic "character," between the geography of the stage and the dramatic "setting," and between the process of acting and the play's dramatic "action."[7] The theater also "identifies" its spectator, casts a form of activity within which subjective significance is created. In and out of the theater, ideologies function neither solely as "bodies of thought that we possess and invest in our actions nor as elaborate texts" but "as *ongoing social processes*" that address us, qualify our actions with meaning, and so continually "constitute and reconstitute who we are."[8] Whether the audience is explicitly characterized (as in Osborne's *The Entertainer* or Griffiths's *Comedians*), symbolically represented (as by the spotlight in Beckett's *Play*), or mysteriously concealed by the brilliant veil of the fourth wall, performance refigures "who we are" in the theater. Our attendance is represented in the "imaginary relationship" between "actors," "characters," and "spectators," where ideology is shaped as theatricality.[9]

Trained as a painter, Fornes is, not surprisingly, attracted to the visual procedures of the mise-en-scène. Her interest in the stage, though, stems from a

theatrical rather than an explicitly political experience, Roger Blin's 1954 production of *Waiting for Godot*: "I didn't know a word of French. I had not read
the play in English. But what was happening in front of me had a profound impact without even understanding a word. Imagine a writer whose theatricality
is so amazing and so important that you could see a play of his, not understand
one word, and be shook up." [10] The theatricality of *Godot* is deeply impressed
on Fornes's pas de deux, *Tango Palace* (1964). Like Beckett, Fornes contests a
rhetorical priority of modern realism: that stage production should represent
an ideal "drama" and conceal the process of performance as a legitimate object
of attention. An "obsession that took the form of a play," [11] *Tango Palace* takes
place in a stage utopia, decked out with a chair, secretary, mirror, water jug,
three teapots, a vase, and a blackboard—theatrical props rather than the signs
of a dramatic "setting." The rear wall contains Isidore's "shrine," an illuminated
recess holding his special props, as well as Isidore himself: a stout, heavily
rouged, high-heeled, androgynous clown. The stage is Isidore's domain: When
he gestures, his shrine is lit; at another gesture, chimes sound. To begin the play,
Isidore creates his antagonist—Leopold, a handsome, business-suited man delivered to the stage in a canvas bag. Isidore introduces him to the set and its
props ("This is my whip. [*Lashing* LEOPOLD] And that is pain"), [12] choreographs
his movements, and gradually encourages him to play the series of routines
that occupy their evening. Like Isidore's furniture, their mutual performances
are classical, "influenced by their significance as distinct types representative
of the best tradition, not only in the style and execution but in the choice of
subject" (130). Isidore's stage is a palace of art, its history contained in its accumulated junk: "the genuine Persian helmet I wore when I fought at Salamis"
(132), a "Queen Anne walnut armchair. Representing the acme of artistic craftsmanship of the Philadelphia school. Circa 1740," a "Louis Quinze secretary"
(130), a "rare seventeenth-century needlework carpet," a "Magnificent marked
Wedgwood vase," a "Gutenberg Bible" (136–37). Consigned to the stage, where
behavior becomes "acting," where objects become props and history a scenario
for role-playing, Isidore and Leopold engage in a fully theatricalized combat,
rehearsing a series of contests ordered not by a coherent plot but by the violent,
sensual rhythms of the tango. [13]

Although the events of *Tango Palace* often seem spontaneous, they are hardly
improvised; the play pays critical attention to the place of the "text" on the
stage. The dramatic text is usually traced into the spectacle, represented not
as text but as acting, movement, speech, and gesture. The text of *Tango Palace*,

though, is assigned a theatrical function, identified as a property of the performance. For Isidore's brilliance is hardly impromptu; his ripostes are scripted, printed on the cards he nonchalantly tosses about the stage.

> These cards contain wisdom. File them away. (*Card*) Know where they are. (*Card*) Have them at hand. (*Card*) Be one upon whom nothing is lost. (*Card*) Memorize them and you'll be where you were. (*Card*) . . . These are not my cards. They are yours. It's you who needs learning, not me. I've learned already. (*Card*) I know all my cards by heart. (*Card*) I can recite them in chronological order and I don't leave one word out. (*Card*) What's more I never say a thing which is not an exact quotation from one of my cards. (*Card*) That's why I never hesitate. (*Card*) Why I'm never short of an answer. (*Card*) Or a question. (*Card*) Or a remark, if a remark is more appropriate. (133–34)

Isidore at once illustrates, parodies, and challenges the absent authority of the text in modern performance: "Study hard, learn your cards, and one day, you too will be able to talk like a parrot" (135). *Tango Palace*, like Beckett's empty stages and Handke's prisons of language, explores the rich tension between the vitality of the performers and the exhausting artifice of their performance, the impoverished dramatic conventions, false furnishings, and parrotlike repetition of words that are the only means of "life" on the stage. Yet Isidore's text also suggests the inadequacy of this dichotomy by demonstrating how the theater insistently textualizes all behavior undertaken within its confines. The more "spontaneously" Leopold struggles to escape Isidore's arty hell, for instance, the more scripted his actions become: "LEOPOLD *executes each of* ISIDORE'S *commands at the same time as it is spoken, but as if* HE *were acting spontaneously rather than obeying*":

> ISIDORE AND LEOPOLD: Anybody there! Anybody there! (*Card*) Let me out. (*Card*) Open up! (*Card*). (136)

Even burning Isidore's cards offers no relief, since to be free of the text on the stage is hardly to be free at all. It is simply to be silent, unrealized, dead:

> LEOPOLD: I'm going to burn those cards.
> ISIDORE: You'll die if you burn them . . . don't take my word for it. Try it.
> (LEOPOLD *sets fire to a card.*)
> What in the world are you doing? Are you crazy?

(ISIDORE *puts the fire out.*)
Are you out of your mind? You're going to die.
Are you dying?
Do you feel awful?
(ISIDORE *trips* LEOPOLD.)
There! You died. (139)

Tango Palace dramatizes the condition of theater—the dialectical tension between fiction and the flesh—and implies the unstable place of theater in the
world that surrounds it, the world that Leopold struggles to rejoin. The theater can offer only illusion, not the gritty reality, the "dirt" that Leopold wants:
"What I want, sir, is to live with that loathsome mess near me, not to flush
it away. To live with it for all those who throw perfume on it. To be so dirty
for those who want to be so clean" (157). Isidore's "cave," like Plato's, can only
provide illusion, yet in *Tango Palace*—as in any theater—artifice is inextricably
wrought into the sense of the real. Even Leopold's final execution of Isidore
serves only to extend their mutual struggle, for Isidore's impossibly stagey death
is followed naturally by his equally stagey resurrection, as he returns dressed
like an angel, carrying his stack of cards and beckoning to Leopold; "LEOPOLD
walks through the door slowly, but with determination. HE *is ready for the next
stage of their battle*" (162).

Tango Palace provides a vision, an allegory perhaps, of how the stage produces
a reality, but produces it as image, performance, theater. Since *Tango Palace*,
and especially since *Fefu and Her Friends*, Fornes's plays have become at once
more explicitly political in theme, more rigorous in exploring the ideological
relation between theatrical and dramatic representation, and more effectively
engaged in repudiating the "burden of psychology, declamation, morality, and
sentimentality" characteristic of American realism.[14] Indeed, Fornes's recent
work frequently frames "realism" in an alienating, critical mise-en-scène that
alters our reading of the performance and of the drama it sustains. *The Danube,*
for instance, presents a love story between an American businessman and a
Hungarian working girl. This parable of East-West relations develops the tentative romance against a distant background of European conflict and against
the immediate physical debilitation of the cast, who seem to suffer from radi-
ation sickness: They develop sores, become crippled, feeble, ragged, and ashen.
Although many scenes in *The Danube* are minutely "realistic" in texture, the
play's staging intervenes between the spectator and the conventions of realistic performance by interrupting the defining moment of realistic rhetoric: the

identification of stage performance with the conventions of social behavior. The play is staged on a platform—not in a stage "room"—held between four posts that serve an openly theatrical function: Postcard-like backdrops are inserted between the rear posts, a curtain is suspended from the downstage pair, and between scenes smoke is released from holes in the platform itself. In its proportions the set is reminiscent of a puppet theater, and much of the action seems to imply that the characters are manipulated by an outside agency. And, as in *Tango Palace,* the text of *The Danube* is again objectified, held apart from the actors' charismatic presence. In fact, it was a "found object" that stimulated Fornes's conception of the use of language in the play:

> Fornes was walking past a thrift shop on West 4th Street, saw some 78 rpm records in a bin, liked the way they looked even before she knew what they were . . . so she bought one for a dollar. Turns out it was a language record, the simplest sentences, first in Hungarian, then in English. "There was such tenderness in those little scenes," she recalls—introducing people, ordering in restaurants, discussing the weather—"that when the Theater for the New City asked me to do an antinuclear piece, I thought of . . . how sorrowful it would be to lose the simple pleasures of our own era."[15]

Many scenes of *The Danube* open with a language-lesson tape recording of the opening lines of stage dialogue: We hear the mechanical inflections of the taped English and Hungarian sentences and then the actors onstage perform the same lines in character, naturally.[16] On the one hand, this technique emphasizes the elocutionary dimension of language, how speech is already textualized in the procedures of social action—"*Unit One. Basic sentences. Paul Green meets Mr. Sandor and his daughter Eve*";[17] "*Unit Three. Basic sentences. Paul and Eve go to the restaurant*" (49). Yet although the tape recordings underscore the "text" of social exchange, the actors' delivery—insofar as it is "naturalistic," spoken "with a different sense, a different emphasis" (42)—necessarily skews our attention from the code of social enactment to the "presence" of "personality" it seems to disclose. Onstage, *The Danube* suspends the identification between language and speech. The performance dramatizes the problematic of "social being," the dialectical encounter between the individual subject and the codes of his or her realization, the "intersection of social formations and . . . personal history."[18] In fact, to speak in an "unscripted" manner is simply to act incomprehensibly, to forego recognition. The characters' infrequent, trancelike monologues are not only spoken out of context, they are apparently unheard by others on the stage.[19] We see the characters physically deteriorate, but they repeatedly deny that their illnesses are out of the ordinary; when they speak textbook patter, they can be realized as "social beings," but when they attempt to speak expressively, they speak to no one, not even to themselves. To be known in *The Danube* is necessarily to "talk like a machine," say only what the "machines" of language and behavior permit one to say (62).

The Danube discovers "the poisons of the nuclear age" in the processes of culture.[20] The machine of language and the cognate conventions of social life—dating, work, medicine, international relations—represent and so inevitably distort the human life they sustain, the life that visibly decays before our eyes. This is the point of the two brilliant pairs of scenes that conclude the play. In Scene 12 Paul's illness finally drives him to the point of leaving Hungary and Eve; the scene is replayed in Scene 13, as "*Paul, Eve, and Mr. Sandor operate puppets whose appearance is identical to theirs.*" Scenes 14 and 15 reverse this procedure, as Scene 14 is played first by puppets and then repeated in Scene 15—culminating in Eve's poetic farewell to the Danube and a blinding flash of white light—by the actors. Like the tape recordings, the puppet scenes disrupt the "natural" assimilation of "character" to the actor through the transparent gestural codes of social behavior. Like the language they speak, the gestures that constitute "character" are shown to be an autonomous text, as effectively—though differently—performed by puppets as by people. The proxemics of performance are shown to occupy the "intersection" between individual subjectivity and the social codes of its representation and recognition. Conventions of politics, codes of conduct, and systems of signification frame the platform of social action in *The Danube*; like invisible hands, they guide the human puppets of the stage.

The formal intricacy of *The Danube* opens a dissonance between speech and language, between the bodies of the performers and the gestures of their enactment, between life and the codes with which we conduct it. This somber play typifies Fornes's current investigation of the languages of the stage, which are given a more explicitly political inflection in *The Conduct of Life*. Set in a Latin American military state, *The Conduct of Life* prismatically reflects the interdependence of politics, power, and gender. The play takes the form of a loose sequence of negotiations between Orlando (a lieutenant in the military) and his wife, Leticia; his commander, Alejo; a domestic servant, Olimpia; and Nena, a girl Orlando keeps in a warehouse and repeatedly rapes. Husband and

wife, torturer and victim, man and woman, master and servant: From the opening moments of the play, when we see Orlando doing jumping jacks in the
dark and vowing to "achieve maximum power" by being "no longer . . . overwhelmed by sexual passion,"[21] the play traces the desire for mastery through a
refracting network of relations—work, marriage, career, politics, sex.

Rape is, however, the defining metaphor of social action in the play, and the
scenes between Orlando and Nena emblematize the play's fusion of sexual and
political relations. Alejo may be rendered "impotent" by Orlando's vicious tor-
turing of an opponent (75), but torturer and victim are bound in an unbreak-
able embrace. Indeed, Orlando speaks to Nena much as he does to justify his
regime: "What I do to you is out of love. Out of want. It's not what you think.
I wish you didn't have to be hurt. I don't do it out of hatred. It is not out of
rage. It is love" (82). Orlando's rhetoric is chilling; that this "love" should be
reciprocated measures the accuracy of Fornes's penetrating examination of the
conduct of social power. Late in the play, Nena recounts her life—sleeping in
the streets, living in a box with her grandfather ("It is a big box. It is big enough
for two" [83])—and how she came to be abducted by Orlando. She concludes:

> I want to conduct each day of my life in the best possible way. I should value
> the things I have. And I should value all those who are near me. And I should
> value the kindness that others bestow upon me. And if someone should treat
> me unkindly, I should not blind myself with rage, but I should see them and
> receive them, since maybe they are in worse pain than me. (84–85)

Rather than taking a resistant, revolutionary posture, Nena accepts a Christian
humility, an attitude that simply enforces her own objectification, her continued abuse. Beaten, raped, owned by Orlando, Nena finally adopts a morality
that—grotesquely—completes her subjection to him and to the social order
that empowers him. Indeed, when Leticia learns how to conduct her own life,
by killing Orlando, she also reveals how inescapably Nena's exploitation lies
at the foundation of this world: She hands the smoking revolver to Nena, who
takes it with *"terror and numb acceptance"* (88).

Finally, *The Conduct of Life* uses the disposition of the stage to reflect and
extend this vision of social corruption. The stage is constructed in a series of
horizontal, tiered planes: The forestage area represents the living room; a low
(eighteen-inch) platform slightly upstage represents the dining room; this platform steps up (eighteen inches) onto the hallway; the hallway is succeeded by a

three-foot drop to the basement, in which are standing two trestle tables; a stair-case leads to the platform farthest upstage, the warehouse. The set provides a visual emblem of the hierarchy of power in the play. More significantly, though, the set constructs a powerful habit of vision for the spectators. The living and dining rooms—those areas of public sociability where Olimpia serves coffee, Leticia and Orlando discuss their marriage, Olimpia and Nena gossip while pre-paring dinner—become transparent to the audience as windows onto the up-stage sets and the occluded "setting" they represent: the warehouses and base-ments where the real life of this society—torture, rape, betrayal—is conducted.

As in _The Danube,_ the staging of _The Conduct of Life_ dislocates the familiar surfaces of stage realism. On occasion, however, Fornes renders the ideologi-cal process of theater visible not simply by disrupting familiar conventions but by dramatizing the audience's implication in the conduct of the spectacle. Indeed, Fornes's most assured play, _Fefu and Her Friends,_ explores the ideol-ogy of stage gender through a sophisticated use of stage space to construct a "dramatic" relation between stage and audience. The play conceives the gender dynamics implicit in the realistic perspective by disclosing the gendered bias of the spectator's interpretive authority, "his" transcendent position above the women of the stage. The play opens at a country house in 1935. The title char-acter has invited a group of women to her home to rehearse a brief series of skits for a charity benefit to raise money for a newly founded organization. In the first scene the women arrive and are introduced. Many seem to have been college friends, two seem to be lovers, or ex-lovers. Much of the action of the scene centers on Julia, who is confined to a wheelchair as the result of a myste-rious hunting accident: Although the bullet missed her, she is paralyzed from the waist down. In Part II, Fornes breaks the audience into four groups that tour Fefu's home—garden, study, bedroom, and kitchen: "These scenes are per-formed simultaneously. When the scenes are completed the audience moves to the next space and the scenes are performed again. This is repeated four times until each group has seen all four scenes." [22] In Part III the audience is returned to the auditorium. The women rehearse and decide the order of their program. Fefu goes outside to clean her shotgun, and suddenly a shot rings out; Julia falls dead, though again she does not seem to have been hit.

In the theater, the play examines the theatrical poetics of the feminine not only as "theme" but in the structuring of the spectacle itself, by unseating the spectator of "realism" and dramatizing "his" controlling authority over the con-struction of stage gender. Early in the play, for instance, Fefu looks offstage and sees her husband approaching: "FEFU *reaches for the gun, aims and shoots.* CHRISTINA *hides behind the couch. She and* CINDY *scream. . . .* FEFU *smiles proudly. She blows on the mouth of the barrel. She puts down the gun and looks out again"* (9). As Fefu explains once Phillip has stood up again, "It's a game we play. I shoot and he falls. Whenever he hears the blast he falls. No matter where he is, he falls." Although Phillip is never seen in the play, his attitudes shape Fefu's stage characterization. For as she remarks in her first line in the play, "My husband married me to have a constant reminder of how loathsome women are" (7). The shooting game provides an emblem for the relation between vision and gender in *Fefu*, for whether the shells are "real" or "imaginary" ("I thought the guns were not loaded," remarks Cindy; "I'm never sure," replies Fefu [12]), the exchange of power takes place through the "sighting" of the other.[23]

The authority of the absent male is everywhere evident in *Fefu*, and particularly is imaged in Julia's paralysis. As Cindy suggests when she describes the accident, Julia's malady is a version of Fefu's "game": "I thought the bullet hit her, but it didn't . . . the hunter aimed . . . at the deer. He shot":

Julia and the deer fell. . . . I screamed for help and the hunter came and examined Julia. He said, "She is not hurt." Julia's forehead was bleeding. He said, "It is a surface wound. I didn't hurt her." I know it wasn't he who hurt her. It was someone else. . . . Apparently there was a spinal nerve injury but the doctors are puzzled because it doesn't seem her spine was hurt when she fell. She hit her head and she suffered a concussion but that would not affect the spinal nerve. So there seems to be no reason for the paralysis. She blanks out and that is caused by the blow on the head. It's a scar in the brain. (14–15)

The women of *Fefu and Her Friends* share Julia's invisible "scar," the mark of their paralyzing subjection to a masculine authority that operates on the "imaginary," ideological plane. The hunter is kin to Julia's hallucinatory "voices" in Part II, the "judges" who enforce her psychic dismemberment: "They clubbed me. They broke my head. They broke my will. They broke my hands. They tore my eyes out. They took away my voice." Julia's bodily identification is broken down and reordered according to the "aesthetic" canons prescribed by the male voice ("He said that . . . to see a woman running creates a disparate and incongruous image in the mind. It's antiaesthetic" [24–25]), the silent voice that characterizes women as "loathsome." This internalized "guardian" rewrites Julia's identity at the interface of the body itself, where the masculine voice materializes itself in the woman's flesh. Other women in the play envy "being like a man.

Thinking like a man. Feeling like a man" (13), but as Julia's coerced "prayer" suggests, to be subject to this representation of the feminine is to resign humanity ("The human being is of the masculine gender"), independence ("The mate for man is woman and that is the cross man must bear"), and sexuality ("Woman's spirit is sexual. That is why after coitus they dwell in nefarious feelings" [25]). The subliminal masculine voice inscribes the deepest levels of psychological and physiological identification with the crippling gesture of submission:

> (*Her head moves as if slapped.*)
> JULIA: Don't hit me. Didn't I just say my prayer?
> (*A smaller slap.*)
> JULIA: I believe it. (25)

Fornes suggests that "Julia is the mind of the play," and Julia's scene articulates the shaping vision of *Fefu* as a whole, as well as organizing the dramatic structure of Part II. In the kitchen scene, for instance, Fornes recalls Julia's torture in Paula's description of the anomie she feels when a relationship breaks up ("the break up takes place in parts. The brain, the heart, the body, mutual things, shared things" [27]); the simultaneity of the two scenes is marked when Sue leaves the kitchen with soup for Julia. Sue's departure also coordinates Julia's prayer with the concluding section of the kitchen scene. Julia's submission to the voice in the bedroom is replaced by Paula and Cecilia's suspension of their unspoken love affair: "Now we look at each other like strangers. We are guarded. I speak and you don't understand my words" (28). This dramatic counterpoint invites us to see Paula and Cecilia's relationship, Cindy's violent dream of strangulation (in the study scene), Emma's thinking "about genitals all the time," and Fefu's constant, nightmarish pain (in the lawn scene) as transformations of Julia's more explicit subjection.

The action of *Fefu and Her Friends* takes place under the watchful eyes of Phillip, of the hunter, of Julia's "guardians," a gaze that constructs, enables, and thwarts the women of the stage: "Our sight is a form they take. That is why we take pleasure in seeing things" (35). In the theater, of course, there is another invisible voyeur whose performance is both powerful and "imaginary"—the spectator. *Fefu and Her Friends* extends the function of the spectator beyond the metaphorical register by decentering "his" implicit ordering of the theatricality of the feminine. First performed by the New York Theatre Strategy in a Soho loft, the play originally invited the spectators to explore the space of Fefu's home. In the American Place Theatre production, the spectators were invited, row by row, to different areas of the theater—a backstage kitchen, an upstairs bedroom, the garden and study sets—before being returned to the auditorium, but not to their original seats.[24] At first glance, Fornes's staging may seem simply a "gimmick," a formalist exercise in "multiple perspective" something like Alan Ayckbourn's *Norman Conquests*.[25] Yet Ayckbourn's trilogy—each play takes a different set of soundings from the events of a single weekend—implies that there could be, in some mammoth play, a single ordering and relation of events, one "drama" expressed by a single plot and visible from a single perspective. In this regard the structure of *The Norman Conquests*, like its philandering hero, Norman, exudes a peculiarly masculine confidence, "The faith the world puts in them and they in turn put in the world," as Christina puts it.[26] Despite Fornes's suggestion that "the style of acting should be film acting,"[27] *Fefu and Her Friends* bears little confidence in the adequacy or authority of the single viewing subject characteristic of both film and fourth-wall realism. In this sense, *Fefu* more closely approximates the decentering disorientation of environmental art than "some adoption by the theater of cinematic flexibility and montage."[28] Different spectators see the drama in a different sequence, and in fact see different plays, as variations invariably enter into the actors' performances. Fornes not only draws the audience into the performance space, she actively challenges and suspends the epistemological structure of realistic vision, predicated as it is on an invisible, singular, motionless, masculine interpreter situated outside the field of dramatic *and* theatrical activity. By reordering our function in the theatrical process, *Fefu* reorders our relation to, and interpretation of, the dramatic process it shapes.[29]

As Cecilia says at the opening of Part III, after we have returned to the auditorium, "we each have our own system of receiving information, placing it, responding to it. That system can function with such a bias that it could take any situation and translate it into one formula" (29). In performance, *Fefu and Her Friends* dramatizes and displaces the theatrical "system" that renders "woman" visible: the predication of feminine identity on the sight of the spectator, a "judge." Fornes regards traditional plot conventions as naturalizing a confining set of feminine roles: "In a plot play the woman is either the mother or the sister or the girlfriend or the daughter. The purpose of the character is to serve the plot."[30] In this sense Fornes's theatrical strategy may be seen as an attempt to retheorize the interpretive operation of theatrical vision. Fornes replaces the "objective" and objectifying relations of masculine vision with the "fluid boundaries" characteristic of feminist epistemology.[31] As Patrocinio Schweickart argues, summarizing Nancy Chodorow and Carol Gilligan, "men define themselves through individuation and separation from others, while women have more flexible ego boundaries and define and experience themselves in terms of their affiliations and relationships with others."[32] The consequences of this distinction have been widely applied and have become recently influential in studies of reading, studies that provide an interpretive analogy to the action of Fornes's dramaturgy. Schweickart suggests that in a feminist, reader-oriented theory, "the central issue is not of control or partition, but of managing the contradictory implications of the desire for relationship . . . and the desire for intimacy."[33] David Bleich, surveying actual readings provided by his students, suggests that "women *enter* the world of the novel, take it as something 'there' for that purpose; men *see* the novel as a result of someone's action and construe its meaning or logic in those terms."[34] Writing the play, Fornes sought to avoid "writing in a linear manner, moving forward," and instead undertook a series of centrifugal experiments, exploring characterization by writing a series of improvisational, extraneous scenes.[35] But while Fornes again disowns political or ideological intent ("I don't mean linear in terms of what the feminists claim about the way the male mind works," she goes on to say), her suspension of plot organization for a more atmospheric or "environmental" procedure articulates the gendered coding of theatrical interpretation. Perhaps as a result, the staging of *Fefu* challenges the institutional "objectivity" of theatrical vision. For the play not only realizes Julia's absent voices, it casts us as their speakers, since we enact the role of her unseen, coercive tormentors. The play reshapes our relation to the drama, setting our interpretive activity within a performance structure that subordinates "plot" to "environment" and that refuses our recourse to a single, external point of view.

The "educational dramatics" of *Fefu and Her Friends* not only alert us to the paralyzing effect of a patriarchal ideology on the dramatic characters; they also imply the degree to which this ideology is replicated in the coercive "formula" of realistic sight.[36] As Emma's speech on the "Environment" suggests ("Environment knocks at the gateway of the senses" [31]), the theatrical activity of Part II reorders the traditional hierarchy of theatrical perception—privileging the drama to its performance—and so suspends the "objective" absence of the masculine eye. *Fefu* criticizes the realistic theater's order of subjection, an order which, like "civilization," is still "A circumscribed order in which the whole has not entered"; even Emma's "environment" is characterized as "him" (32). In *Fefu and Her Friends,* vision is achieved only through a strategy of displacement, by standing outside the theatrical "formula" of realism in order to witness its "bias." The play undertakes to dramatize both the results of that bias—in the various deformations suffered by Julia, Fefu, and their friends—and to enact the "other" formula that has been suppressed, the formula that becomes the audience's mode of vision in the theater. To see *Fefu* is not to imagine an ideal order, a single, causal "plot" constituted specifically by our absence from the performance. For *Fefu and Her Friends* decenters the absent "spectator" as the site of authentic interpretation, replacing "him" with a self-evidently the-atricalized body, an "audience," a community sharing irreconcilable yet inter-dependent experiences. The perspective offered by the realistic box set appears to construct a community of witnesses, but is in fact grounded in the sight of a single observer; the realistic audience sees with a single eye. *Fefu* challenges the "theory" of realistic theater at its source by dramatizing—and displacing—the covert authority of the constitutive *theoros* of naturalism and the social order it reproduces: the offstage man.[37] In so doing, *Fefu* provides an experience con-sonant with the play's climactic dramatic event. Much as we are returned to the auditorium in Part III, to assume the role of "spectator" with a fuller sense of the social legitimacy embodied in that perspective, so Fefu finally appropriates the objectifying "bias" of the unseen man in order to defend herself—and free Julia—from its oppressive view. Fefu cleans the play's central "apparatus" and then assumes the hunter's part, the "sight" that subjects the women of the stage:

(*There is the sound of a shot.* CHRISTINA *and* CECILIA *run out.* JULIA *puts her hand to her forehead. Her hand goes down slowly. There is blood on her forehead. Her head falls back.* FEFU *enters holding a dead rabbit in her arms. She stands behind* JULIA.

FEFU: I killed it . . . I just shot . . . and killed it . . . Julia. (41)

Despite the success of *Fefu and Her Friends* and of several later plays—*Evelyn Brown* (1980), *Mud* (1983), *Sarita* (1984)—addressing gender and power issues, Fornes refuses to be identified solely as a "feminist" playwright.[38] Spanning the range of contemporary theatrical style (experimental theater, realism, "absurd" drama, musical theater, satiric revue), Fornes's drama resists formal or thematic categorization. What pervades her writing is a delicate, sometimes rueful, occa-sionally explosive irony, a witty moral toughness replacing the "heavy, slow, laborious and pedestrian" didacticism we may expect of "ideological" drama. Brecht was right, of course, to encourage the members of his cast to play against such a sense of political theater: "We must keep the tempo of a run-through and infect it with quiet strength, with our own fun. In the dialogue the exchanges must not be offered reluctantly, as when offering somebody one's last pair of boots, but must be tossed like so many balls."[39] Like Brecht's, Fornes's theater generates the "fun," the infectious sophistication of a popular art. Juggling the dialectic between "theater for pleasure" and "theater for instruction," Fornes is still—earnestly, politically, theatrically—"playing games."

WATER UNDER THE BRIDGE

From Tango Palace *to* Mud

I LIKED the other title better, *There! You Died,* but Irene wanted to change it because, as she wrote me before we met, others had found it confusing. She actually wrote "incomprehensible," which I couldn't understand at all, though they apparently thought it meant "there (not here) and that something went wrong with the punctuation." I still prefer the other title because of its exclamatory point, which—it still seems pretty clear—deploys the adverbial there to stress what happened here, whether it happened or not, though even if it didn't sooner or later it will. "Are you out of your mind? You're going to die. Are you dying? Do you feel awful?"[1] If not, you probably should. Despite the odds on that, and the impeccable punctuation, the title was changed to *Tango Palace* after we did the play, in 1963, at The Actor's Workshop of San Francisco.

Since that's water under the bridge, as Isidore might say, tossing one of his cards, I should probably let it pass, but reading the text after many years I'm struck, once more, by Leopold's remark, "I know there is a way out because there have been moments when I've been away from here" (*Tango,* 143). Where those moments were is not exactly clear, for like Gertrude Stein's Oakland, across the bridge from San Francisco, there's no there there, and when he walks through the door at the end, determined as he's ever been, the implication is that wherever he thinks he's going it's nowhere else but here. One is tempted to say, of course, that in the capricious vicinity of Isidore's shrine that is neither here nor there, which might have occurred to Leopold when he first emerged from a sack, as from a uterine dream, to the strains of "A Sleepy Lagoon." It may be a tempest in one of the teapots among the properties on stage, but with Isidore as a pudgy Ariel about to become a malignant Prospero—pedagogue, wizard, master of the revels—"this music crept by me upon the waters" (*The Tempest*, I.2.394) back to the metaphysics around the grammar of *There! You Died*. For, enchanting as the song may be, it is merely the derisive accompaniment to the parody of a birth. "Look what the stork has brought me," says the enraptured Isidore (*Tango*, 129), who might even be thrilled at the thought that we die into this world, though the prospect was, I'm sure, always already there, written on one of his cards.

Needless to say, he dismisses the voice coming from elsewhere that Leopold claims to hear, and as for the inscription tattooed on Leopold's chest—"This is man. Heaven or bust."—he considers it in "terrible taste" (133). With the logos out of the picture and teleology itself a bust, collapsing the bridge from here to there, Isidore himself is ready to fill the breach, declaring himself (in falsetto) the one and only voice: "It's me . . . me . . . It's me . . . and only me" (135). Unfortunately for Leopold, all that this establishes—as Isidore cheerfully admits— is that he's way down at the bottom, while Isidore's at the top, with the space around them infinite, "enclosed as it may be, because there is not a third person. And if the space around us is infinite, so is, necessarily, the space between us" (138). Which is not exactly a void but more like an extension or echo chamber of the narcissist's lagoon. "The memory of / the moments of love / will haunt us forever . . . ," but the spatial dynamics are tricky, as to where (or when) that was, so no sense dwelling on the water into which, like the Greek's imponderable river, you can't step twice. But wait: To whom does that *you* refer? for there must surely be a card saying, "Never say you can't." Or, in another language, *"Dime con quien andas y te dire quien eres . . . (Card)* Spanish proverb meaning . . . You know what it means" (135). What it means is that, if it can even be imagined, Isidore might attempt it, as if what was really in the cards were, for all their scattered redundancy, a Word Perfect program to the Eternal Return.

"Memorize them and you'll be where you were *(Card)*. Be where you are. Then and now" (133), transferring to the plane of the temporal the problematics of "there (not here)." As it is, even before he returns as an angel to end the play beginning again, Isidore seems to determine events that are going to happen twice: once in thought, then sooner or later done, though the inevitable seems to occur as if, being remembered, it were merely improvised (which may be, *pace* Heidegger, what we mean by being itself). A typical scenario, or case in point: "I'm supposed to sit there imagining a field of orange blossoms and then you're going to pour a bucket of water on my head" (143). Which is precisely what Leopold does—is it water from under the bridge?—when Isidore can't erase the boundless orange grove that, prompted to imagine an elsewhere, he invented to forget. Never mind that old conundrum of stepping into the river twice: In those "thousands and thousands of acres" (145) with their infinite mess of rotting oranges, how one steps at all is a matter for chaos theory, as it is on a smaller scale when Isidore is teaching Leopold the Argentine tango, and reminds him that dancing "is the art whereby the feelings of the mind are expressed by measured steps." Here the problem would seem to be that, whatever the feelings are, the habits of Isidore's mind incline to the immeasurable, though with a certain fastidiousness in his profligacy there's always a lesson in that.

The entire play is pedagogical, but Isidore's demonstration is a sort of catechism in "the poetry of motion," by which, moving from here to there, "One . . . two . . . three . . . dip," you can easily lose your step, as indeed they dip and do, in a rather semiological way: not here, *there!* not there, *here!* When I think of Isidore now he seems to be, *avant la lettre,* an avatar of what, since Saussure's revival in Barthes, we've been fussing about for years, "One . . . two . . . three . . . rotate" (130), the metonymic play or circuitous prattle of the slippery signifier itself. A little retard in the tango, but what else is Isidore? "Does the text have human form, is it a figure, an anagram of the body? Yes," says Barthes, "but of our erotic body."[2] With Isidore, however, it's the erotic body itself that seems to have found its form, androgynous, polymorphous, overcome with itself, or so profusely what it is that the anagram *is* a body, displaying in human flesh something like the "text of bliss" (*Pleasure,* 14). To which the cards are, then, a copious annotation.

"I read on, I skip, I look up, I dip in again" (*Pleasure,* 12), which, though it may sound like him, is not Isidore doing the dipping, for that's more like skinny dipping, and Isidore is "stout" (*Tango,* 129), if nothing but his babble, the figure of plenitude. What Barthes was describing in that series is the desultoriness of reading. Such intermittencies, however, have "nothing to do with the deep laceration the text of bliss inflicts upon language," nor—in the *brio* of Isidore, manic obsessive as it is, his *"will to bliss"* (*Pleasure,* 13)—upon the baffled Leopold. What is captivating in the cruelty, as in the fervor of children's games, is not "the winnowing out of truths, but the layering of significance"—the excitement coming, however, as "the hole, the gap, is created and carries off the subject of the game" (*Pleasure*, 13). "Look, everything is moving," says Isidore, when Leopold is about to thrust. "But I am steady as a rock." But if the rules of the game require it, even rocks have holes, like the moon is a piece of cheese. "(*Leopold lifts the sword slowly, points it to Isidore's heart, and pushes it into his body*." There! you died. "Say you're sorry and my wound will heal" (*Tango*, 161). For which the rules don't quite provide, neither an apology nor the healing, as the game comes round again.

Actually, in a previous letter, asking what I thought, Irene said she was feeling "more and more" that either *The Machine* or *The Wise Parrot*, two still earlier titles, was preferable to *There! You Died*. She didn't say anything about the parrot, though there's parroting in the play (and a toy parrot too), but in the same letter in which she explained what troubled her about the title, she said that in her "original conception of the play, Isidore was not a man, but an IBM machine who communicated with Leopold by means of printed cards, lights, and sounds. The IBM machine was, to put it in very simple terms, the master mind of society." While that idea was displaced in the actual writing of the play, she went on to say that "if an IBM machine were a man, he would be like Isidore. This would, I imagine, be helpful to the actor." As Isidore's charm is quite infectious, even on the page, I was not so sure about that at the time we were doing the play. But as I am writing this now, shortly after Deep Blue, in winning the match with Kasparov, actually laid claim to being the master mind, it's not altogether far-fetched to believe it will become like Isidore. That there is in the machine, along with a certain mystery, "a very human sense of danger,"[3] as Kasparov has indicated, may not be quite enough. But who can tell what's in the cards? It may be that, in the accretion of human qualities upon artificial intelligence, it will be impulsive, fantastic, bizarre, and in the erotics of digital process, polymorphous perverse, with Isidore's almost demonic gift for exploiting the sense of danger. But then there's another prospect that comes up in the letter, which may be already within the scope of the redoubtable Deep Blue. It arises from a somewhat conflicted statement of what, for Irene, was "a main theme" or "a message perhaps," or what at the time she "wanted to say": "Be able, be willing to be alone. Be able to relinquish all."

Maybe with additional human qualities that will be a problem for the machine, but at the moment, surely, it is still a problem for us, and for all his virtuosity, maybe more for Isidore. As it turns out, while he seems to know "what it is to be alone. It's horribly . . . lonely" (*Tango*, 160), it's not entirely certain that he is able, in the finality only imagined, to really relinquish all, unless relinquishing means possessing, as it appears to do with his death. He can instruct Leopold in the necessity of giving up what he wants, but Isidore himself is, dressed for vogueing, "throwing shade,"[4] a virtual figure of desire. With that word almost exhausted by the "discourse of desire" (or subsequent theorizations, such as the notion of "performativity") his lust for living, the *brio,* almost requires another name. In Barthes's terms (anticipating some of that discourse), Isidore refuses the textual mandate to arrive at bliss by "subtraction," or to accept the consummate loss that is the "zero of the signified" (*Pleasure,* 41): in short, with absence as more than metaphor, the mortal fact of having vanished. "Vanished? I have never vanished" (*Tango,* 143).

Now the same might be said for the devil, which in defining her theme around Isidore, Irene's letter said he is, which then elides into her statement, "Solitude is God. Destroying the devil is not enough, because it always lives. One must be capable of destroying it and also of living with it." Who is doing what to whom is, among the slippery signifiers (in and out of the play), well worth thinking about, and as she approached the dilemma of the title, she seemed to be doing that: "Perhaps I am getting a little carried away, but I just thought that this play is an homage to destruction. Not destruction for itself, but because of the renovation that follows." No wonder, at the time, I inclined to *There! You Died:* With the homage culminating in a rather kitschy aphanisis, it seemed conceived by Isidore, the triumph of his stagecraft. It wasn't entirely clear, however, what the renovation was, unless it was the enlivening prospect of dying over again.

As for the other titles, *The Machine* or *The Wise Parrot,* not only do I prefer *Tango Palace* to either of them, but now that I think it over, almost thirty-five years later, it probably best conveys the quality I had in mind when someone asked, back in San Francisco, what I was rehearsing at the time. I said a new play by a woman born in Cuba who had lived in France and was, at least in her dramaturgy, a sort of exotic Beckett. (I might have described it as "magical realism," if that omnibus term for anything Latin had been current at the time.) The feeling of the exotic abated as, in the homage to destruction, the tango lost its footing, dipping down and out, and the house of cards collapsed eventually into *Mud.* There are significant differences, obviously, but what Fornes still shares with Beckett, aside from a sense of "the muck" (his term for *How It Is*), is the knowledge that play is deadly, really a dirty game. There is a certain paraplegic momentum in Beckett, and the autistic spectacle of dismembered bodies, at which, perhaps, we laugh too readily now. That was not yet the reaction to Beckett at the time we discovered Fornes; nor could we deal with the political impasse ("Nothing to be done")[5] as the ideological inadequacy that, compounded by nostalgia, came with the end of modernism. When it wasn't merely nervous, what made the laughter so painful is that, visceral, inarguable, it could only be ontological, what he called the *risus purus* (the laugh laughing at the laugh), out of the abyss defined by Pozzo as giving birth astride of a grave. It is by no means to diminish the cultural politics of Fornes, or the gender and ethnic concerns of the later plays, to suggest that they proceed from a similar datum: even if not explainable, something lethal at the heart of things, as in *Fefu and Her Friends*. This is no mere cultural construct, nor is it to be encompassed, psychosexually, by an "epistemology of the closet."[6] (Fornes actually wrote, relative to the physical appearance of the characters: "Whether this is a play about two homosexuals who are giving each other a hard time or a play about entirely different matters, depends greatly on the aspect and behavior of the actors.") As for the quality of play in *Tango Palace*, some of it is very funny, as when Isidore first trips Leopold, exclaiming, "There! You died"; but when push comes to shove, as after the mock bullfight—when Leopold is impaled, then kissed by Isidore—what's laughable is "putrid with death" (161) and up to its neck in rot.

Or so we may gather from Leopold's assessment of Isidore, which is also, in utter revulsion, a judgment upon himself. It follows upon Isidore's story of the man who, because he lost his beloved rat, virtually worshiped its picture until, as if "summoning his own death," he picked up his ax to smash it, only to find the rat, trapped in the wires behind it, dead of starvation there. "The dead rat turned his head to face the man and said (*As if imitating a ghost*) 'If you had not been satisfied with my picture you could have had me. You chicken-hearted bastard,' and then disintegrated into dust" (153). It is this parable that leads to the moral about relinquishing all, but Leopold, frightened by whatever it implies about him, is impelled to a diagnosis of what, for all his mesmerizing affection, is the malice in Isidore. So far as there is an issue of authenticity that asks to be understood, there is really little to choose between the picture and the rat: "I understand one thing," says Leopold. "There is something that moves you. There is something that makes you tender and loving, only one thing: nastiness . . . and meanness and abuse" (154). As for the immanence of the muck, Leopold himself appears to be the dead-level expert on that, his whole being given up to crawling, like the creature of *How It Is*, in the dirt that comes from everywhere, the universal filth: "And it comes to us from within us. It comes out through each pore. Then we wash it away, we flush it away, we drown it, we bury it, we incinerate it, and then we perfume ourselves. We put odors in our toilets, medicinal odors, terrible odors, but all these odors seem sweet next to our own. What I want, sir, is to live with that loathsome mess near me, not to flush it away" (157). Isidore mocks him, of course, but this is the one time he seems to be taking instruction—in the nightmarish scene where, after his propaedeutic on beetles (versatile and invasive, and also the most fertile of insects), they perform a ritual dance wearing beetle masks. "To make the dirt come out through the mouth," Leopold says, crawling in the dance, "you have to make your holes very tight, and let the dirt rot inside you. Then it will come out through any opening" (158).

As a contribution to the ethos of play, the intensity of self-contempt was a considerable qualification in the 1960s, when games were all the rage in the forms of alternative theater, and polymorphous perversity was, as defined in Norman O. Brown's *Love's Body,* often self-edifying as the stuff of celebration. There is, if the actors are up to it, a bizarre hilarity even in the morbidity of these scenes. Nor have I meant to minimize, in my emphasis on the dying, the quotient of vivid living that goes into imagining that. Which is, to say the least, hard to miss in Isidore. His teachings may not exactly add up to the model of a model curriculum, but it is an anticipatory paradigm for the pedagogy in later plays, and not merely for the process but its mortifying substance as well. Like some of her characters, Fornes seems blessed with a passion for knowledge, which has not abated over the years in which she's been doing her own teaching. Her work has moved in various directions, from the brain damage of *The Danube* to the Dantesque transcendence of *Abingdon Square,* but whatever the subjects she's writing about, some very valuable part of her drama is still down there in the muck, where somehow the love of learning may energize desperation.

So it is most specifically with the indefatigable Mae in *Mud.* With Lloyd bloated, puky, rotten, dying "like a pig in the mud," so that not even the flies will go near, she is determined "to die in a hospital. In white sheets. You hear? . . . I'm going to die clean."[7] That's going to be accomplished by her going to school and learning things, and while she's only "intermediate" (21), not at all advanced, the more advanced the text the better, as with the inscrutable medical terms. The text may need more study, but what does seem apparent, as she listens with *"an air of serenity"* to Henry reading aloud, is her pleasure in the text and, even when it's read at high speed, her ability to get the point: "perineal pain, irritative voiding, aching of the perineum, sexual impotency, painful ejaculation, and intermittent dysuria, or bloody ejaculation." Here the issue of gender is focused in a "chronic bacterial infection" of the masculine prostate gland (21–22), but the rottenness spreads through the play, with Mae struggling against it, like an existential condition.

When Henry asks her why, since there's no binding blood relation, she's so attached to Lloyd, and why she doesn't do something about it, she says: "There's nothing I can do and there is nothing Lloyd can do. He's always been here, since he was little" (28). Here is a "wooden room, which sits on an earth promontory," whose earth is "red and soft" and, though without greenery, "so is the earth around it." The wood, by contrast, "has the color and texture of bone that has dried in the sun. It is ashen and cold" (15). With a "vast blue sky" behind the promontory, one has a sense—despite the brutal immediacy of behavior, itself frozen like a still photograph at the end of each scene—of something not merely alienated, historicized, but unaccountably remote. Thus it is with Mae's story of her father's bringing Lloyd to keep her company. There is something primordial about it, like the base opposite—in memory encrusted by mud—of Miranda imagining Ferdinand through the dark backward and abysm of time: "I don't know what we are. We are related but I don't know what to call it. We are not brother and sister. We are like animals who grew up together and mate" (28). Henry's coming is another matter, first enlightening, then crippling. If the space between Isidore and Leopold is infinite, because there are only two, the situation in *Mud* is impacted by successive degradations in the unsuccessful life of three. When the whole thing becomes intolerable—with both men exploiting her, cheating and lying, soiling even the muck, constituting an offense, not only to each other, but to high heaven if it were really there, or to the last dwindling promise of a "decent life" here (38)—Mae herself is almost murderous and resolves to break away. But it's more than the drama's plot that makes it seem too late.

Is it that the learning curve is a problem? "I feel grace in my heart," says Mae, when she hears Henry recite grace. And while she can give as good as she gets, in the tawdry agons with Lloyd, part of her life has been lived in a kind of active forgetting. "I feel fresh inside as if a breeze had just gone inside my heart." But "what were these words?" she asks, because she finds it hard to remember. "I have no memory," she says, and (whoever he happens to be) her teacher seconds that. "Not enough to pass the test. But I rejoice with the knowledge that I get" (26). Her desire is extremely moving, and her capacity to love or cry with joy, but in the accretion of reality around her, its grievous tedium, the ironing, the protoplasmic irritation, it's as if there's something else she has forgotten: Something is very sick, something is rotting away, somebody is going to die. Unfortunately, even when her reading improves—as with the inspired passage about the starfish that "keep[s] the water clean"—it doesn't protect her from that, as if she failed the test. The memory of / the moments of love / will haunt us forever . . . , but what the "starfish's eye cannot see" (27) is that, clean as the waters are, the sleepy lagoon is also inhabited by bloodsuckers and hermit crabs—which, as the discourse sometimes forgets, but Fornes certainly doesn't, are also moved by desire.

FEFU AND HER FRIENDS

The View from the Stone

I

IN THE WORLD of *Fefu and Her Friends,* the men possess the outside world. Fefu's unseen husband Phillip, her brother John, and the gardener Tom walk the grounds "in the fresh air and the sun."[1] The women gather in the house, "in the dark" (13), venturing forth only so far as a garden lawn near the house. There are three breaches of this divided genderscape: Emma's exuberant leap out the door to greet the men, the ominous invasion of dead leaves into Julia's bedroom, Fefu's catastrophic foray with the gun in the last scene. It is not accidental that it is these three characters who "cross over."

If Fornes genders the out-of-doors male in *Fefu,* she genders the interior, with its depth, penetrability, and comfort—its domestic spaces figured as body parts and inner organs—female.[2] The division between house and grounds is one of several variations on Fefu's parable of the stone, offered early in Part I. The story metaphorically describes a chief organizing pattern of the play.

Have you ever turned a stone over in damp soil? . . . And when you turn it over there are worms crawling on it? . . . And it's damp and full of fungus? . . . You see, that which is exposed to the exterior . . . is smooth and dry and clean. That which is not . . . underneath, is slimy and filled with fungus and crawling with worms. It is another life that is parallel to the one we manifest. . . . If you don't recognize it . . . (*Whispering*) it eats you. (9)

The stone, Fefu immediately makes clear, is not simply a metaphor for the difference between life and the grave. It is a metaphor for the crucial, characterological difference between men and women. Women, like the undersides of stones, are "loathsome." Phillip, Fefu's husband, thinks so, and Fefu agrees. Men, she says, "are well together." They seek fresh air and the sun. But women are not wholesome; they either chatter to avoid contact or avert their eyes. The closest they can come to feeling wholesome is the stupor they experience in the presence of men (13).

The inner life of *Fefu and Her Friends* is governed by the rule of the stone: Its bright upper side is matched, indeed virtually overwhelmed, by the parallel underside hidden from view. As it is with the out-of-doors and the interior of the house, so is it with the men and women who inhabit those spaces. But by the same rule, the house differs from itself. It is the locus of human warmth and social affirmation, but also the site of human and animal functions that should remain unseen, such as the broken upstairs toilet, or the black cat's explosion of diarrhea in the kitchen.[3]

The community of women may also be divided by the rule of the stone. The ecstatic Emma, who sings hymns to the body, sexuality, the "Divine Urge," and the "glorious light" is the upper side of Julia's horrific depths. It is Emma who, joyously ignoring tragedy, throws herself on Julia's wheelchair lap and begs for a ride. The stone divides women from themselves as well. Julia, who above all the other women "knew so much" and "was afraid of nothing" (15), is the one who is now most shockingly abject. Paralyzed, she suffers hallucinations, more real than life, of being beaten, tortured, and condemned to humiliating recitations about the "stinking" and "revolting" parts of the female body (24). She is viscerally abject in Julia Kristeva's sense of "death infecting life," subject to and of "[t]hese body fluids, this defilement, this shit."[4] Fefu may be the most divided figure of all. She enjoys "being like a man," fixes toilets, and shoots a gun, but is hypnotically pulled toward Julia's female abyss (13).

Viewed through this sickening vortex, the source of all disgust, disease, revulsion, and death is the female body. The underside of the stone, that which is "loathsome," is not just women, as Fefu teasingly asserts early in Part I, but specifically the sexual organs of the female body. The reason Fornes set her play in 1935 was to create women freshly naive to the source of this accepted "truth."[5] "Women are inferior beings," Octavio Paz wrote in *The Labyrinth of Solitude* in 1950. "Their inferiority is constitutional and resides in their sex . . . which is a wound that never heals."[6] It is surprising that twenty years of criticism about this play have produced greater attention to the capacity for positive bonding among the group of eight women—itself a kind of bandage over a perennial wound—than to the bottomless negative sublime of Fefu's distaste for the female body, the horrifying bodily images of Julia's hallucinations, and Julia's almost biblical suffering.

While the men discuss the lawnmower, the talk in the house circles back again and again to women's bodies. It begins discreetly. In Part I, which takes place in the living room, the public portion of Fefu's house, the references to female bodies emerge for the most part in veiled allusion and literary device. In addition to the metaphor of the stone, there is the curious reference to Voltairine de Cleyre, the figure on whom Fefu has just recently given the talk that Paula heard and Emma was sorry to miss.

De Cleyre, a late-nineteenth-century American anarchist and feminist, attacked church, state, and the institution of marriage as colluding in the bondage of women. In a tract entitled "Sex Slavery," de Cleyre called the married woman "a bonded slave, who takes her master's name, her master's bread, her master's commands, and serves her master's passion." Contesting the common prejudice of her time, de Cleyre attacked the fictional "Mrs. Grundy" for declaring that women's bodies are "obscene" and should be hidden from view. Young girls, wrote de Cleyre, should swim, climb trees, dress freely, and live fearlessly.[7]

Like Emma Sheridan Fry, the educator of a generation later who is quoted in Part III, de Cleyre emerges from the apparently desultory chatter as a kind of bulwark against the forms of feminine (un)consciousness represented in the play, as if to say that somewhere, in the background of women's history, lay the possibility for a different path. Had Fefu not been in thrall to Phillip, had Julia not been vulnerable to the mysterious accident, they might have been Voltairine de Cleyres. Perhaps Paula could be a Voltairine de Cleyre, but Paula, like Masha in *The Seagull*, is in mourning for her life.

The culminating event of Part I is the description of Julia's accident. Up to this moment, Fefu has seized the stage with her shooting game, her toilet repair, and her playful riffs on the superiority of men to women. Her own superiority as a masculine woman is underscored by her condescending good humor to the more conventional women, Cindy and Christina. By these means, she mostly keeps herself, and the tone of the play, on the sunny side of the stone. But suddenly we enter the nightmare of the body. A young woman arrives in a wheelchair, the victim of an objective event and a subjective state of mind. The most painful details are at this point obscured. We know Julia has a "scar in the brain." There were symptoms of a spinal nerve injury, but no injury. She has "petit mal" (15). She cannot walk. She was not struck by the hunter's shot that left her with a bleeding forehead. From now on in the play, the fearless host Fefu will fear herself "host" to Julia's mysterious female contamination.

One must pause at the surrealistic image: A shot kills a deer, a woman falls with blood on her forehead. Julia is, or was, a deer and a woman, for a strike at one brought down the other. If they were at some level the same being, the deer must be associated with the powers she has lost. For she was once afraid of nothing and wise beyond her young years, Fefu tells us, and now, like Wagner's Klingsor, she is wounded without end.

The traditional iconography of the deer as a purifier of venom, poison, and sin—of the "loathsome" in short—would seem to operate in Fornes's play as well. From ancient times, the deer was thought to leap toward purifying water after devouring the venomous snake, of which it was the antidotal creature. An entry in the Biedermann *Dictionary of Symbolism* figures the deer as an emblem of rebirth because of its capacity to purify venom. In Christian mythology, by extension, the deer becomes the enemy of "the great serpent, the devil" and of "filthy sin." Biedermann points out that the carved reliefs on Christian baptismal fonts for that reason often included representations of deer.[8] Finally Christ himself was linked to the image of the "stricken deer." I will return to this link later, at Julia's final catastrophe.

I I

With the announcement to the spectators that they will be divided into four groups, circulating through four locations in Fefu's house to witness the scenes of Part II, the alternate, compensating pattern of the play begins to emerge.[9] We soon learn that there is no correct, linear order in which to perceive the central scenes of the play. Despite the hoary device of the gun of the first scene going off in the last, the dramatic model in *Fefu* will not be linear and progressive, but circulatory and cyclical. The second deep pattern of the play, then, is not, like the "stone," one of binary opposites, but of organic and biological circularity. At the levels of text, dramaturgy, and reception, the play is em-bodied.

Not content merely to align her spectators and her actors on facing planes, Fornes now welcomes her audience into the very body of Fefu's house. Like the body, and unlike most stage sets, the house has a depth and scale matched to our own offstage bodies. Its rooms are tied to the needs of the body—the kitchen, the stomach; the bedroom, sleep and sex. But beyond such familiar associations, spectators begin to discover something unfamiliar, the specificity of their own bodies in the theater.

In the American Place Theatre production, where I first saw the play, spectators were invited at the beginning of Part II to cross the mainstage living room set and walk through an upstage door. There we found our way to the kitchen on the left, to the lawn at the rear, and to the bedroom up a few steps to the right. (The study scene in this production was played on a side level of the mainstage, bringing one-fourth of the audience back into the auditorium.) With this staging, I was no longer separated from the actors by the ontological divide of theater—the "house" and the stage. Since the actors and I now shared the same "house," their bodies became real bodies instead of the stand-ins for the imagined bodies of characters that most audiences make of actors. Even more remarkable in making me aware of my own body in the theater was the acquiring of new seating companions for each segment: next to me in each scene, new elbows, knees, rates of breathing. I was bodily alive to my environment in more senses than "spectator" or "audience" suggest. In the theater (as Emma says in Part II of people and their genitals at business meetings), spectators do have bodies, they just pretend they don't.

But if Part II reveals the often literally organic concern with bodies and embodiment that is part of *Fefu*'s design, it does so in pieces: Plot, dramaturgy, and the poetry of Fornes's dramatic world—as well as the setting of the house that is their expression—all follow a trajectory from dis- to re-memberment. Part II marks the stage of dismemberment in this process, a centrifugal motion that fragments the audience, cast, and setting, while stories of the individual characters' shatterings are being revealed. It is in this part of the play that Fornes breaks her group of eight women into twos and ones. In the scenes that follow, the talk turns again and again to the dismembered female body.

The eight women of the play fall into three groups, the more conventional heterosexuals, the lesbians, and the three androgynous women, whom Fornes develops as figures with mythic imaginations. Some critics of *Fefu* treat the eight as a chorus united in their experience of men, violence, and fear. Rather, they appear to me to live out distinct trajectories within what Fornes depicts as the wounded world of women. The conventional women, Cindy, Christina, and Sue, lend balance and order to that world. Sue, the treasurer of the group effort rehearsed in Part III, stitches the world together with soup and tea, good cheer and practicality. Of these three, she alone is apparently not uncomfortable in her body, and makes no reference to its needs, longings, or vulnerability, although in Part III we learn she went through an unhealthy episode in college. Sue makes only fleeting appearances in the scenes of Part II.

The Women in the Study

Christina, a confessed "conventional," is timid and unimaginative. The two unruly scenes, Fefu's shooting at Phillip in Part I and the anarchic water fight in Part III, flatten her weakly on the sofa, the second time with a pillow over her head for protection. "One can die of fright, you know" (10). Yet only she musters an appropriate level of concern over Fefu's outrageous shooting "game" with Phillip, and about Fefu's keeping lethal weapons in the house. Fefu, she observes, may not be "careful with life" (22).

Christina and Cindy now share a scene in the study, which, with its books and neutral furnishings, is the safest—safest in the sense of the least gender- or sex-encoded—of the four intimate spaces that provide the settings for Part II. In this scene, Christina uneasily discusses Fefu, whose dangerous shooting game had earlier left her "all shreds inside" (13). Cindy, who is closer to Fefu and to Julia in friendship, is also somewhat nearer to them in psychic potential. She reports a disturbing dream populated by male authority figures. At first paternalistically friendly, and then apparently indifferent, these figures become menacing in a way that mixes seduction and physical threat. A policeman, Cindy relates, "grabbed me and felt my throat from behind with his thumbs while he rubbed my nipples with his pinkies. Then, he pushed me out the door. Then, the young doctor started cursing me" (23).

Cindy is not without resources in this dream. From the height of a balcony she slows down the now furious doctor with the words "Stop and listen to me," and when he does so, she manages to command, "Restrain yourself." Her sister is present as support. Cindy is unable to say what she wants to say, however, which is "Respect me." With the help of a friendly man the two women run to a taxi "before the young man tried to kill me" (23). The dream ends in unresolved panic, with Cindy waking up as the doctor is on the verge of wrenching open the taxi door.

Stacy Wolf suggests that the dominant force in the play is male violence— either fear of it, enactment of it in the background story, or performance of it by Fefu and Cecilia in their masculine aspects.[10] But such a reading does not take account of differences in planes and degrees. Julia suffers hallucinations as real as life and actual physical symptoms, Fefu is visited by daytime terrors of death and alarming portents of infirmity, but Cindy's more complacent imagination only dreams of a malevolent doctor treating her for an indistinct health problem. Cindy's fears are walled off in dreams from which she can awaken. She can use her waking life to counter her nightmares, even as she is capable of making positive efforts to save herself within the dream.

The Women in the Kitchen

The two lesbians seem not to share the fear and dependency that is particular to heterosexuals in the play, but they also differ from each other. The frosty Cecilia, who at some point in the past jilted Paula, has a shrunken emotional life and speaks in intellectual abstractions. On the other hand, one senses that, more than any of the others, she identifies herself as a woman with a career. Cecilia makes aggressive, even cruel, sexual advances to the still-wounded Paula in the course of the play, but for better or for worse she utters no word of connection to either her body or her feelings. Paula, on the other hand, can be seen as the strongest, and most fully alive, woman in the play.

Fornes distinguishes Paula from the other women in a number of ways. She is the only character from a working-class background, and the only one capable of class analysis, glimpsing her upper-class friends in political and economic dimensions of which they themselves are unaware. Paula expresses no terror of predatory males or the encroachment of a mysterious female malaise, nor does she express, as does Fefu, an envy of the male role in the world. If this comfort with her situation in the world does not leave her immune to suffering, hers is the only suffering in the play that is scaled to a full emotional and sexual life. When Paula speaks of her body, as she does in effect in describing the unraveling of her love affair—the phases undergone "in parts" by the brain, the heart, the body, the mind, the memory—she anchors these successive stages in terms of intimate, lived-in space ("You move your things out of the apartment but the mind stays behind," etc. [27])

Paula here echoes the structure of the play that sets up a correspondence between body and domicile. However, in Paula's account there is no hint of descent into the basement or foundation, the hell realm of pathological disgust and terror "underneath the stone" that Julia inhabits, Fefu dreads, and Cindy— in her dream effort to take control of her destiny by standing on a balcony— distantly sights and flees. (Fornes's later *The Conduct of Life* again makes such an association by placing Nena, the young girl kept as a sexual slave by the Latin American torturer Orlando, in a basement room of a house whose upper rooms respectably house a wife and a domestic servant. It is no accident that the scene with the most emotionally complete of the women—and the competent and caring Sue, who is also briefly in this scene—is staged in Fefu's kitchen, the sustaining core, or stomach, as it were, of Fefu's house.

The Women on the Lawn

The other scenes of Part II, those involving Fefu, Emma, and Julia, are set in a less realistic, more symbolic world. Fefu and Emma play croquet on the lawn, in effect on the "clean, dry, and smooth" upper side of the stone. This is the only represented scene that abandons the house for the sunlight and air Fefu associates with men. And they are doing somewhat mannish things for 1930s women: They are talking openly about sex while swinging at croquet balls. As in the other scenes, the talk is of body parts, but these parts are curiously detached from bodies and unmarked by gender. The subject is genitals, and anybody's will do. "Do you think about genitals all the time?" Emma asks. "Each person I see in the street, anywhere at all . . . I keep thinking of their genitals. . . . I think it's odd that everyone has them. Don't you?" (19). Fefu's response is ever so slightly embarrassed, "No. I think it would be odder if they didn't have them." But in her sudden "Oh, Emma, Emma, Emma, Emma," she strikes other notes we had begun to hear in Part I. The tone is affectionately patronizing, like that of an adult speaking to a favorite child. In Part I, Fefu had greeted Emma, "How are you, Emma, my child?" (16). Now she will add, again as if to a child, "You always bring joy to me" (20).

Emma may clean up sex and sexuality all she wants, clean up in the sense of rescuing sex from the slimy side of the stone by imagining a lovers' heaven in which only the most devoted sexual enthusiasts, "religiously delivered" (20) to the act, are admitted. But with the repeated "Emma"s, Fefu may be signaling that Emma is too young, naive, inexperienced, or shallow to understand the dark side of life and the trap of female sexuality. Yet isn't Fefu signaling as well a strand of sexual attraction between the women? Emma is the only one of her visitors Fefu embraces in Part I. Now, at the end of the scene on the lawn comes the stage direction: "Emma kisses Fefu." Fornes may be posing the question, as a kind of grace note here, whether a sexual relationship between two women not afraid, symbolically, to leave the house, yet still heterosexually identified, would result in a refreshing cleansing of the "slime" of conventional sexuality; or whether it would result in adding another layer of confusion to the slime-fungus-worm-filled imaginative space in which their sexuality is culturally inscribed.

Immediately following Emma's ecstatic riff on sexual performance Fefu blurts out a confession: "I am in constant pain." She describes the beginning of a kind of breakdown, evidencing itself—she speaks in quasi-erotic terms—through the disappearance of a "spiritual lubricant" in her life, without which "everything is distorted." Fefu then tells the story of the mangled and diseased black cat who appeared one day in her kitchen, an animal she felt obliged to feed. "One day he came and shat all over my kitchen. Foul diarrhea." Though she fears him, "He still comes and I still feed him" (20).

The relationship with the cat sounds suspiciously like Fefu's relationship with her husband Phillip, but with the roles reversed. In the reversal, Fefu becomes the black cat, in effect her own familiar, haunting herself and Phillip from hell. "I exhaust him"—she explains her tortured marriage to Julia in Part III— "I torment him and I torment myself . . . I need him . . . I need his touch . . . I can't give him up" (39). Just as Phillip (Fefu's first line of the play) "married me to have a constant reminder of how loathsome women are," so Fefu adopted the cat because of his monstrosity. "At first I was repelled by him, but then I thought this is a monster that has been sent to me and I must feed him" (20).

After her disturbing tale about the cat, Fefu goes off to assemble lemonade. Emma is left alone on the lawn, reciting Shakespeare's fourteenth sonnet, dedicated to the gaze of the sonneteer's lover. It is the second of three important moments in the play in which Fornes draws attention to the revelatory force of the human gaze.

But from thine eyes my knowledge I derive.
And, constant stars, in them I read such art
As truth and beauty shall together thrive (20–21)

In Part I, in her comparison of men and women, Fefu had said that women "keep themselves from making contact . . . they avert their eyes . . . like Orpheus"

(13). In Part III, the entire confrontation between Fefu and Julia turns on their ability, or failure, to meet each other's gaze. Here, in the setting of the lawn, which Fornes has ironically established as the realm of the wholesome and the "masculine," Fornes offers the fullest statement of the ideal of direct, unashamed, human exchange. The aspiration, which is really the aspiration to the highest form of human love, is stated in two ways, in the ideal of equal, conscious sexual union, and in the ideal of the silent, profound, speech of the eyes. Emma, in her riff on the "divine registry of sexual performance," and in her own performance of Shakespeare, is thus far the bearer of both messages.

In the play's manner of delicate indirection, the scene hints at a culture of feminine freedom, of women able to leave the house-world that demands entrapment as the price of protection. The implication is not that women must henceforth discuss the new lawnmower, so to speak, but that they internalize a principle of freedom that protects women's minds and spirits, as Fefu tells Christina in Part I. However, this attainment is not within the reach of any of Fornes's women, not even Emma, who is too charmingly blind to the dark side, or Paula, who hurts too much.

The Woman in the Bedroom

Julia's world is the hell to Emma's heaven. In an interview published in *TDR* shortly after *Fefu* was first produced, Fornes described her manner of working on the play. Each day, she explained, she would need to recreate a certain kind of heaven and hell for herself before beginning to write. She would listen to the recordings of the "passionate and sensuous" Cuban singer, Olga Guillot. And she would also read passages from her folder of "sufferings."

> A playwright has a different distance from each script. Some are two feet away, and some are two hundred feet away. *Fefu* was not even two inches away. It is right where I am. That is difficult to do when one feels close. A different kind of delicacy enters into the writing. Each day I had to put myself into the mood to write the play. . . . Each day I would start the day by reading my old folder . . . where I have all my sufferings, personal sufferings: the times when I was in love and not, the times I did badly, all those anguishes which were really very profound. . . . It was writing for the sake of exorcism. A lot of those things had been in this folder for many years. I had never looked at them. That was where the cockroaches were, so to speak. I would start the day by reading something from that folder. . . . [I]t would put me into that very, very personal, intimate mood

to write. I never before set up any kind of environment to write a play! This was the first time that I did that because the play was different. I had to reinforce the intimacy of the play.[11]

Julia is as deep a portrait of the feminine subterranean "where the cockroaches are" as exists in modern dramatic literature, and its dramaturgy and staging are similarly radical. The scene in the Bedroom moves off the realistic continuum of the play. Julia's problems are not those of the dream (Cindy), the ecstasy (Emma), or the portent (Fefu), where bridges back to the realistic imagination are allowed to stand. In this scene, the bridges are gone for the character, and even for the spectator, on whom Fornes imposes physical and psychic discomfort.

The spectators are not given seats, but stand surrounding the "patient," who lies on her mattress on the floor, wearing a medical gown. We are like medical students at one of the famous lecture-demonstrations, Rembrandt's anatomy lesson perhaps, or Dr. Charcot's medical circus of female hysterics at Salt-pêtrière. But there is no Dr. Charcot here to exhibit the patient, place her in what might pass for an objective frame, and assure us that boundaries are in place. The experience of Julia's hallucination melts and slips across boundaries, those between spectator and actor, between character and invisible persecutors, and even between character and spectator. Can we be certain that it is not we, the surrounding audience, to whom Julia is describing her journey through hell? As close observers in an undivided theater space, we have become uneasily implicated in the medical and spiritual experiment that is this character's fate.[12]

Of the four intimate scenes of Part II, the bedroom scene is the only one that is not in the form of a dialogue between women. Though Julia appears to be in intense relationship with her unseen male interrogators, no other character of the play joins her until Sue arrives with soup at the end. Putting Julia's hallucination in the form of soliloquy without an authorized observer or receiver is Fornes's chief means of creating its surreal effect.

This scene is also the only one to depart from realism in its setting. It is a sunny day in late spring or early summer, with cold drinks being served and the new lawnmower under inspection, yet in the Bedroom—stage directions tell us that it is a bare and unpainted storeroom that has been converted into a sleeping room for Julia—there are dead leaves on the floor. The leaves offer a symbolic contrast with the bright lawn of the Emma–Fefu scene. The incursion of the woods into the space of the house ironically recalls Julia's last moment of independence, when, in or near the forest, she was felled by the hunter's shot that killed a deer. Fefu and Emma are capable, within limits, of appropriating the masculine preserves of fresh air and sunshine. Julia, once the most independent of women, who moved as if unimpeded in the male world, is now a captive in the house-world of women, her former freedom reduced to a handful of dead leaves. These leaves expressionistically portend her losing battle with death.

Expecting an expansion on her "folder of sufferings," I asked Fornes how the Julia figure came into being. Fornes's surprising reply was something out of a feminist Brothers Grimm. In the 1960s, she relates, she had been thinking of writing a mystery play about scary, fairy-tale "gremlins" who abduct the spirits of women. At some point this story attached itself to her consciousness-raising group experience in the feminist movement of the 1970s. Julia was born of this combination.

I had thought at some point that I wanted to write a murder mystery. I imagined certain judges, non-existent in flesh and blood, but in my mind they were these little people, with animal-like faces. They had a determination to destroy the desire in women to be intelligent, to be adventurous, to be courageous, to be curious. They abducted the spirit of any woman who dared to break the rule of modesty and discretion, and would take the woman into their world for a trial. They would condemn these women to death, or if the women repented they would be left in a brain-washed state. These "gremlins" were small and vicious like rats, but were more terrifying than Nazis. They were like animals, you could not reach them. Or like squirrels—they had that fast movement. All of that is how I connected the idea of writing a murder mystery with what happened with the feminist movement in the 70s. At the group I could discuss things I thought all my life. These thoughts were maybe in the category of a woman who has short legs, she is conscious of it, but she doesn't think of it all the time. But these thoughts are in the "reserve room" because you think there is something odd about feeling that way, especially when we live in a century when women's freedom is absolute. We have public rights, yet we feel these other things. So it kind of lives in a mysterious place and we don't understand it. Something made us not talk about our feelings of this kind of inferiority. We didn't want to recognize our sense of inferiority.[13]

The overlay of Fornes's personal experience in the women's movement on something akin to a comic-strip playwriting experiment evolved into the complexity of Julia, whose mutilation is both socially imposed and regulated, but also strangely self-generated.[14] It is because Julia both exemplifies and grasps this ambivalent condition of women better than any other character in the play that Fornes once identified her as "the mind of the play—the seer, the visionary."[15]

Fornes places her torture victim in a setting that extends the motif already well established in the play, the body-as-house. The setting is a domestic version of the *locus classicus* of torture described in Elaine Scarry's *The Body in Pain*.

> In torture, the world is reduced to a single room or set of rooms. . . . The torture room is not just the setting in which the torture occurs. . . . It is itself literally converted into another weapon, into an agent of pain. . . . The domestic act of protecting becomes an act of hurting and in hurting, the [room] becomes what it is not, an expression of individual contraction, of the retreat into the most self-absorbed and self-experiencing of human feelings.[16]

Scarry draws the telling contrast that Fornes dramatizes in the four domestic variations that comprise the middle movement of her play.

> In normal contexts, the room, the simplest form of shelter, expresses the most benign potential of human life. It is, on the one hand, an enlargement of the body: it keeps warm and safe the individual it houses in the same way the body encloses and protects the individual within. . . . But while the room is a magnification of the body, it is simultaneously a miniaturization of the world, of civilization. . . . It is only when the body is comfortable, when it has ceased to be an obsessive object of perception and concern, that consciousness develops other objects. (40–41)

If I were to put *The Body in Pain* and *Fefu and Her Friends* into conversation with each other, the play might tell the book to get a little gender. It would say that to some of its women the body cannot cease to be an "obsessive object of perception and concern," that such concern is forced back on them by this same "civilization," and that they are not simply protected by their house but crippled in it. Nonetheless, Scarry's distinction between settings that affirm and support life, and those that extinguish it, is valuable in illuminating Julia's radical separation from the organic assurances of normal life.

In three of the four scenes of Part II, the spectators have shared the domestic trials of the play's characters in just such benign settings as Scarry suggests. But in what should be the most intimate of settings, a room intended to shelter sleep and sexual love, the most exposed and defenseless of human acts, Julia hallucinates a scene of physical and psychological annihilation. Though all four scenes develop the motif of female dismemberment, Julia's goes far beyond the others to an imaginative limit that approaches the literature of apocalypse. But the apocalypse here is inward, taking the form that Kristeva calls abjection.[17] Abjection, says Kristeva, is at bottom the appalling process of "death infecting life." Kristeva describes the soul-shaking spectacle of abjection in a meditation on this collapse of boundaries.

> I behold the breaking down of a world that has erased its borders, fainting away. . . . The body's inside . . . shows up in order to compensate for the collapse of the border between inside and outside. It is as if the skin, a fragile container, no longer guaranteed the integrity of one's "own and clean self" but . . . gave way before the dejection of its contents. Urine, blood, sperm, excrement then show up.[18]

Julia lucidly reports—resists—succumbs to—the particular horror of this loss of integrity. The narrative is not entirely clear. As I read it, in her hallucination Julia is speaking, and mostly responding, to one or more male interrogators who have trained her in the recitation of a prayer. She is explaining to them, once more in the language of dismemberment, what another set of inquisitors did to her body. These were the implacable judges, who claimed to love her, but threatened to cut her throat if she resisted.

> They clubbed me. They broke my head. They broke my will. They broke my hands. They tore my eyes out. They took my voice away. They didn't do anything to my heart because I didn't bring my heart with me. They clubbed me again . . . I never dropped my smile. I smiled to everyone. If I stopped smiling I would get clubbed because they love me. They say they love me. (23–24)

In a grotesque parody of Paula's lament for the love affair that ends "in parts" associated with the higher human functions, the heart, the brain, the mind, the memory, and the body (as if that were just one "part"), Julia reports the instructions of one of her tormentors on how to contain the material enormity of the female body. The "stinking" parts—the genitals, the anus, the mouth, the armpit —"must be kept clean and put away" (24). The bottom is "revolting" and must be kept concealed in a cushion. The worst part of all is a woman's "entrails." "He said that women's entrails are heavier than anything on earth. . . . Isadora Duncan had entrails, that's why she should not have danced. But she danced and for this reason became crazy" (24). But when Julia in a confident aside defends Duncan (whose dancing was known in part for its new emphasis on gravity, on connection of the lower body with the ground),[19] an unseen interlocutor threatens to slap her face. "She moves her hand as if guarding from a blow" (24).

And now comes the strange language of religious inquisition. To defend herself, Julia hastily mumbles her "prayer." She says she has "repented." She defends Fefu, receives several invisible blows, then says the prayer aloud. The prayer is a catechism of gender that might have been written by Otto Weininger in 1903, directing the believer-in-training in the meaning of the first rule of the universe: "The human being is of the masculine gender."[20] "They say when I believe the prayer I will forget the judges. And when I forget the judges I will believe the prayer. They say . . . all women have done it. Why can't I?" (25). Julia's problem, within the dramaturgy of the hallucination, is that of all religious heretics, a refusal of belief. For her resistance, yet also for her failure to resist enough, Julia is sacrificed. *Fefu* finally crystallizes as a feminist Passion Play.

III

If Part I is about gathering, Part II is about dismemberment—in text, dramaturgy, staging, and spectatorship. The "smooth, dry" affirmative level of the characters as social beings enjoying the community of women is undermined by the "loathsome" fantasies and terrors that arise when they are splintered into their own individual existences. In Part III the motion runs the other way, toward reintegration, although at a terrible price, as it will appear. All the characters now return to the group scene of Part I, while the audience returns to the auditorium, enacting its own reunion in a movement that parallels the reassembly onstage. The spectators are beginning to experience in their bodies the motions of dis- and re-memberment that move the play and its characters.

This third part of the play—musical movement is almost more appropriate a term—contains two group scenes with all characters present that formalize in circular tableaux the circular shape of the play. However, in their opposed motions of life and death, growth and decay, these scenes represent yet one more version of Fefu's parable of the stone. In between are the several scene fragments that comprise the joyous rondo of the water fight, as well as the confrontation between Fefu and Julia that precedes the play's mysterious, surreal end.

The first of the group scenes is the women's run-through of their appeal for support of what appears to be a primary school arts project. The women position themselves in a semicircle, then one by one five of them step forward to walk through their parts. Emma, at the center of this performance, just as her ecstatic ideology is at the center of the school program the women are collaborating on, performs her part in a flowing floor-length robe. Paula imitates Emma affectionately, bringing her hands together, opening her arms, and throwing her head back to speak. Ah-ha, it is Isadora Duncan! Or perhaps Duncan doing Delsarte. In the performance within the rehearsal, the speech Emma performs is taken from the writings of Emma Sheridan Fry. Emma does indeed perform with the expressive gestures of a Duncan. It is a layered double or triple image, recalling the turn-of-the-century performing arts theories celebrating "Expression," in which progressive women of the 1930s continued to educate their children.

Emma Sheridan Fry was one of the remarkable arts educators of the first two decades of the twentieth century, teaching children dramatic expression in the same years in which Duncan's reputation was at its height.[21] At the Educational Alliance in New York City, she founded and ran the Children's Educational Theatre. In an influential short book, *Educational Dramatics*, published in 1913 and again in a revised edition in 1917, Fry set forth the vitalistic principles, so close to those of Duncan, which governed her work. The high calling of the dramatic educator, wrote Fry, was not mere preparation for a show, but the development of the entire human being through the cultivation of the Dramatic Instinct, a reflection of the consciousness of God.[22] Fry thought of dramatic expression as Duncan thought of dance expression, as the individual "interconnected with the cosmos." Duncan wrote that the dancer's soul could "merge with the universe" if it was "awakened" to the universal by means of either music or nature.[23] The "environment" of Fry's theory, battering at the gates of the soul to wake it up, was equivalent to Duncan's music or nature.

Fry is the last of the three historical "foremothers" invoked by Fornes's women: Fefu is linked with Voltairine de Cleyre in Part I, Julia with Duncan in Part II, and now Emma with her namesake, Emma Sheridan Fry. The three turn-of-the-century women, models of feminine activity and independence, might be seen as a chorus of resistance to the nightmarish male patrols who perform surveillance on the world of women. (Their representatives in the play are Phillip, who loads the gun, the mysterious hunter who shoots the deer and fells Julia, the malevolent doctor and policeman of Cindy's dream, and Julia's evil interrogators.) Even if their understanding of gender may seem limited by contemporary insights, as the following example from Fry will show, yet these female historical figures would seem to belong among Julia's benign "guardians," figures or faculties that protect women from death.

Fornes adapted Emma's "Environment Knocks at the Gateway" speech from the introduction to Fry's 1917 edition of *Educational Dramatics*. With its celebration of an exuberant surge into life, the speech is the culmination of the Emma-motif in Fornes's composition. Celebrating the Divine, or Eternal, Urge, the speech contemplates no serious barrier to the achievement of what Fry calls the Whole or the All. "What is Civilization?" asks Emma as she quotes Fry, "A circumscribed order in which the whole has not entered" (32).

In the universe of both Emmas, the restraints of civilization can be transcended by those who tap into the ever-present inner energy of the Divine Urge. But both are blind to the worm of gender within the ecstatic drama. Fry teaches that each individual's Divine Urge is locked inside "Center"—the individual's Being, narrowly conceived. Environment, the active principle outside ourselves, batters at Center, striving to be admitted. "Never was a suitor more insistent than Environment . . . shouting to be heard," exclaims Emma-quoting-Fry. "And through the ages we sit inside ourselves, deaf, dumb, and blind, and will not stir" (31). Does this not sound suspiciously like Fefu's Part I description of the difference between men and women, the "wholesome" males appropriating the sun and air, "while we sit here in the dark?"

Fornes has Emma repeat the unwitting language in Fry that makes the gender rules of the Environment/Center courtship very clear. Eternal Urge "pushes through the stupor of our senses, making paths to meet the challenging suitor, windows through which to see him, ears through which to hear him. Environment shouting "Where are you?" and Center . . . battering at the inside of the wall . . . dragging down bars, wrenching gates, prying at port-holes. . . . The gates are open!" (31–32).

No doubt the "suitor" of Emma's recitation, the external, active principle, is gendered male, while the female partner, eager though she may be to be awakened, is trapped inside the walls of her body/house, unable to see the light. (This love affair of opposites moves toward the extremes of Kokoschka's proto-expressionist one-act play, *Murderer, the Hope of Woman,* written in the same decade in which Fry began her teaching in New York and Duncan had her first triumphal tour of the United States.)

Emma seemed earlier to embody a route to freedom from the curse of Fefu's stone, but here she unconsciously recapitulates it. The "glorious light" she extols, implicitly gendered as a male sun, cannot penetrate Julia's persecutory death-realm. And to Julia, now trained in the ways of that realm, such light is not the result of "life universal" chasing "life individual" out of its dark retreats, but is inborn in fearless women who haven't (yet) noticed that they are "loathsome." The light is inner: It is what such women lose if they "get too smart" (24). "Oh, dear, dear, my dear, they want your light. Your light my dear. Your precious light," moans Julia in imaginary dialogue with Fefu from the depth of her hallucination (25).

It is not possible finally for Emma to wish away the underside of the stone, the slime, worms, and darkness, with a religion of light. Julia's prayer teaches the doctrine of another religion, an enormous machinery of gender-darkness. Like Emma's it is a cosmic system, and like hers, it has its higher universal principle and its lower individual one. In Julia's system, the difference between those planes turns on sex, or more precisely, on projections of male fear onto female sexuality. Man's "spirit is pure," as the prayer insists, but "women's spirit is sexual." "[Women's] sexual feelings remain with them till they die. And they take those feelings with them to the afterlife where they corrupt the heavens, and they are sent to hell where through suffering they may shed those feelings and return to earth as man" (25).

The Sacrifice

Throughout the play, Fefu has adopted two more or less unmediated gestures toward the world. She has playfully, even swaggeringly, performed the man, shooting at Phillip, fixing the toilet, and making macho pronouncements about women to scare the "girls," or she collapses into fear and anxiety. Only in the final moments of the play does she attempt to move beyond this alternation. After Julia is seen walking in a scene that may very well be Fefu's own hallucination or a piece of Fornes's domestic surrealism, Fefu confronts her in a new guise, assuming the role of the very Orpheus she prophetically invoked in Part I. Like the gun in the first act that goes off in the last, every vagrant reference in Fornes's seemingly nondirectional text assumes a precise place in a dense poetic structure. So it is in this culminating scene that Fefu attempts the recognition that will "blow the world apart."

As Orpheus, Fefu seeks to break the law of the underworld and the grip of death. She will do this not by sticking to the rules and avoiding Julia's gaze, but by breaking them and actively seeking it. She and death's captive must urgently understand each other, must speak honestly and exchange a fearless gaze. In mythic style, the attempt is made three times:

JULIA: What is the matter?
FEFU: I don't know, Julia. Every breath is painful for me. I don't know. (FEFU *turns* JULIA's *head to look into her eyes.*) I think you know. (39)

But "Julia looks away," and answers evasively. Fefu describes the trouble with Phillip: Their relationship is in the second phase described earlier by Paula, "His body is here but the rest is gone." Fefu tries again.

FEFU: (*She looks into* JULIA's *eyes.*) I look into your eyes and I know what you see. (JULIA *closes her eyes.*) It's death. (39)

This Eurydice will not join Fefu in rewriting the myth. She pleads exhaustion even as Fefu demands a response: "What is it you see! . . . What is it you see!" (40). Fefu charges Julia with lack of courage, but a moment later her own courage fails. "I want to put my mind at rest. I am frightened." With this confession the roles reverse. Now the stage direction: "JULIA *looks at* FEFU." And Fefu's surprising response:

FEFU: Don't look at me. (*She covers* JULIA's *eyes with her hand.*) I lose my courage when you look at me. (40)

The opportunity to "blow the world apart" is lost. Between them, the women cannot sustain an honest gaze. It is not clear whether it is Julia's failure to look when asked, or her willingness to look when not asked, that seals her fate. Whichever it is, she has now passed from being rescued from death every minute by her "guardians" (among which she had earlier named eyesight itself [35]), back into the kingdom of death. From there she delivers a final "blessing" over Fefu, wishing her protection from the shattering dismemberment that she herself has suffered.

Fefu is a map of the dismembered female body. Julia's account of her sufferings in Part II may be the most frightening version of this theme, but it appears again in Paula's account of the death of a love affair, in Emma's obsession with "genitals," in Cindy's dream about the policeman's menacing grip on her neck and nipples, in Christina's having been reduced to "all shreds inside," and in the implications of Fefu's parable of the stone. Now the last long speech of the play, Julia's blessing of Fefu, repeats the threat of dismemberment as an *apotropaion*— a ritual charm to ward off evil. As Fefu cries "Fight!" to the exhausted Julia, Julia makes a last, heroic effort to stitch her endangered friend back together: "May no harm come to your head . . . May no harm come to your will . . . May no harm come to your hands . . . May no harm come to your eyes . . . May no harm come to your voice . . . May no harm come to your heart" (40).

In the famously disputed ending that follows, Fefu takes the gun outside to clean it, fires, and Julia is "struck." The play ends in a circular tableau, the final gathering-in of women. Julia sits center in her wheelchair, her head thrown back with a bloody wound in the forehead. Fefu stands behind her. The other women circle around. It is a group portrait, a final re-membering as the lights fade. I believe the ending hints at much more, as I shall develop in a moment.

I am sympathetic to Assunta Bartolomucci Kent's probing questions directed to the liberatory assumptions of many of the readings of this enigmatic, if shocking, ending.[24] To believe that Fefu's shot can symbolically free the women from self-representations as victim is to read Fefu's conflicted character too uncritically, and especially, to weigh Julia's "lucid" (Fornes's word) understanding of how-things-are-for-women too lightly. It molds the eight women into a group identity that erases the differences Fornes has carefully inflected. And it forces on the ending an ideological purity, a sudden lack of what Fornes calls "delicacy" that the play does not support. Finally, behind many of the positive, emancipatory, readings of the ending has been the (excessive) anxiety that without them Fornes would be suspect as a feminist.

I earlier suggested that there were two dominant organizing patterns of the play. Perhaps from them further meaning can be discovered. The codings threaded through the play by the potent images of the upper and hidden sides of the stone and of the membered and dismembered body are sustained to the end, but they are ultimately lifted entirely out of realism.

It is of course almost overdetermined that Fefu must seize the gun and go out-of-doors to the men in order to find a safe "smooth" place after Julia's incantation promised an approaching descent into the hell of female dismemberment. And it is similarly determined that the final resolution—the rabbit dead, Julia "dead," the wound on her forehead, the group circled in a gesture of concern and mourning—would once more cast doubt on the efficacy of these same masculine gestures. The hunt, presumably one of the activities in which men are "wholesome" together, nevertheless really kills, as Fefu had already decided in giving it up before this backsliding. (Christina is right: Fefu is not careful with life.) "I'm game," Julia had said earlier with an attempt at gaiety, standing in for the class of women who are "eaten"—Fefu's dark prophecy of Part I.

The ending of the play is a riddle to most readers and spectators. Why, first of all, a rabbit? No one speaks of it in reading *Fefu*, but there is something vaguely disappointing, dare one say almost *comic*, in Julia's "dying" as a rabbit. One wonders whether Fornes is pulling a rabbit joke out of her playwriting hat. The rabbit has a homely association with reproduction. If it has benefited from its annual appointment with Easter, it is only as the dumb and earthbound manifestation of Easter's regenerative theme. It may be a mark of Julia's decline and weakness that while she earlier fell as a deer, she has now succumbed as a rabbit. The mystery of the rabbit is intensified by the formality and seeming solemnity of the context in which it appears. In Fornes's original published version of the play, with which I am working here, the stage direction has Fefu entering with the dead animal in her arms. She continues to hold the animal in this fashion as she stands behind the prostrate Julia. There is a symbolic dissonance here: The pathetic creature takes its place in a tableau that echoes the iconography of the Pietà.

Like the dead Jesus, Julia has acquired a stigmata-like wound. She has received the bullet hole as saints develop such insignia, by some process of intense and mysterious identification. Julia sits center in her wheelchair, feet forward, body falling back. Like the Madonna in traditional representations of the Pietà, Fefu is positioned behind the sacrificed figure—Fornes is very clear in these directions—and like her, she is holding the sacrificed, in this case Fornes's peculiar sacrificial surrogate, the dead rabbit. Surrounding the mortified body, flanking "Mary," is the familiar circle of mourning women. It is a Passion Play in mythic-domestic double image. As the dying god, Julia becomes heroic, and through an overlay with Christ (the "stricken deer") she has in her martyrdom moved beyond the punishment of gender. "The corpse, seen without God and outside of science, is the utmost of abjection," writes Kristeva.[25] But at the last moment Fornes mysteriously transforms the scene with a touch of "God."

Other associations may be brought to this impacted moment. Perhaps Julia is the dying, dismembered Orpheus, torn apart by women who could not hear his music. The felling of Julia was, if truth be told, not Fefu's doing alone, but a group enterprise. Phillip loaded the bullet, Christina hid the gun but then weakly revealed it again, Julia removed the remaining slug from the gun and dropped it on the floor, yet Cindy was careful to reload it. So whether the women are, as a group, simply the mourners of Julia, or covert collaborators in this second and perhaps fatal "accident" is an unresolved question.

One can read the scene with different emphases, but such a complex, simultaneous image may be distorted by cumbersome linear explication. It speaks through methods unfamiliar in our still realistic theater. Fornes's nonrealism has been called "absurdist" and "metatheatrical,"[26] but I sense she is functioning here as a painter. Fornes was a painter before she was a playwright, and it should not surprise that she sometimes speaks on the stage in the compressed visual language of the painter's art. It is futile to work such stage language for certain meaning. It acquires meaning through context, every detail signifying, nothing excluded, which is no doubt why Fornes directs her own work. In the final scene, Fornes is "painterly" both in creating a stationary tableau and in staging the scene in reference to a high tradition of European religious painting. She may have gone even further, and wickedly combined one of the most sacred motifs of religious painting with a secular tradition that strikes today's museumgoer as vaguely comic—the Dutch genre painting of the seventeenth century in which the trophies of the hunt became the central adornment of the domestic scene. I recall numerous paintings by forgotten painters in which dead rabbits, draped for skinning and cooking, were displayed with deadpan reverence. Fornes may have administered the rabbit to the audience to counter its inflationary appetite for symbols.[27]

Fornes writes a realism that is both underpinned and interrupted by what we could call surrealism. Or in honor of Fornes's Cuban origins, perhaps a more Latin American inflection, magic realism, should be brought into service. The Latin American painter whose work especially illuminates Fornes's in *Fefu* is Frida Kahlo. Just as magical, intensely visualized eruptions—Julia as prey, the hallucinations, the black cat—break the seemingly realist domestic world of *Fefu*, so Kahlo combines autobiographical and domestic motifs with fantastic, often savage, depictions of psychological and physical suffering. This abrupt combination of discontinuous planes has led to confusion about Fornes's method and intentions. Around Kahlo's work too has swirled a classification debate, some critics agreeing with Breton's enthusiastic embrace of Kahlo as a New World surrealist, and others pointing to the autobiographical and domestic elements as proof of her difference from European surrealists.[28]

Kahlo's imaginative world has strong and sometimes uncanny resonances with the world of *Fefu*. Kahlo depicted herself as a kind of Julia, surrounded by dismembered parts of her own body, identifying herself with animals, religious martyrdom, and images of death. Like a Madonna of suffering, Kahlo represented herself in fierce self-portraits with a "wound" in her forehead, the source of suffering being located, as in Fornes, within and outside the subject. In the 1943 portrait *Thinking About Death* the emblem on the forehead becomes a dark circle containing a skull and crossbones. Like Julia's bloody circle of a bullet wound, Kahlo's marks are located at the "third eye," the seat of superior, spiritual, vision.

Both in the Fornes of *Fefu* and in Kahlo the gaze or its absence is significant. In Kahlo, the painter's unwavering gaze is often depicted above a broken body, an arresting of affect that deflects sentimentality and encourages critical thought. A particularly striking image of this type is the Kahlo painting most uncannily suggestive of Julia, the *Little Deer* of 1946. This well-known painting depicts a deer pierced with arrows like Saint Sebastian. On its bleeding body is superimposed the painter's head, wearing antlers. Her eyes gaze with steadfast intelligence at the viewer. Julia, as stricken deer and as "lucid" narrator of her own disaster, incorporates both aspects.

Another Kahlo painting that powerfully suggests the nightmare of Julia is one in which it is precisely the subject's averted gaze that reduces her to total abjection. It depicts a naked woman in a room that could be the bedroom setting of Julia's hallucinations. The painting, ironically entitled *Unos Cuantos Piquetitos!* (A Few Small Nips!), shows a woman's body, still wearing a shoe and a rumpled stocking, sprawled on a low hospital-like cot in a windowless and doorless room that is as frighteningly isolated from the outside world as any setting Scarry could imagine for the infliction of physical torture. The only colorful element is the woman's blood, splattered on her body, the sheets, the floor. Like Fornes, who implicates the spectator in Julia's persecution by gathering us into the same cramped physical space she inhabits, Kahlo brings her scene of mutilation into the viewer's world by spilling the blood of the painting out over its wooden frame. In both cases, boundaries "bleed."

Standing over the woman in Kahlo's painting is a fully clothed man in a blood-spattered shirt. His expression is cruel and detached. He has the woman completely in his power. One hand rests easily in his pocket, a menacing detail. The other holds the knife that has chipped away at the woman's face, torso, legs, arms, and breasts as if she were a cheese. The woman's face is turned away and her eyes are closed. But a surrealist element in the painting gives the viewer perspective. The ironic title, *Unos Cuantos Piquetitos*, floats on a ribbon held above the scene by a pair of doves.

The distancing device of the title helps to locate the female perspective of the artist: She is not in masochistic or voyeuristic collusion with the male perpetrator; she criticizes male violence against women as well as male denial or rationalization of that violence. The case of Julia, like the case of the wretched woman in *Piquetitos,* is also double-coded. Julia falls into the "concentrationary universe" of her male judges, yet brings back a clear-eyed, even subversive, report from the abyss. Kahlo has inserted a surrealist element into a scene of brutal realism; Fornes creates a grotesque world of the imagination, then anchors it with characterological realism. In both Kahlo and Fornes, a response of some complexity is mobilized by the layered, often conflicting, representations before us.

We do not finally know what happens at the end of this play, not even whether Julia has actually died, though many critics declare this as a certainty. The pattern of affirmative circularity does not rescue the women from their invisible oppression, nor us from the dilemma of uncertain agency and meaning. The re-membering of the female community has occurred, but the community is nonetheless broken. A message of hope may be taken from the reassembly of dramaturgy, spectators, and characters that drives the play's last movement. (The dismembered Orpheus, after all, was gathered up and restored by women.) But the "recognition scene" that Fefu longs for in her Orpheus speech—the confirmation that the torn fabric of women's existence can be made whole— refuses to take place. There is a hint of religious iconography, but Julia does not finally "die for our sins" and redeem the group. Tragedy and hope circle uneasily and perpetually, and no easy resolutions are possible. The dilemma of gender will not lift like a cloud. Fefu's stone must split or erode, and old fault lines crumble away from long disuse, before the circle of women can find its full freedom and strength. In this, Fornes is a strict realist.

Promenade. Directed by Lawrence Kornfeld at Judson Poets Theatre (New York), 1965.
Left to right: Gretel Cummings (Miss I), Crystal Field (Miss O), Christopher Jones (Mr. S), George Bartenieff (105), David Vaughan (106).

Dr. Kheal. Directed by Remy Charlip at Judson Poets Theatre (New York), 1968. *Pictured:* David Tice (Dr. Kheal).

Molly's Dream. Directed by the author at New Dramatists (New York), 1968. *Foreground, left to right:* Julie Bovasso (Molly), Leonard Hicks (John), Ray Barry (Jim), Jim Cashman (Mack).

Fefu and Her Friends. Directed by the author at the American Place Theatre (New York), 1978. *Left to right:* Margaret Harrington (Julia) and Rebecca Schull (Fefu). Photograph by Martha Holmes.

Fefu and Her Friends. Directed by the author at the American Place Theatre (New York), 1978. *Left to right:* Connie LoCurto (Paula) and Arleigh Richards (Sue). Photograph by Martha Holmes.

Eyes on the Harem. Directed by the author at INTAR (New York), 1979. *Left to right:* Cliff Seidman (Abdul Hamid), Janet Leuchter, Lucinda Hitchcock Cone, Mary Lou Rogers, Robert Daniel, Michael Kemmering. Photograph by Rafael Llerena.

A Visit. Directed by the author at Theater for the New City (New York), 1981. *Left to right:* Mary Beth Lerner (Rachel) and Penelope Bodry (Margery). Photograph by Carol Halebian.

The Danube. Directed by the author at Theater for the New City (New York), 1983.
Pictured: Margaret Harrington (Eve) and Michael Sean Edwards (Paul). Photograph
by Carol Halebian.

The Danube. Directed by the author at Theater for the New City (New York), 1983.
Left to right: Michael Sean Edwards (Paul), Margaret Harrington (Eve), Arthur Williams
(Mr. Sandor). Photograph by Carol Halebian.

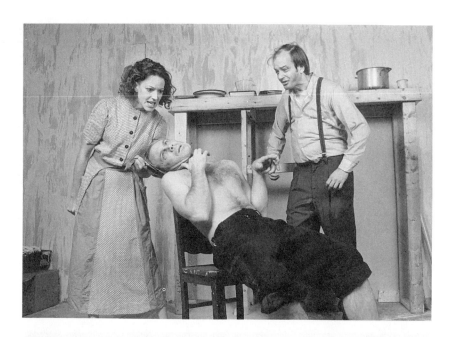

Mud. Directed by the author at Theater for the New City (New York), 1983.
Left to right: Patricia Mattick (Mae), Alan Nebelthau (Henry), Michael Sollenberger
(Lloyd). Photograph by Carol Halebian.

Sarita. Directed by the author at INTAR (New York), 1984. *Left to right:* Blanca Camacho
(Yeye), Sheila Dabney (Sarita), Carmen Rosario (Fela), Bambu (Juan), Rodolfo Diaz
(Fernando). Photograph by Carol Halebian.

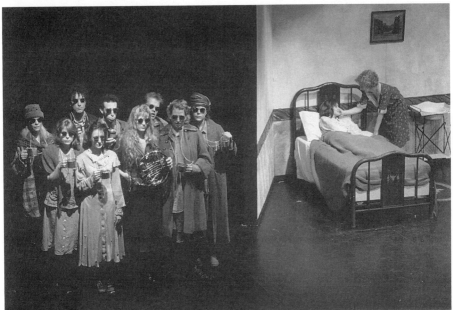

Lovers and Keepers. Directed by the author at INTAR (New York), 1986.
Left to right: Sheila Dabney (Toña) and Tomas Milian (Nick).

And What of the Night? Directed by the author at the Milwaukee Repertory Theater, 1989.
Left to right: Ensemble (Panhandlers), Catherine Lynn Davis (Greta), Kelly Maurer
(Rainbow). Photograph by Mark Avery.

Abingdon Square. Directed by the author at the Women's Project and Productions/
American Place Theatre (New York), 1987. *Pictured:* John David Cullum (Michael),
Madeleine Potter (Marion), John Seitz (Juster). Photograph by Martha Holmes.

Oscar and Bertha. Directed by the author at the Magic Theatre (San Francisco), 1992.
Left to right: Regina Saisi (Eve) and Patricia Mattick (Bertha). Photograph by David Allen.

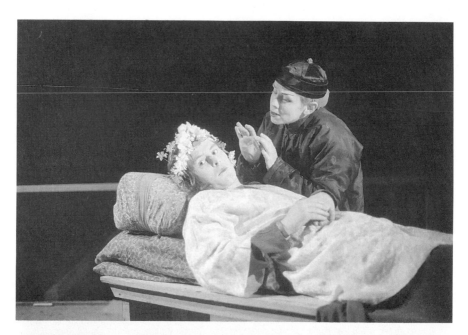

Enter THE NIGHT. Directed by the author at New City Theater (Seattle), 1993. *Left to right:* Brian Faker (Jack) and Mary Ewald (Tressa). Photograph by John Kazanjian.

The Summer in Gossensass. Directed by the author at the Women's Project and Productions / Judith Anderson Theater (New York), 1998. *Left to right:* Clea Rivera (Marion) and Molly Powell (Elizabeth). Photograph by Martha Holmes.

To speak and to reflect is their real vocation.
—Hugo von Hofmannsthal, "The People in Ibsen's Drama"

THE SUMMER IN GOSSENSASS

Fornes and Criticism

HARDLY A profile of her appears without the familiar anecdote: Maria Irene Fornes had not read a single play except *Hedda Gabler* before she began writing in 1963. The journalists are usually making a point about Fornes's precocious-ness, as if after this one reading experience she had both mastered the rules of dramaturgy and been emboldened to challenge them. Others use the infor-mation to depict her as an idiot savant—original because she didn't know any better. One of her admirers goes even further, finding Ibsenite touches in many of Fornes's own plays: trapped women, volatile sexual tension, suffocating con-vention, and so forth.[1] None of these interpretations is necessarily wrong. (In-deed, one of the more amusing signs of Ibsen's influence is in *Fefu and Her Friends,* where Fefu, firing her rifle out the French doors and just missing her husband, mirrors Hedda firing out her own French doors at Judge Brack.) But the correspondences tell only part of the story. Among the many themes that may have occurred to Fornes as she read *Hedda Gabler,* the most powerful would probably have surfaced whatever the play. Reading itself, and by exten-sion all the other ways of experiencing a work of art, became her enduring preoccupation—an expansive idea of such experience, in which the work of reading (or listening to music, or watching a play) captures in miniature all the duties and demands of life in the outside world.

Fornes has regularly revisited this primary, almost magical scene of reading from her artistic education. In *Mud, The Conduct of Life,* and *Abingdon Square,* among other plays, a woman cut off from more direct avenues of inquiry pores over a letter, an old pamphlet, a scrap of poetry, or, if she's lucky, a whole book—each one the only available source of knowledge in an indifferent land-scape—and won't relinquish it until she has wrung out the last drop of nourish-ment.[2] This kind of reading is not just mere acquisition of facts, enjoyment of stories, or admiration of beautiful images. It includes everything that happens more actively alongside the book and after it is put down: interpretation, curi-osity about the author's life and personality, and finally self-questioning, as the reader watches how the book changes his or her own angle of vision, sense of beauty, and moral compass. In readings begin responsibilities, Fornes argues, as she envisions an obligation that, if properly managed, can never be fulfilled. The best readers in her plays can't stop responding to a text, never feel they've exhausted its possible applications.

So it is with Fornes's relationship to *Hedda Gabler.* The play won't settle into place for her, its importance taken for granted. When she's reading it, it won't consent even to be fully understood. Fornes makes sure it won't, for the play works like a whetstone on her senses, sharpening them for future days of read-ing and writing. *The Summer in Gossensass* recreates this exercise, and honors the obsession behind it: Fornes dramatizes the efforts of Elizabeth Robins and Marion Lea—the American actors living in London at the turn of the century—to produce the British premiere of *Hedda Gabler.* The women become surro-gates for Fornes, recalling her own deep attachment to the play, and helping her understand what made that early act of reading the standard by which she would judge all subsequent artistic encounters.

But for all its personal significance, *The Summer in Gossensass* is not a private play. As she dramatizes her reading temperament through the actions of her characters, Fornes also addresses her own readers, as if she hoped to break us of old habits and help us rediscover the less guarded, more innocent attitudes in which we used to read, before one or another esthetic ideology claimed us. To a certain kind of reader, in fact, Fornes focuses her analysis even more directly. For them, *The Summer in Gossensass* is less about Ibsen, or theater in general, or disinterested reading than it is about the mechanics of criticism. Fornes en-visions an ideal style of analysis, and hopes to cultivate it in her critic-readers. She even seems to agitate for such a style, while maintaining her customary tact: The play imagines a critic who will be as feverish as the reading characters in

Fornes's other plays, yet as single-minded as Elizabeth Robins and Marion Lea —someone managing to combine the two temperaments so that the art under examination will regain its original force from the force of its reader's attention.

Fornes publicly confronted _Hedda Gabler,_ and her memory of first reading it, once before, in 1987, when she directed the play at the Milwaukee Repertory Theater. From that experience, she has said, came the idea for _The Summer in Gossensass._ In rehearsal, she found herself coming to terms with more than the text. As with every director before her, she also had to contend with the history of its interpretation—its many productions, the criticism by Ibsenites and anti-Ibsenites, and the sometimes killing love of generations of actors. The more meddlesome of those readers, Fornes believed, had prematurely answered questions that Ibsen meant to leave open—questions about Hedda most of all. Ibsen's protagonist had been softened by generations of actors and directors who had never met a character they couldn't explain. In their mad hunt for motivation and justification, these and other readers wasted time that would have been better spent (Fornes argues) looking at what is in plain sight—the play itself, however outrageous or disquieting its events may be.

To reach that bottommost layer of _Hedda Gabler_ herself, and revive something of its original power to disturb, Fornes began asking a series of provocative, even perverse, questions: Each of them, she hoped, would act upon the text like a corrosive agent, dissolving the accumulated responses of previous readers. Why do we assume that Hedda is pregnant? Fornes began.[3] Are the repeated references to her "filling out" anything more than Aunt Julie's wishful thinking, Tesman's inept try at intimacy, and, after the burning of the manuscript, Hedda's own attempt to explain away her actions as those of an "unreliable" mother-to-be? Maybe, Fornes suggested, we've interpolated a pregnancy into a play where none existed, using it to domesticate an otherwise alien character. In her own production, Fornes wanted to discover what we've missed by clinging to this standard interpretation, and so she cut all references to Hedda's possible pregnancy.

Other provocations followed easily from this one. Why do we always picture Lovborg as sexually irresistible, she asked, or at least imagine a powerful erotic current beneath all his scenes with Hedda? If there were one, of course, then Hedda's destructiveness could be put down to jealousy, envy, or frustrated passion. But might the play be more interesting if Lovborg weren't so tempting, and if, as a result, Hedda's actions didn't make so much sense? (In the Milwaukee production, Lovborg was fat and sweaty.) Fornes's next question: Why do we assign so much significance to the facts of Hedda's upbringing: the horse riding, the absent mother, the overpowering general who raised her as a boy, then left her penniless? ("The title of the play is: *Hedda Gabler.* I intended to indicate thereby that . . . she is to be regarded rather as her father's daughter than as her husband's wife." Ibsen's famous comment is partly responsible for influencing our judgments.)[4] None of these facts is unimportant, of course, but we turn to them, Fornes believes, out of fear and helplessness, when it becomes too disturbing to imagine Hedda in the present tense, shorn of the extenuating circumstances of her biography, acting without motivation.

Hedda's perversities must remain perverse, Fornes insists, otherwise the play is a mere soap opera and our responses are limited to pity. Pity is hard to resist, for we're accustomed to turning all characters into people "like us," or at least wanting to find persuasive reasons for their idiosyncrasies. But Hedda isn't like us, shouldn't be made to fit our patterns; and we gain a richer, less sentimental understanding of human psychology—ours as much as Hedda Gabler's—if we let ourselves face a character whose scorn for our sympathies makes her attractiveness all the stronger.

So says Fornes. Of course, many artists and spectators would dispute her eccentric interpretation. There is ample evidence in *Hedda Gabler* and Ibsen's notebooks to support the standard conclusions about Hedda's pregnancy and her feelings for Lovborg; and all the characters emphasize Hedda's background so as to make it impossible to ignore. But the persuasiveness of Fornes's argument matters less than the fact that she is arguing at all. Any ridicule she might have to endure is a small price to pay, she reasons, for the pleasure of making us look afresh at an overfamiliar text. After considering Fornes's version, we may end up returning to the standard interpretation; but if we do, we do so voluntarily—not because convention requires it. Fornes puts her audience on the spot and makes us defend our assumptions, which requires us to attend anew to the actual dialogue, map out the play's structure, and demonstrate its mechanics. We become active readers once more, no longer waiting for the play to trigger the predictable nods, gasps, and knowing smiles. We will be reading or watching with the kind of heightened interest that we hadn't felt since we encountered *Hedda Gabler* for the first time—when we didn't know who was who, didn't have actors in mind dictating how we imagined the scene, and didn't know how the story would end. We could be as amazed as Thea, Aunt Julie, or Tesman is by Hedda's behavior; as horrified as Brack is by her suicide.

—I ask. That's good, you know . . .
—Why?
—It starts action.
—MARIA IRENE FORNES, *The Successful Life of 3*

Suspense isn't the only pleasure Fornes hopes to recover. She also wants us to feel the need to learn all we can about *Hedda Gabler*—a need felt most during a first reading, when, until the last page disillusions us, we trust the play to tell us everything necessary to understand it. This kind of trust is the subject of *The Summer in Gossensass.* Fornes's plot, in its essentials, is based on fact: By 1891, when the story opens, Ibsen had become a cause among the English intelligentsia, and the object of fear and distaste to almost everyone else. Productions of *A Doll House* (1889, with Robins as Kristine) and *Ghosts* (1891) were met, in some quarters, with the kind of vitriol that assures fame; when word reached London that Ibsen had finished a new play, the race was on among his defenders to produce it, sight unseen. Rival impresarios fought for the rights. Translators vied for Ibsen's approval. And two actors hoped to create the title role—Lillie Langtry (put forward by her lover, Prince Edward) and Elizabeth Robins. When one producer's plans for the premiere collapsed, Robins and Lea saw their chance. They pawned some jewelry to fund a private production, in which Robins played Hedda and Lea played Thea. Shaw, Wilde, Hardy, and Henry James attended its opening on April 20, 1891, and wrote enthusiastic responses. Lesser lights called the play "a visit to the Morgue," a "tedious turmoil of knaves and fools," and "a bad escape of moral sewage-gas." [5]

So much is history, but in *The Summer in Gossensass* history stays in the background: The play isn't a documentary, a lesson, or an impersonal tribute to Ibsen. Fornes's scale is smaller: She studies relationships between readers and texts, and in the process suggests how a text affects the relationship of its readers to one another. The play begins, appropriately, with a scene of reading, in which the first line announces Fornes's theme: understanding. "Ibsen said that anyone who wished to understand him must understand Norway," Elizabeth says, as she and Marion pore over books about Ibsen and Norway, looking for clues about a play that no one in London has yet read, while their friend Lady Florence Bell reads another book in the background. More scenes of reading follow. Marion steals a few pages of the translation used by the Langtry company and shares it with her own colleagues. Lady Bell reads in the company of Vernon, Elizabeth's brother, who carries his own book. The women and some friends read to one another from Ibsen's and Emilie Bardach's letters and diaries about their summer in Gossensass (the resort where Ibsen presumably began planning *Hedda Gabler*). At one point or another, everyone in Fornes's play holds a book, newspaper, or other printed matter. But Fornes isn't simply celebrating a love of literature, nor is she echoing the reading episodes in her earlier works. In those plays, the reader is usually alone. (Even in company, as in several scenes in *Abingdon Square*, the characters are isolated by their books.) Here, Fornes dramatizes reading together. With each approach to a text, the characters approach one another, the reading giving structure and purpose to intimacies that would otherwise be clumsy, or never risked at all. More important, as they grow closer to one another, they see things in texts invisible to those who read alone.

Their temperaments also change. Instead of feeling the sense of entitlement typical of the solitary reader, who can't help feeling that a book's contents are meant just for him or her, the reader in the company of other readers is both humbler and more assertive. She shares her book *and* her opinions. She stakes a claim on a text, but also agrees to revise that claim in the light of her companions' own responses. Discussion—confirming or challenging her instincts—secures her relationship to the book and extends its reach. At the same time, discussion loosens the book's own authority. Moreover, Fornes shows the workings of a familiar paradox: A reader's sense of privacy deepens in the company of another reader. Reading the same book together, they collaborate in establishing and protecting one another's solitude. What had been mere isolation to the lone reader now becomes intimacy—a richer and more secure privacy.

These transactions are nothing new to students in a classroom, or families reading to one another. But the give-and-take often disappears when the reader becomes a critic. At least Fornes fears it can: The scenes of careful reading in *The Summer in Gossensass*, structured by Elizabeth's and Marion's questions and answers, seem her rebuttal to those other readers for whom toying with abstractions replaces considered observation and hands-on analysis—readers (she would argue) who haven't the patience needed to let the book have its say before being interrupted. Such deference comes from strength. Fornes hopes for critics whose self-confidence allows them to throw away as many opinions as they cherish—who won't make up their minds about a text until faced with it, when its vigor encourages them to read as vigorously, and match its subtlety in their own prose.

The virtues of this approach are also well known to the actor; and it is in rehearsal—a synonym for reading together, as David Cole reminds us in *Act-*

ing as Reading—that Fornes finds her ideal for all forms of interpretation. Unsure of Ibsen's new play, yet determined to know it intimately, Elizabeth and Marion have the right combination of purpose and restraint—passionate tact—that Fornes deems essential to good criticism. The actors make careful guesses about the play with only scraps of evidence to go on. Lady Bell quotes a review of the Munich premiere that describes a "horrid" protagonist. What is horrid about her? the women ask, sketching their own portrait of Hedda derived from their books, their own experiences, and their instincts, then wondering if they would share the critics' definition of "horrid." They rely on this skepticism to keep them tethered to the text when they later acquire a few pages of the first English translation. The longest scene in *The Summer in Gossensass* is an impromptu rehearsal of these pages—a fragment of Hedda and Thea's first conversation about their school days. For the time being, they have no hope of getting the rest of the play, but their limited resources—twenty-eight lines of dialogue—disciplines them. Unable to get caught up in the story or become enchanted by a fully formed character, they have no choice but to go over every inch of their scene-fragment, then go over it again, and still once more, like archeologists or optimistic beachcombers, hoping to hit upon buried insight if they approach the same square of land from a new angle or cross it at a different speed. Individual words, the placement of pauses, the phrasing of one character's question, the timing of another's entrance: Ibsen's smallest decisions, mere craft in the context of a complete, action-filled play, have an overwhelming, almost magical significance for the women. They ponder the details—pottery shards of a play—as if they held crucial clues to the mystery of the whole—as if one of them, in fact, might be the answer to a riddle they have yet to hear.

Elizabeth and Marion's first run-through is cautious, inquisitive, precise; they seem reluctant to move much for fear of losing their sense of the words. But afterwards, encouraged by the sheer fact of getting through the scene—the fact that Ibsen's words have become theirs—they try again. Now they act more confidently—"more direct," Elizabeth suggests, "less guarded." The scene kindles. Hedda seems already consumed by a plan of attack; Thea parries her, as she simultaneously regrets saying more than she should about herself. Ideas about roles that seemed persuasive in discussion have begun to fall apart now that the women are moving: The body quickly contradicts what the intellect had insisted upon. As actors, they can no longer wonder about symbols or subtexts; now the words themselves—and their literal meanings—demand all their attention. What they discover compels a third run-through. Their acting becomes "extreme," Fornes notes; and indeed, in her own production of *The Summer in Gossensass* (at the Women's Project in New York in April 1998), the actors approached caricature—as if they were in a campy silent film. When Molly Powell, playing Robins-as-Hedda, said "we are going to renew our friendship," she moved on Thea aggressively. "There now!" she said, and gave Thea an emphatic kiss on the cheek. She then pulled Thea up by her hair, grabbed at her ankles, threw her over one knee to spank her, and squeezed her in a bear hug. When Thea tried to extricate herself, Hedda hugged harder. Thea was caught: All she could say was "Oh, you're so kind."

Elizabeth and Marion feel they are nearing a nuanced performance of the scene—because, not in spite of, their belligerent acting. But Fornes is not making points about right and wrong Ibsen interpretations. She is more interested in the development of those ideas—the "labor of thought," as Susan Sontag calls it, rather than the thoughts themselves. The sequence of the actors' revisions is what holds our interest. The Ibsen scene, after all, is well known. (Indeed, the link here between acting and thinking has a parallel in the life of the real Elizabeth Robins: Mrs. Patrick Campbell once praised Robins's acting for the "swiftness with which she succeeded in sending *thought* across the footlights.")[6]

With so little to work with, the women become experts at a task that has faced many Fornes heroines: making distinctions. As Cecilia says in *Fefu and Her Friends*, "The main reason for stupidity or even madness [is] not being able to tell the difference between things."[7] The typical Fornes heroine inhabits a disintegrating world, in which she is at the mercy of various superhuman adversaries: environmental catastrophe in *The Danube*; economic disaster in *Hunger*; illness in *Enter* THE NIGHT and *Springtime*; torturers in *The Conduct of Life*, *Mud*, and *Tango Palace*. For some characters, the disarray comes from within: Marion's own restless desire (in *Abingdon Square*) and Julia's visions and fears (in *Fefu and Her Friends*) upset a simple moral order the women once trusted unthinkingly. Even in Fornes's lighter plays—*Promenade, A Visit, Oscar and Bertha*—the screwball energy is enough to overwhelm the wide-eyed character who stumbles into its current. In each case, the Fornes heroine struggles to remember her goals and withstand humiliations both physical and psychological. But just as important, she tries to protect her own sensibility—her taste, idea of decency, spiritual priorities. The world may be crumbling and those around her may be violating everything she holds sacred, but at least she can evaluate the damage and pass judgment; at least she can respond to the few surviving pockets of beauty. In the act of assigning things their proper place in a moral or esthetic scheme, Forness's characters recover their own dignity—orienting themselves as they organize their world.

The same process consumes Marion and Elizabeth, as they face a far less severe disarray—the strange new world of _Hedda Gabler_, its pieces in their hands, no guide to its structure anywhere in sight. How can they rebuild the play, they ask themselves, and then enter and occupy it comfortably? How can they learn the language and codes of manners appropriate to their new environment? _The Summer in Gossensass_ is filled with their efforts to be as discerning as Forness's earlier characters. Conversation helps them develop the skills of accurate seeing: "She is wild, isn't she?" Marion says about Hedda. "Yes," says Elizabeth, "and yet she's very conventional. . . . She's wild at home. In the parlor . . . But she would not be wild in public." "Thea is different," Elizabeth says later. "She's kind. . . . But she doesn't fascinate us." Marion agrees, but then corrects Elizabeth's interpretation of that difference: "Thea is different, realistic. She has her feet on the ground. But she's not dull."[8]

Their attentiveness to such distinctions ensures that their reading remains flexible. Not for these Ibsenites the arrogance that considers reading mere preamble, an unpleasant obligation to be discharged quickly so the glorious analysis can begin at last. In _The Summer in Gossensass,_ reading and thinking about reading are inseparable: Each determines the other's fate, moment to moment. A new page prompts the analysis to change direction, just as a line of argument, once pursued, colors their memory of all previous pages. Elizabeth and Marion welcome the shifts—a kind of analytic turbulence—for in the effort to steady themselves they learn how to attach themselves more securely to the text. They catch its rhythms, moving as it moves, thinking in concert with the writing. Analysis, for Fornes, is a process of perpetual adjustment, demanding an alert ease—true readiness—denied those who consider analysis a form of legislation. Others have made this point before (and probably few critics, if pressed, would disagree), but Fornes reaffirms a core principle of interpretation with a grace that makes it seem newly persuasive—makes us see that any other way of reading can obscure the text, if not ruin it beyond repair.

In fact, the word "interpretation" may itself be an imprecise way of describing Elizabeth and Marion's work. "Inquiry" is more in keeping with the spirit of their discussions and rehearsals, which obey no agenda, in the hope of covering more ground. Inquiry connotes more curiosity and fewer assumptions than interpretation; it calls up images of direct engagement, even the physical approach of acting—the reader crossing the distance separating him or her from the text and asking to be admitted—rather than detached, and often smug, assignment of value. Elizabeth and Marion are not relying on any system; they belong to no school. As they read, they seek their own language, one suited to the occasion, complementary to the writer's words and capable of preserving their memory.

In this respect, Fornes's reading characters, Elizabeth and Marion included, are like all her characters: Whether they are considering a lovely object, a fascinating person, some phenomenon in the natural world, the prospect of an exciting experience or the memory of a confusing one, they are interpreting—mustering the same concentration they bring to a text, and then hoping that an appropriate language of response will emerge, unforced, as if created by the object itself. Indeed, criticism, for Fornes, is as much a form of anticipation as of intervention—the reader trying out words and phrases, but retracting them without complaint if they don't sound right in the presence of the thing itself. Much of this inquiry is a matter of ridding oneself of old language—overused ways of describing something, explanations that harmonized with other texts, but here sound off-key. Without the patience to wait for these words to be shed, readers will only idle, circling themselves and their overfamiliar opinions instead of actually advancing into the text.

Fornes doesn't underestimate how difficult it is for readers (and writers) to break out of familiar patterns of thought. As the characters in *The Summer in Gossensass* develop the skills needed to recognize their instincts, then scan their vocabulary for sufficiently vivid ways of expressing them, they are, in fact, learning to read all over again. Fornes traces every stage of that education, so that, as we listen to her characters, we enter into their minds, seeming to witness the birth of ideas and, even more important, the struggle to sustain them, make them intelligible to others, and translate them into action. This is literalized in the play's translation scene, when Elizabeth sits with dictionary, script, and notebook, and slowly works through a single, simple Norwegian sentence, considering all its possible variations in English, and despairing of ever being able to settle on one. But her struggle is experienced throughout *The Summer in Gossensass*, even at the molecular level of speech, and gives the play its distinctive pulse. The efforts of one character, an actor named David, to describe Ibsen are representative:

He's old . . . Strong . . . Physically strong . . . Mentally strong . . . he's passionate . . . Stubborn. Suspicious and cautious. Yet he's trusting, naive. He is rigid.

There is an impotent side to him and a side where he is unfathomable. He is on fire. He leads many lives in his mind. He feels a sword will be put through him and crack a hole in him. He's made of glass. He is a coward. As a man he is a coward. As a writer he is courageous. Courageous! He delves in delicate, mysterious, and dangerous things. (sc. 5, p. 18)

One image coaxes another to come forward. Adjectives breed adjectives. Declarations require qualifications, which in turn reveal new subjects, as the act of speaking leads the character to unfamiliar terrain, where the whole challenge to describe a thing adequately is sounded again. The particular temperament of these Fornes characters—fastidious but excited—suggests someone scanning a horizon, monitoring and recording every variation on what is only apparently a static landscape. These characters also challenge a common generalization about Fornes: Instead of stripping thought and behavior down to its essentials, as she does in many of her other plays, Fornes here presents a study in accumulation. Characters seem unaware of what they are saying until they fall silent—and even then, the process doesn't really end: The speaker only rests in a long journey toward mastery of his or her subject—a goal that seems less desirable to Fornes's characters the more adventurous they become with their language.

The liveliest passages in *The Summer in Gossensass* all have the exploratory syntax of David's description of Ibsen. The incremental structure of individual speeches is mirrored, and elaborated, in the structure of whole conversations. A typical scene starts out tentatively, sometimes even lazily, as Elizabeth asks one of her many questions ("Is she hiding something?" "Is she intelligent?" "Was he a Bohemian?"), which hangs in the air a moment before it is acknowledged, giving us time to feel its weight and the full force of the speaker's curiosity; or when Marion parses a line, not yet sure of its context, and in her patience escorts us closer to the sentence, until we seem to be reading (or watching) the play from the inside. During the seconds following any utterance in *The Summer in Gossensass,* characters listen for their own echo, as if they were waiting to see how successfully their sentences captured their subjects. We can almost see a speaker cooling down, recovering her balance after speaking, then summoning the necessary energy for a new approach; meanwhile her companion begins her own cycle. Finally, after a few rounds of conversation, the characters' hesitant rhythm changes. The scene seems to bolt forward, spending the energy accumulated over the past few minutes. It is as if Fornes's characters had all along been pushing against a door that suddenly gave. Individual lines are dwarfed when seen in this context; each one serves only as a kind of marker, something by which we can locate the complex thinking that surrounds it.

As they talk their way toward clarity, Fornes's characters also reveal something of her own process—a link that she acknowledges directly in *The Summer in Gossensass*, when Vernon describes the writing philosophy of an unnamed friend who sounds a lot like Irene Fornes.

> A play is a riddle. A riddle that's in the head of the author. *(Pause)* Something that intrigues the author but doesn't have a shape yet. It doesn't even have a question. And a riddle must have a question. The question is an important part of the riddle. How can you have a riddle without a question? She says that in the beginning all the author has is that there is something to be discovered. That is all she has. And the writing of the play is its discovery. She says that by the time the author gets halfway through, she knows what the question is. Then, answering the question begins to shape the play. She says every answer creates another question. And each answer makes the play grow. (sc. 6, p. 2)

Writing as careful, attentive address: Fornes's emphasis on the step-by-step work of writing—rather than the rapture of inspiration—keeps her definition free of romanticism. Fornes is, if anything, even more rigorous than her spokesman. Vernon's friend imagines an ending to this process: "When the questions began to dwindle," he says, "that meant the play was coming to an end. The last question is the one whose answer doesn't invite another question. At the start, the subject haunts the writer. And at the end, the writer is in a state of bliss." But Fornes, for whom directing is an extension of writing, knows better. The "state of bliss" is tantalizing, but in rehearsal it grows ever more elusive.

In "How Should One Read a Book?" Virginia Woolf envisions a collaborative relationship between reader and text—the reader "completing" the book (as Woolf writes) by thinking about it. The image would seem to have obvious appeal to Fornes. But it's another matter when Woolf argues that reading ends in separation—that moment when a book, read through, reveals its value and meaning only to those readers who let go, stand back, and watch the book, hitherto just a series of pages, coalesce in the light of memory.

> The first process, to receive impressions with the utmost understanding, is only half the process of reading; it must be completed, if we are to get the whole pleasure from a book, by another. We must pass judgment on those multitudinous impressions; we must make of these fleeting shapes one that is hard and

lasting. But not directly. Wait for the dust of reading to settle; for the conflict and questioning to die down; walk, talk, pull the dead petals from a rose, or fall asleep. Then . . . the book will return, but differently. It will float to the top of the mind as a whole. . . . We see the shape from start to finish; it is a barn, a pigsty, or a cathedral.[9]

In every respect, Woolf itemizes what Fornes, in *The Summer in Gossensass*, is determined to prevent. Fornes doesn't want the "dust to settle" or the "conflict and questioning to die down." The skirmish is evidence of true engagement; the contest of questioning makes for more persuasive analyses. Someone forced to sort through "multitudinous impressions," trying to register each one without slighting the others, is a better reader than one content with a single view, just as one forced to chase after a story's "fleeting shapes" can't afford to be complacent about their meaning. In *The Summer in Gossensass*, Elizabeth and Marion keep deferring the moment of "passing judgment," waiting instead for understanding to deepen into sympathy, and knowledge to expand into sensibility, by which time no judgment is possible, because no distance remains between subject and student.

Such unmapped reading, long but never tedious, humbles Elizabeth and Marion. Their intellect is at the mercy of their instinct; ideas about Hedda give way to images of her, more disconcerting but more reliable, and visible only to those who hold off claiming the play as their own. The women are jolted out of one thought and into another at every juncture, never allowed to settle for a concise description or a seamless explanation. These jolts are crucial events for Fornes, who values surprise as an essential part of criticism. The most sensitive readers, she argues, enjoy in analysis the same suspense to be found in a well-crafted play. They wonder what will happen next in their own drama of inquiry. Where will thinking take them? What conclusion might they stumble upon unawares? The merely competent reader grows more knowledgeable the longer he or she stays inside a text. The reader in Fornes, by contrast, grows more baffled, as the mysterious tendencies of his or her mind mirror and seem to honor the mysteries of the text. The book or play ends—has to end—but the inquiry goes on, at least it will as long as the reader, especially the critic-reader, believes that he or she hasn't seen it all.

Reading happens in time, the time it takes to turn the pages of a book, which controls our access and conditions our response to its contents. The simple point bears repeating, Fornes believes, for too many of us discuss books as if they could be apprehended all at once, the way a painting is, its structure apparent and fully formed from the moment we first look at it. It has always been somewhat misleading to suggest, as many critics have, that Fornes's realist plays are like a series of photographs (or daguerreotypes, as the actor John Seitz remembered them in a discussion of his work on *Abingdon Square*).[10] True, many of those plays consist of discrete episodes framing small yet psychologically crucial parts of a larger condition, the gaps between them as highly charged as the scenes themselves. (*Mud* is the prime example, with its freezes at the end of scenes.) But the photography analogy deprives the plays of their momentum — something impossible to ignore in *The Summer in Gossensass,* organized as it is by the rhythms of deduction. A better metaphor for this play might be of *one* photograph, slowly developing. The presence and pressures of time are everywhere apparent, both on the play's surface (the story of Elizabeth and Marion acquiring and translating the script in installments, then racing to produce it before anyone else does) and in its interior (the intellectual and psychological processes of discovery, analysis, and reconsideration: the growth of ideas). Each scene in *The Summer in Gossensass* fills in a section of its landscape, but also clarifies what remains to be dramatized, setting the next task for the characters and the playwright. For in depicting the gestation of Elizabeth and Marion's interpretation, Fornes restores *Hedda Gabler* itself to its history. The women seek new scenes and make decisions about the play (who's who, what's what) in such a way as to suggest Ibsen's own search, his own decision making, when planning, writing, and rewriting. *Hedda Gabler* recovers its livelier life *as* writing, not as something written.

In this respect, the rehearsal scenes in *The Summer in Gossensass* recall a key passage in *Seven Types of Ambiguity.* William Empson describes going to a Constable exhibit at a London museum where alongside the painter's mature landscapes hang a few preliminary studies for the same paintings. As Empson reports, the juxtaposition forces many viewers to revise their scale of value: Compared to the finished works, the studies seem far superior. They owe their power to their incompleteness — to their failure, in fact, to mean anything outside the context of Constable's development. They are reference points for the more compelling image of an artist in the midst of working. Uninterested for the moment in perfection, the Constable of the studies has a more urgent, more adventurous hand. The brushstrokes have all the energy of a first thought or risky guess — a wildness he tamed with technique and sometimes denied outright in subsequent days of virtuoso painting. The studies retain time: A viewer can see how they emerged from the painter's instinct and how they led to his later, larger works. The effort that produced them seems to continue before our eyes. Constable's racing imagination barely touches down on the sketchbook, as he hopes to record a flash of insight with an equally brisk style, before lifting up again on the wave of his curiosity. The finished paintings, for all their grandeur, have been uprooted from this temporal context. In exchange for immortality they have sacrificed some of their vitality.

The studies interest Empson in two ways—first, as an object of criticism; second, as a form that criticism might take. As an object of criticism (Empson implies), these works hang in a privileged place—outside the circle of masterpieces, and so free of the critical language of mere approval. There is more room for the critic—for Empson himself—to maneuver, fewer constraints on the style of his analysis: The terms of the discussion are his to invent. In this regard (and this is the second reason for the studies' appeal), Empson the critic strives to match Constable the experimenting painter. Each man sketches a response to phenomena on which no one has yet forced a label, scorning virtuosity if it prevents bold, untried expression. Fornes provides the theatrical parallel: In *The Summer in Gossensass*, Elizabeth's and Marion's first tentative questions about *Hedda Gabler,* their embryonic interpretations, and their earliest rehearsals have all the life that a long history of theatrical production, critical exegesis, and sheer familiarity have since drained from the play. The women's run-throughs are their own sketches. They are mostly erasure, negative space, and half-gestures; but to Fornes they are more expressive than a fluent, thoroughly argued analysis.

These criteria are assumed by the actor, whose insight into a role deepens the longer he or she can keep experimenting, but they are often forgotten by the reader, particularly the reader as critic. Even the most discreet must fight the temptation to freeze the art they admire in the mold of their responses. Those thinking theatrically win this fight, for they know that all interpretations are, at their core, ambivalent. It's not just that good actors are haunted throughout a performance by all the other ways a role could be imagined or even a line delivered. Nor is Fornes merely writing a variation on the old theater cliché about no two performances being the same. She imagines a more severe condition. Even if a performance is so powerful as to erase, for an evening, the memory of past productions and the possibility of future ones, it still lives in flux, its current shape only one stage in a long evolution toward a continually deferred completion. The most committed actors work in a state of chronic disorientation and uncertainty that carries through the actual performance. The same is true, she suggests, of the most vital criticism. In the moment-to-moment unfolding of a single essay, its subject seems capable of falling apart at every juncture. Only the thrust of the critic's attention keeps it viable.

Implicit in Fornes's vision of interpretation is an appreciation of the value of error. Empson acknowledged its usefulness in art when he praised Constable's studies. Others have argued for its place in reading. Randall Jarrell called the best critics "fallible creatures," who approach literature with a "terrible nakedness" and whose awareness of their vulnerability keeps them from turning complacent.[11] Harold Bloom famously celebrated a strong misreading as the poet's surest route to originality. Fornes has her own, related idea about error. Elizabeth and Marion see deeply into *Hedda Gabler* because they have no settled ideas of how or where to look. Misinterpreting Ibsen's art (at least at the start), they gain the confidence to make their own. The actors come to all sorts of wrong conclusions in their attempt to realize *Hedda Gabler*—about plot directions, a character's importance, the consequences of an event. At various points before they acquire a complete script, Vernon thinks Tesman is a servant; Elizabeth wonders if Hedda and Thea are sisters; David insists that one of the characters is based on Ibsen. "Responsible" readers correct these errors before they close the book; Fornes, however, seems to want her characters (and by extension her readers, too) to remember them, even if they can't prefer them to mature impressions. A play's characters have more life, are capable of surprising and shocking us more, when they are distorted in the awkwardness of a first meeting. Before they settle into habit, they can still jump the tracks. Their passion is all on the surface and shining bright—nothing has found its proper level; to our ears they don't yet harmonize with the other characters. In fact, they haven't become characters at all, in any reliable sense—figures with legible behavior and recognizable temperaments.

As a result of their passion, a reader's own passion on meeting them is just as strong. *The Summer in Gossensass* is full of moments where the delight of reading is so intense, and the behavior of Ibsen's characters so unexpected, that Fornes's own characters can only swoon. In the Women's Project production, Molly Powell did a celebratory little dance after her character figured something out about Hedda. When she hit a stumbling block in her translating, Powell embraced the Norwegian script and kissed it, hoping perhaps to break down its resistance. ("I have the play . . . in my hands," Robins says, "but I can't read it.") Vernon does something similar on seeing the pages Marion stole: He crushes one against his face, eager to smell the print, as if it were some forbidden drug.

When Elizabeth and Marion hear that Langtry may have beaten them to the play, all they can say, in unison, is "Oh! oh! oh! oh!" Later, when Vernon brings them a complete English translation, they can only breathe out a long, shared sigh. In each scene, reasoned speech only partly captures what they feel in the presence of a revered text. The balance—something larger, more forceful, and ultimately more personal—must come through action and exclamation.

The Summer in Gossensass is perhaps most refreshing for these scenes, in which Fornes demolishes a hardy perennial in critical debates: the divide between the so-called appreciative and analytic critics. Those were Empson's terms. T. S. Eliot, for his part, called the two camps impressionistic and scientific (in _The Sacred Wood_). To our ears, the debate may sound old-fashioned, even quaint, but in this age of critics disdaining one another for either their indifference to theory or their indifference to art, the split remains unbridgeable, whatever the terminology. At least it does for those critics who can't imagine a response to art that draws on both the intellect and the emotions. Empson and Eliot, of course, along with their more sensible students, understood the artificiality of the split, but the history of these arguments continues to influence many critics, for whom evaluating a work of art becomes either a sentimental journey or, at the other extreme, an exercise in mere problem solving.

Fornes has no use for this debate, and insists we finally outgrow it. Elizabeth and Marion illustrate her belief that the best critics are both disciplined _and_ passionate—focusing on only the text, like good close readers, but engaging it with generous spirit. They aren't "impressionistic" (as in all her plays, Fornes insists on the value of concrete things, empirical truths), but neither are they clinical (Fornes reminds us that we can never know or explain everything about a text; those who think otherwise turn writing into mere evidence). By depicting characters who, in their enthusiasm for their subject, agitate for, chase after, and eventually steal a text, then treat it as a fetish, Fornes expands our usual narrow idea of critical engagement. The pleasures of reading, her Ibsenites show, are more than a matter of wonderful stories and beguiling characters—the lure of unknown experience and the music of its representation. Reading is a sensual act in itself, with its own value that survives even a disappointing book. Such an encounter, Fornes understands, doesn't begin on page one. By the time the reader gets there, the romance has been under way for some time, ever since he or she first acknowledged an interest in a subject, an author, or a style; and then tried to satisfy it, settling on one of many untouched books to read next. The relationship with the text tightens as readers next ask themselves all the familiar questions, no less exhilarating for being asked over and over: Which edition should I read? Which translation? In which bookstore should I start my search? Fornes acknowledges the risk of sentimentality in this idea of reading—even its corniness—but the sentiment is true to the unguarded curiosity of the engaged mind. Some of the most endearing (yet least "significant") passages in *The Summer in Gossensass* give the characters time to discuss the 1870s Bohemian movement, or the Archer–Gosse debate, or, preeminently, Ibsen's and Emilie Bardach's views of one another. The reader doesn't disappear in reading, Fornes insists. The world in the book doesn't obliterate the world *of* the book.

> *One reads poetry with one's nerves.*
> —WALLACE STEVENS, "Materia Poetica"

This line of Stevens sums up the spirit of *The Summer in Gossensass,* and Fornes's own theory of reading. So, too, does his understanding of the value of emotion: The reader (or writer) who shuts down his or her emotion for fear of sentimentality forgets that (as Stevens writes) "the origin of sentimentality . . . is a *failure* of feeling." [12] On both occasions, Stevens envisions a fearless, even reckless reader, who goes far beyond mere sympathy for a book's characters and involvement in their actions.

The characters in *The Summer in Gossensass* lead the way. As Elizabeth and Marion risk insupportable interpretations in discussion, then follow them up with aggressive performances in rehearsal, all the while raging at their rivals and overflowing with delight in Ibsen's art, they do far more than merely reforge the link between thought and feeling. (Although that, as we've seen, is an essential first step.) Elizabeth and Marion's form of nerve-reading leads them to outrageousness, which in turn brings them closer to understanding Hedda's psychology than do their most discerning, compassionate analyses.

The outrageousness is a corrective to a durable cliché about Fornes's theater. To those critics for whom the realist Fornes is the true Fornes, she will always and only be a meditative writer—all Chekhovian indirection, small gestures, nuanced speech. But such an emphasis misrepresents even her most measured plays—like *Abingdon Square*—in which characters shatter the surrounding calm, exposing its phoniness and protesting its suffocation. Marion's protest is sexual—her affair with the window glazier, her evenings spent in bars and out dancing, the fantasies explored in her diary—as it is for the protagonists of many of Fornes plays: Emma, in *Fefu and Her Friends,* insisting that we pay more attention to our genitals, Rachel submitting to the porcelain penises worn by most of the male characters in *A Visit,* Jack speaking feverishly about violent sex in *Enter THE NIGHT.* As Jack proves, the results aren't always, or even often, liberating: Abjection follows uplift, and lasts longer. Moreover, the orderliness these characters worked so hard to establish with their reason and taste crumbles in the wake of an unexpected enemy: their own unruly bodies. But the more resilient of them welcome the damage. Fornes's characters do seek esthetic pleasure and solace, but not at the price of feeling, nor of truth. An estheticised world can be just as dehumanizing as a chaotic, ugly one—a point often lost on those readers enchanted by Fornes's delicacy. These are the same readers who value Fornes only for her stillnesses—the rarefied atmosphere where she lets us hear the inflections of experience drowned out in louder, busier art. True enough, up to a point. But stillness can be stifling, as so many Fornes heroines discover. Their grace carries in it the longing for bad manners; their silences hum with the sound of imminent speech.

This is the world of *Hedda Gabler* as well. Like many of Fornes's heroines, Hedda walks a line between tranquillity and chaos, unable to feel at ease or fully herself on either side. She longs to break out of the deadly Tesman parlor and speak her mind, but she also fears what the servants will say (as she repeatedly tells anyone tempting her to ignore convention). She complains that "everything I touch turns mean and ludicrous" (this, too, is echoed in many Fornes plays), yet can't keep from reaching out for more, as her relationship with Lovborg shows. Their interviews following Lovborg's brothel visits summarize Hedda's contradictions. Demanding more and more detail of Lovborg's experiences, Hedda hopes to immerse herself in a seamy world she'd never dare visit: Her fear only makes her more curious. The desire for forbidden knowledge (a final link with Fornes characters, from Leopold, in *Tango Palace,* to Marion)—this is more outrageous (in Hedda's world) than any of her petty cruelties to Thea, mockeries of Tesman, or insults of Aunt Julie. She's following her instincts against her better judgment. Reason gives way to passion—the passion of the mind.

Elizabeth Robins, as Fornes imagines her, would recognize the behavior as her own. The real Robins, in fact, put this outrageousness at the center of her performance. In Robins's essay *Ibsen and the Actress* (some of which is quoted at the end of *The Summer in Gossensass*), Fornes found support for her impatience with the tradition of sentimental Heddas. In Robins's view, Hedda cannot find any middle ground between the two extremes of recklessness and paralysis.

"It was never any wish of mine to whitewash General Gabler's somewhat lurid daughter," she wrote, "to mitigate [her] corrosive qualities." Yet Robins also acknowledges that, for Hedda, "there was no deadlier enemy than Fear."[13] It, more than any innate cruelty or selfishness, motivates her transgressions: She offends, because not to offend would be to risk having no feeling, no opinions.

When one remembers the age-old prejudice against theater—the common belief in the vulgarity of actors, most of all—then Fornes's study of outrageousness comes full circle. How different is Hedda's out-of-place, excessive candor, one could ask, from an actor's bold impersonations of his or her character? How different is Hedda interrogating Lovborg from an actor's own relentless questioning? More to the point, how different is Hedda's hunger for knowledge from that of the reader or critic envisioned in *The Summer in Gossensass?* Just as Fornes hopes we will learn from Elizabeth and Marion's example, so too might Ibsen hope his own readers will learn from Hedda's example. Her willingness to pry, her inability to censor her first thoughts, her uncouth replies and disarming directness: Behavior that seems vulgar to the Tesmans is liberating to the critic, at least to one at ease with excess and possible error, if in the effort his or her senses catch fire, and the play loses its forbidding, thought-blinding aura.

In fact, *Hedda Gabler* abounds in models and antimodels for productive reading. Tesman's pedantry, Lovborg's brilliant unpredictability—these are only two styles in a play in which (as in *The Summer in Gossensass*) almost every relationship is forged over a book. Thea and Lovborg come together to create their "baby"; Lovborg and Tesman reunite on the occasion of the baby's birth and seal their friendship by reading the manuscript aloud; Hedda and Lovborg rekindle their own relationship as they look through the honeymoon scrapbook; and finally Thea and Tesman find happiness together as they pore over Lovborg's notes.

It's this last coupling that Fornes stages near the end of *The Summer in Gossensass,* in a scene from Elizabeth and Marion's finished production. The excerpt functions as an image, in negative, of everything that had gone before: a cautionary tableau. Thea and Tesman sift through the fragments of a masterpiece, hoping to rebuild it, just as Elizabeth and Marion had sifted through the fragments of *Hedda Gabler.* Both pairs of readers must make educated guesses on the basis of limited evidence: They interpret the text, whether they want to or not, as they rewrite or stage it. Like Elizabeth and Marion, Thea and Tesman lose themselves in their text, and in the process find one another. But there the similarities end. On a deeper level—that of temperament—the two pairs have nothing in common. Tesman and Thea are worshipful, even obsequious. They take for granted the manuscript's brilliance; they keep their distance even as they reassemble it, so as not to break the spell it has cast over them.

Elizabeth and Marion don't have the means to be so complacent. Even if they had the entire script of *Hedda Gabler* to work with, and a history of critical response to guide them, they wouldn't be polite readers. Their enthusiasm never becomes awe—a rigid state, derived from fear. If they fear anything, it's this paralyzed condition—just as Hedda fears the consequences of an overcautious life more than the fallout of any single indiscretion. It's to overcome this fear that Elizabeth and Marion welcome excess in their rehearsals—welcome conditions, in fact, that should make them feel anxious. Only by lingering in confusion, where mastery is a distant and probably unreachable goal, or risking an occasional indefensible acting choice, which might upset all their earlier achievements, will they experience the workings of Ibsen's mind and art. He will come alive for them, whereas for Thea and Tesman their own beloved author recedes, untouchable in the glow of their idealization.

Fornes's heroines want order, but not if it is this forced, and not if it is drained of humanity. The tired assumption about reading—that it offers a retreat from life—has never seemed more false after this play. Fornes's characters discover and try out modes of living as they read. Not in the usual way—learning lessons from a story, modeling their behavior on that of the story's characters. Instead, Fornes's reading characters make their discoveries on a more basic, almost structural level: How they read, more than what they read, suggests how to live. Just as Tesman's failure and Lovborg's tragedy are summarized in how they read (and how they interpret what they read), and just as Thea's loyalty and Hedda's passion are clearest to us as they fight for Lovborg's manuscript, so it is (with happier results) for Elizabeth and Marion. It's not simply that the women suggest a braver kind of living in their unsocialized reading of *Hedda Gabler*. Perhaps that is what they *want* to think, but Fornes is more ambivalent, unwilling to minimize the difficulty of both living and reading. The women are constantly trying to keep their balance: As they interpret *Hedda Gabler* they want to be respectful but not servile; vigorous but not invasive. This balance is more active than ordinary poise. This is poise besieged by the restless mind.

SOME THOUGHTS ABOUT
MARIA IRENE FORNES

FIVE WOMEN shaped my theater work: Caryl Churchill, JoAnne Akalaitis, Maria Irene Fornes, my dramaturg/collaborator Kimberly Flynn, and my mother, Sylvia Deutscher Kushner, a bassoonist who moonlighted as a reigning trage-dienne of the community theater in my hometown, Lake Charles, Louisiana. Of my mother's influence and of Kimberly's I have written elsewhere. Churchill is a great playwright; Akalaitis is a great director. Fornes is both. *Fefu, Eyes on the Harem, Evelyn Brown (A Diary)* were formative evenings. I left the theater on each of these nights wanting to make theater, to write it and design it and direct it. *Mud, The Danube, Conduct of Life:* I wanted to *be* Fornes. I wanted to understand the Fornes magic: Politics, psychology, and formal experimentation cohabit in the house of Narrative Realism as if nothing were more natural. Play-fulness effortlessly joined to neo-classical austerity and asperity, as they are in Churchill, as they were in Akalaitis's Kroetz productions, as they are in Brecht: But Maria Irene Fornes isn't a British Socialist nor a history-infested German, she's a Cubana, a New Yorker, and these are American plays. The Fornes oeuvre is one of American drama's most important achievements.

In an interview she gave several years ago, Fornes made a point which has come to stand for me as a sort of First Principle of playwrighterly faith: The play is yours, only you can fix it, only you will defend it. Others may offer sage advice, but the ultimate responsibility for the text is yours, your brainchild, your burden. If *you and you alone* can't make it work, it will never be made to work. I try not to believe in "you alone," I believe in collaboration and in collective creation, I am a socialist and I don't know what Fornes is—I mean, I know she's a progressively minded person but she's also obviously a tough individualist, and I suspect she is in some sense a real (and *entirely* nonreactionary, non-Republican) conservative, as wary and suspicious of degraded outdated liberalism and its prodigal offspring as of misogyny, bigotry, fascism, and colonialism; like Hannah Arendt, like Susan Sontag: a crankily elitist, conservative progressive. I treasure her unsentimental, enterprising, and no-nonsense-responsible spirit, her gravitas and graviloquence. I'd like to be capable (at least at times) of such classical conservatism, a necessary leaven for my mushy murky utopian pink political daydreaming. All five of my theatrical matriarchs are considerably tougher than I. Women are so much tougher than men. From Fornes I have learned to regard playwriting as a playful/grave moral responsibility.

In 1996 she and I participated in a panel discussion at the Wilma Theater in Philadelphia. At the dinner before the discussion she said to me, with a kind of appalled fascination, her high-pitched voice rising higher and higher, "I have something to ask you. Did you *really* tell your students to write *arrogantly* and *pretentiously?*" She and I are both teaching at New York University / Tisch School of the Arts Dramatic Writing Program, and I'm afraid I had to respond "guilty as charged." When I'd told my students I wanted them to stop being timid, careful, neat, and polite, to embrace their bombastic American birthright, several of them worried at the time that the pitch to which I was exhorting them was utterly dissonant with the music they were making for Fornes: Learn humility before your subject, lose rather than aggrandize the Self.

Fornes has had a direct impact, through teaching, on subsequent generations of American playwrights which is greater by far than any other important American playwright, the only one who can list pedagogy as a primary accomplishment. Her students revere her; even the ones who find her critical or unapproachable or unimpressed with their work. *All* of them speak of her having made a new way of writing possible for them, or as one of our mutual students reported to me, "Irene has taught me how to fly." Usually I get queasy when people say things like that to me, but this man *had* in fact learned to fly, his writing is wonderful, and he gives Fornes much credit for it.

I want American playwriting to be noisier, more sloppy, more argumentative, more daring, more sophisticated, more politically and culturally critical than it usually is—the last three of which qualities are certainly exemplified in the works of Fornes. It makes me crazy and sad that the writers I teach, many of whom are spectacularly talented, don't know critical historical facts, haven't read essential works of philosophy and history, or literature, even dramatic literature; they seem often to be ignorant of the events detailed in the daily papers. Several of them, English-language playwriting graduate students, don't know what iambic pentameter is. Jeez, I sound like Bill Bennett (which Godforbida-milliontimes) and I don't intend to mock or belittle the smart, dedicated writers I teach. But I'm catastrophically less well-educated than the generations that precede me, and the subsequent generations seem to me to be lacking critical information for which computer literacy seems a very poor recompense.

I agree with Fornes, if I understand her correctly, that the unfettered irresponsible Unconscious is a better artist, a better Prime Mover and shaper of the little world a playwright creates when she writes a play, than the clackery quotidian guilt-ridden inelegant Ego. But the Unconscious, it seems to me, also needs schooling. Fornes is vastly read, has lived and worked through some of the most exciting and productive years in all of theater history, has seen and participated in the masterworks of her fellow giants, has slept with and argued with remarkable people. Her Unconscious is Politically Correct (she is going to *hate* this!), by which I mean that she is not merely well informed and well intentioned, but actually deeply wise; justice is not dogma or cant for her, it's molecular, it's bone-marrow; and that's rare and getting rarer in these confused times. Hmmmm. Maybe I'm already more conservative than I need to be.

The Big Problem of American Playwriting as I see it? Nobody's read enough, everyone keeps trying to reinvent the wheel. We are talented and passionate and occasionally technically skilled, but we haven't done our homework, and several of us have reading- and attention-deficit disorders. So while Fornes is teaching our students to fly, I am running behind them pelting them with the books they've left behind, hoping I'm not causing irreparable damage to their pinfeathers when, from time to time, one of these books strikes a flapping wing. I just don't want them to be little writers, and I know Fornes doesn't want that, either, though perhaps she feels, like Lenin felt about vanguard political parties, small and good is preferable to elephantine-ogreish and inept. Who could argue? But isn't ogreish and inept preferable, or at least more enjoyable, than small and inept? Shouldn't a playwright at least recognize the possibility of making of oneself a mighty disaster, a big stench rather than a little stink?

The question I suppose might be called the Walt Whitman conundrum: Are you more likely or less likely to Contain Multitudes if you go about declaring yourself chock-full?

The first time I ever laid eyes on her was years ago during the final dress rehearsal of a friend's production of one of her plays. He had directed it—beautifully, I thought—and Fornes was coming to watch the final dress; I came to watch Fornes. She was terrifying. With an extraordinary mildness of tone and an absolute incontrovertability of will she devastated the participants afterwards. Everything was wrong, either too self-indulgent or too feckless, too pandering or not entertaining enough. She wasn't mean, or mocking, or dismissive. She enunciated principles for a theater of impossible perfection, any falling away from which was too hideous to contemplate, the attainment of which was both necessary and, for her, absolutely plausible. That the production was manifestly deficient in financial and technical support, its venue some maladapted warehouse, its cast young and uneven, its rehearsal time and run extremely limited—all this seemed beneath her notice. *This was her play* and she simply insisted, with elegant and precise and steely good manners, that the interpreters cease to fail her. I have attempted in every production ever since to emulate her, but I fear the attitude has suffered in translation. I don't know how to keep the esthetic and intellectual struggle so serene, so free of competition and S&M. Every time I listen to Fornes, or read or see one of her plays, I feel this: She breathes, has always breathed, a finer, purer, sharper air.

PART II

FORNES

IN PERFORMANCE

RICHARD GILMAN

ON *THE SUCCESSFUL LIFE OF 3*

& OTHER EARLY PLAYS

IN THE SPRING of 1965 I directed Maria Irene Fornes's *Successful Life of 3* for The Open Theater. The other members of the company and I had been unhappy with a production of the play that the group had done earlier, and felt in need of some principle of performance and presentation that would do justice to Miss Fornes's imagination and dramatic powers. And so I queried myself about just what kind of imagination she had and about her particular strengths as a playwright, and I thought I knew. She was "absurd" (the term was still new enough for you to think it told you something), blessed with a sense of the incongruities and discontinuities of language, zany, fruitfully illogical, and tuned in to social inanity as a kind of radical parodist. All of which advanced textbook notions were of course entirely useless for knowing how to stage her work.

And then something happened during an early rehearsal, one of those windfalls that a director had better be able to recognize, that gave me the clue I needed. In the scene in the doctor's office at the beginning of the play, one of the men is ushered into an inner room; we assume he is seeing the doctor but learn,

Originally published as the Introduction to the first edition of *Promenade and Other Plays* by Maria Irene Fornes (New York: Winter House, 1971).

when he comes back, that he has "banged" the nurse who led him in. The script merely indicates that they return, but our actors came back instantly, which suggested that the act had been consummated with blinding, unheard-of speed. It struck us all as wonderfully funny and, more than that, as being exactly true to the way Irene Fornes organizes her stage time and, by extension, her stage space. Things happen outside chronologies and beyond known boundaries; the center of the action is sometimes in language, sometimes in gesture or sheer mise-en-scène, but always in a dimension unlocatable by any of our ordinary means of determining the whereabouts of what we consider truths.

This may be simply to say that Miss Fornes is a dramatist of almost pure imagination (as pure as imagination can be in an age of mixed media and life-styles contending with those of art) whose interest in writing plays has little to do with making reports on what she's observed, in parodying society or behavior, or in "dramatizing" what already exists in the form of ordinary emotion or experience. But if this is a simple thing to say about her, it isn't any less important, because there are exceedingly few playwrights, particularly in America, of whom it can be said. Our genuine avant-garde is for the most part heavily implicated in the uses of the stage for therapy or social action, while our surrogate avant-garde goes on turning out its little "human" playlets about people who can't communicate, and so on.

In any case, we staged *Successful Life of 3* as a lucidly demented paradigm of human relationships, doing it as though it were a movie (Keaton, the Marx Brothers, the Keystone Kops: nothing to be imitated, but a spirit to assimilate) with the film's freedom precisely from the oppressions of finite time and space. We speeded up the action to a whirlwind pace, eliminating all the integuments, the texture of verisimilitude and logical connection which, to be sure, Miss Fornes had excluded as part of her principle of writing but which conventional theater wisdom would have put right back in. At other times we slowed things down to a crawl, violently exaggerating that emptiness, that duration in which nothing *active* happens, which the same received wisdom would have regarded as fatal to theatricality. In other words, we staged the play as it had been written, only we had to find out this manner for ourselves; like any true and confident artist, Miss Fornes doesn't tell you what she is doing, she does it.

Successful Life of 3 remains one of my favorites among Irene Fornes's works, along with *Dr. Kheal* and *A Vietnamese Wedding*. I admire to one major degree or another each of the other four plays in this volume—*Molly's Dream* and *The Red Burning Light* are especially interesting for the new density and range of the former and the surreal political intelligence of the latter—but the three works I mentioned above seem to me the essential products of Miss Fornes's dramatic imagination so far.

All three plays exhibit in very different ways her occupation of a domain strategically removed from our own not by extravagant fantasy but by a simplicity and matter-of-factness that are much more mysterious. *Successful Life of 3* organizes the "story" of a shifting triangle whose members behave much the way we do—once our behavior has been stripped of rationalizations. The play abstracts behavior patterns from ordinary life, removing the illusion of continuity, the sense of fitness that we too often suppose to be truth itself. *Dr. Kheal* is an exercise in plausibility, a seeming parody of pedagogy but in fact a brilliant investigation of the myths of knowledge itself. Reminiscent (but by no means derivative) of the professor in Ionesco's *The Lesson*, its single character is a lecturer for whom "poetry is for the most part a waste of time, and so is politics . . . and history . . . and philosophy"—in short, everything sanctified—and who proceeds to offer a wholly new epistemology, logical, convincing, aggressive, far-seeing . . . and entirely unreal.

A Vietnamese Wedding is the play of Irene Fornes that least resembles conventional drama, even of a radical kind, yet it is also the quietest and seemingly most artless of all. Constructed in the form of a reenactment of a traditional Vietnamese betrothal and marriage ceremony, it calls upon members of the audience to participate in its rites, without having to learn any roles or indeed to "act" at all, and upon the rest of the spectators to imagine themselves present at something historical and actual. Yet from this sober summons to reality, so lacking in the superficies of drama, we experience a strange displacement; in imitating an exotic social custom and limning it as though it were an actual event, we find ourselves in the very heart of the country of the dramatic. For theater is the imagining of possible worlds, not the imitation of real ones, and what could be more unreal to us than a ceremony like this play? In enacting it we learn not how other people live but how we are able to imagine ourselves as others, which is what drama is about. If Maria Irene Fornes had given us nothing else, it would be a remarkable thing to have accomplished. But of course she has given us much more.

SUSAN LETZLER COLE

"TO BE QUIET ON THE STAGE"

Fornes as Director

IN THE LATE fall of 1987 I was allowed to observe rehearsals of Maria Irene Fornes's production of *Uncle Vanya*. The rehearsals were held in the fifth-floor La MaMa studio at 47 Great Jones Street, New York, in preparation for performance at the Classic Stage Company (CSC Repertory) theater from December 13, 1987, through January 2, 1988. The cast included actors who have performed on and off Broadway as well as in regional and repertory theater, film, and television; at least one actor, Austin Pendleton, has also directed. If there was a tendency toward a predominant acting style among the principal members of the company, it was that of Method acting. Fornes used Marian Fell's 1912 translation of *Uncle Vanya*, which she revised along with Chekhov's stage directions.[1] A few months before the *Vanya* rehearsals, I also observed Fornes direct her own play, *Abingdon Square,* performed at the American Place Theatre in New York from October 7 through October 25, 1987. Since these rehearsals illuminate each other, I make reference to both in the following pages.

Originally published as "Maria Irene Fornes Directs *Uncle Vanya* and *Abingdon Square:* To be quiet on the stage" in Cole's *Directors in Rehearsal: A Hidden World* (New York: Routledge, 1992) The essay has been slightly abridged and revised for publication here.

During a break in the *Vanya* rehearsal on November 20, 1987, Fornes tells me that she was originally asked to direct a Shakespeare play at the CSC Repertory but demurred, suggesting instead *The Three Sisters* and eventually agreeing to direct *Uncle Vanya*. When I ask if she admires Chekhov, she responds, "Chekhov is the writer I *most* admire." Fornes elaborates, characteristically choosing her words with care: "[Chekhov is] so delicate. I don't mean 'polite.' [He] understands things with a refinement. . . . This play is like a fabric that is woven . . . [with] so many delicate threads." She continues, "I never know whether we're doing the first act or the second," adding with emphasis, "The *actors* always know what act they're in. . . . You feel as if any scene could be in any act, but it isn't so." (She clarifies later that "it isn't so" is a supposition.) "I'm not too sure that we couldn't reshuffle scenes. Maybe it . . . [is only necessary] that the play . . . end with Yelena and the Professor's departure."

Fornes's sense of Chekhov's delicately woven fabric clearly does not imply an inevitable narrative sequence, although her musing on reshuffling scenes remains merely musing.[2] Earlier this same day she tells me, "What I'm pursuing is a kind of clarity," but adds, "I think what other directors are pursuing is tension, emotional energy whether it is natural to the scene or not. But I'm finding out from the text what is going on. . . . I think directors and actors are afraid to be quiet on the stage, afraid to be boring, but to be quiet on the stage is as beautiful as it is in life."

This concern for a kind of quiet on the stage, clearly important to Fornes as playwright and director, poses certain difficulties for actors and theater critics alike.[3] A week later, describing for me what she wishes from the actors in rehearsal, Fornes says: "*For the actor to put himself a little more at rest* than the usual performance requires . . . so [the actor's] thinking process and emotional changes can be seen or sensed by the audience. The moment [the actor's] emotions are pushed, the audience is less aware of what is happening inside" (emphasis added).[4] "I know if a voice comes softer, it will have some music in it. I feel as if the air starts building up the spirit of the time, the place, the author. If a voice is too loud, it can shatter it or destroy it."

On my first day of observing the *Uncle Vanya* rehearsal, Fornes is directing a scene near the beginning of Act 3. Vanya speaks of the "autumn roses, beautiful, sorrowful roses" and exits.[5] The phrase is repeated by his niece Sonia and then her young stepmother Yelena delivers two lines whose juxtaposition gives trouble: "September already! How shall we live through the long winter here?"[6] Alma Cuervo, playing Yelena, at first wonders if her lines are facetious, for the two thoughts seem to her contradictory. The director, sitting without script in hand, rephrases the speech, "The dreary winter is coming too soon. No matter how much time has passed, it appears that winter has arrived too soon," and suggests that this speech is connected to, and "in the same key" as, the repeated reference to the autumn roses. The actress replies, "So it's all one thought," as if the speech of a single consciousness were a kind of verbal sigh emitted by a group of actors. Following this discussion of the text, the actress delivers her brief speech four times. Each rendering is slightly different, the final version seemingly incorporating something of the earlier explorations so that in these simple, haunting lines, even now, as later in performance, the implied contradictions of loveliness and sadness, of time passing too quickly and lingering oppressively, become part of the carefully woven fabric, its delicate colors softly subdued in the actress's voicing.

During Yelena's long soliloquy at the end of this scene, the actress has tears on her cheeks. But Fornes focuses on arms and hands, telling the actress not to let them "take it away." As she stills her hands, the actress's voice becomes stronger. Fornes's emphasis on an exterior stillness, the physical marker of the kind of quietness she often seeks, is quietly challenged. The actress makes the realistic point that at times the human body involuntarily takes over, becomes dominant, and she wishes to show this during Yelena's soliloquy. Fornes's view is different, and is elaborated at various points throughout the rehearsals of *Vanya* and *Abingdon Square*. She says of Yelena, "It's happening inside her, here," touching the actress's face and upper chest just beneath her neck. Afterwards Fornes tells me, "The hands and arms become expressive, but they are taking over, putting a lid on, the emotions."[7] She adds that, in a different scene rehearsed the previous day, she asked the actress "to sit on the edge of the sofa as if she were applying to a convent school . . . very quiet . . . very vulnerable," "just to speak very quietly": "It came out beautifully."

Sitting quietly is as difficult on the stage as elsewhere. Often it is simply a practical necessity, especially in ensemble acting. For example, a week later, rehearsing Act 1, an actress, having been instructed to sit on a bench until the next pause in the action, repeatedly asks the director, "Irene, what am I *doing* on the bench?" The jokes that surround this incident range from one actor's mock-Stanislavski reply, "You're acting, baby. Never forget that," to the remark of another that in sitting on the bench the actress is not really *working* and that perhaps she ought to be building the bench.[8] Fornes, who has previously asked the Nurse not to give significant looks to Astroff while Telegin tells his tale of woe, says with a smile: "There's something about movement that attracts the eye. I don't know why."

On the one hand, these directorial notes are different versions of the convention that an actor avoid upstaging another actor. On the other hand, Fornes is trying to encourage an active stillness, particularly appropriate to Chekhov as well as to *Abingdon Square*. How difficult an achievement this is, to create and to evaluate, is illustrated at the end of the third week of rehearsal, ten days before the first preview. Fornes asks one actor to "go very still" after the conclusion of his speech. The actress whose speech follows his asks, "Should I wait longer before I say that line?" Fornes responds, "I don't know, because there's never been enough stillness to tell."

The director asks that the scene be repeated. The actor protests, saying, "I can just be quiet." And indeed his line coincides with this promise. It is: "I am silent. I apologize and am silent."[9] But Fornes needs to see the stillness enacted. They rehearse the scene again, and this time an actress moves in the space of the stillness. Fornes stops the scene, points this out, restarts the scene. Now the actor finishing his speech reaches for his tea. They repeat the scene. The actress who had previously moved delivers her lines and immediately immobilizes herself, arms outstretched. Fornes stops the scene again, saying, "A stillness, not a freeze." Once again the scene is rehearsed. This time I see the hands of yet another actress move but Fornes allows the rehearsal to continue.

In her rehearsals of her own play, in a small studio on the second floor of the Applecorps Theater on West 20th Street in New York, Fornes personalizes that "place" of active stillness. On September 18, 1987, my first day of observing the *Abingdon Square* rehearsals, Fornes says quietly to the actress playing Marion, Madeleine Potter, who is sitting on the floor beside the director's chair: "You have to find that hollow, that space, inside you, that place where I am when I write." Fornes is speaking of a long climactic monologue at the end of the second scene of the play in which, according to the playwright's stage direction, "As the . . . speech progresses Marion speaks rapidly as if in an emotional trance."[10] Fornes says to the actress who has now moved into the playing area: "You're transformed now. As if you've suddenly grown into a very tall person," a directorial reinscribing of her own authorial reference to a state of trance. The actress, who has previously been in physical contact with the other actor in the scene, now moves away from him and, in fact, slows down her delivery of the lines. Fornes comments, "Don't move unless you have to." The actress responds, "I have to," but nonetheless moves less as she continues her speech.

Earlier, Fornes suggests to John David Cullum (playing Michael) that he be less physically active while the actress delivers her monologue. The actor, with some irony, asks: "You just want a body here?" and the director replies, "A body with ears." The actor initially plays this scene as inert and insentient but gradually he becomes "a body with ears." [11] It is doubtful that an audience watching his later performance of lying still on the stage would believe the amount of work required to realize what seems so effortless.

Stillness, seeming nonmovement, is an essential condition of all of Robert Wilson's theater work. While Fornes, unlike Wilson, occasionally makes use of the rhetoric of psychological realism in her discussion with actors in rehearsal, her concern with slowed-down stage time, states of seeming immobility, characters in the presence of characters whose presence they do not seem to acknowledge is, in some ways, as Wilsonian as it is Chekhovian.

Only once has Fornes ever acted. She performed a silent role in a Judson Church production: She "didn't move, just wore a dress, loved it, being there on the stage, in the dark." This experience has some connection with the works she writes as well as the author she most admires and her directorial privileging of stillness on the stage. In discussing a workshop production of *Abingdon Square* at the Seattle Repertory Theatre in 1984, Fornes tells the actors that she wanted "a pleasant scene at home, a serenity that comes from people just being together in a room." She eventually wrote Scene 6, a scene of reading and writing: Marion, the young wife of Juster, sits at a desk writing in her diary; her stepbrother, Michael, the same age as Marion, sits cross-legged on the floor, reading a book; Juster, the patriarch of the family, sits reading aloud an excerpt that Fornes has taken verbatim from *My Garden in Autumn and Winter,* a book by E. A. Bowles.[12] The artistic director at that time had suggested that the playwright include a scene, possibly sexual in nature, with Marion and Juster alone together. Fornes chose instead to write a scene in which people who are "not supportive of each other and not necessarily understanding of each other . . . [are] in the same room together trying to deal with the same problem," a scene in which simply being in the same place conveys a sense of being connected. This is a characteristic situation in Chekhov as it is in Fornes's own plays. It is also a telling description of the rehearsal situation itself, and, in a metaphoric sense, it is the situation of the playwright in the process of creating the play.[13] It is what Wallace Stevens describes at the close of his revealingly titled poem, "Final Soliloquy of the Interior Paramour," in which the speaker of the soliloquy is consistently plural: "We make a dwelling . . . / In which being there together is enough." [14]

This sense of characters just being there together in a room suggests the difficulties for both cast and director of knowing which verbal, visual, spatial, and emotional fields are operating at any given moment in a scene of ensemble acting. In practical terms, this can simply take the form of an actor's not knowing "where to look."

In rehearsing Scene 18 of *Abingdon Square,* actor John Seitz, playing Juster, says to Fornes: "This text is . . . not naturalistic. There is a spare, formal, austere approach. I'm asking as an actor: Do I look at her? [his wife, Marion, who sits silent, staring at the floor] at him? [his son, Michael, whom he seems to be addressing and who responds in a single line at the end of the scene]. I hate to talk in these terms because in a way it's talking about results but it helps me." Fornes seems to respond first as playwright: "I feel the sense of spareness is inevitable," and then, perhaps, as director: "But I think it *is* what would have happened." The actor continues, "I really think of . . . [the scene] as daguerreotypes, formal poses for a picture," and the director replies, "But it has to do with how you *feel* about speaking with Michael, not just how it looks." This is a complicated moment in which several issues are overlaid: naturalistic versus non-naturalistic depiction of "reality," results versus process, "how you feel" versus "how it looks." And there is a further potential source of tension. The actor's candid admission, "What I'm trying to do is to reduce the possibilities," is met by the director's frank reply: "If I had directed the play fifteen times, probably we could trust that there is something rich in certain physical positions. . . . But when I direct a play once, I usually change it, in both the writing and in the directing, because the possibilities do not contain the essence: There are enormous possibilities." The question of "where to look" uncovers the *enormous* possibilities in the minimalist situation of characters simply present in the same space.[15] In this case the actor continues to rehearse the speech, in the presence of the author-director, exploring and shedding various physical movements and overt contact with other actors.

At times Fornes intervenes in an actor's decision to address, explicitly or implicitly, a particular speech to another character in the scene. An idiosyncratic example is the rehearsal of the opening scene of Act 3 of *Uncle Vanya,* in which Sonia tells her young stepmother, "You feel miserable and restless, and can't seem to fit into this life, and your restlessness is catching."[16] While Sonia's lines in the text seem clearly directed to Yelena and are initially delivered that way, Fornes suggests to Patricia Mattick, playing Sonia, that she not direct this speech to Yelena as if to blame Yelena for the boredom that is "everyone's internal state" in the play. This may seem a disputable interpretation of a speech that ends by characterizing Yelena as a woman who bewitches those around her ("You must be a witch"), but it is an important sign of Fornes's directorial disruptions of literalistic readings of the play text. Later in rehearsal, Sonia defends Astroff's avid interest in preserving forests against Yelena's criticism of it as an uninteresting preoccupation. Fornes alienates the initially naturalistic delivery of Sonia's speech to Yelena by placing a screen between the chair on which Sonia sits and the bench where her stepmother is seated. When the actress rises from her chair as she continues speaking, Fornes interrupts, saying to her, "Softer, Patty. To yourself."

An earlier, more clearly text-centered illustration of the problem of where to address a speech occurs in the first act, when Vanya repeats the word "yes" as he enters a scene of which he has not been a part. Austin Pendleton first addresses his "yes" to the room from which he comes.[17] After Fornes asks the actor to enter more quickly and comments briefly on the state of consciousness of someone just awakening from sleep, Vanya's repeated explosive "yes" is heard ambiguously as a remark to himself, a reply to unseen others in the room where he has been napping, a "choric comment" on the conversation of the old nurse and doctor to whom he enters.

One last example occurs in rehearsal of a two-person scene in *Abingdon Square*. Fornes says to John Seitz playing Juster: "I imagine this is very hard to do because you are speaking but not *to* somebody."

Actors in rehearsal of *Abingdon Square* characterize Fornes as having very firm ideas yet always remaining open to exploration. In the *Vanya* rehearsals, I hear her say to the actress playing Yelena, "Try anything that seems possible." At another point she asks Michael O'Keefe, playing Astroff, to "make a movement," and in response to his question, "Make a movement?" says, "Yes, we'll see where it goes." Working later with the same actor, Fornes says, "As long as something is kept mysterious, and a little bit beyond our reach, the character is whole."[18]

At one point in Act 2 Astroff is described in the stage directions as slightly inebriated. During a two-hour rehearsal of this brief scene, Michael O'Keefe, as directed by Fornes, creates a far spookier state of altered consciousness than that of literal drunkenness, a state physicalized at times by the kind of semi-immobility that often accompanies inner activity. The actor's voice begins to lose its previous naturalistic inflections after Fornes says of the repeated word, "Play!" (Astroff's instruction to Telegin to strum his guitar):[19] "Think of it less as a *command* than as a necessity, as if you were a pilot. It's what you need for the evening or the scene to work, to get the script open at the right page!" As the scene is rehearsed, Fornes interrupts Astroff: "Be less affectionate toward Vanya. It's more as if you're hearing an inner voice that is inviting you into an inner voyage with clues like this playing of the guitar and song, like a ritual." The actor agrees. The scene becomes both weirder and truer. After Astroff's speech, "I feel capable of anything. I attempt the most difficult operations and do them magnificently. . . . Play, Waffles!"[20] Fornes comments: "It's almost there, but let it be true. You're telling about something that really does happen. . . . 'Play' still needs to be said as if you *need* that sound of the guitar. That playfulness keeps coming back in. I think it has to do with habitual vocal tones and voice patterns. You *are* in that place [of inner voyage] that we discussed but you need to break the vocal patterns. In order to break the vocal patterns, you have to really think of the *necessity* of every element." Fornes's interpretation of the instruction to *play* as arranging necessities rather than issuing commands is suggestive of her view of the directorial role in rehearsal.

To Ralph Williams playing Telegin (Waffles), Fornes says, "Ralph, the scene is very different now. It's not just drunk any more. Astroff has gotten darker. You have to be more subdued now in what you're doing . . . because it's gotten more serious. In a way you have to be more concerned about him than about the others, more concerned about what is happening to him than about a person who is drunk and making too much noise." Similarly, after the actress playing Sonia enters the playing area, Fornes tells her that "the scene is now changed, . . . is much darker."

A parallel moment, and one of the most striking acting adjustments I ever witness in any single rehearsal session, is the collaborative re-creation of Juster's long monologue in Scene 20 of *Abingdon Square*. The knowingly cuckolded husband enters his house and, in the presence of his wife and son, begins to describe a difficult day of work at his office. His speech is simultaneously banal and strange, especially as he focuses on the state of his own clothing:

(*He sits down and . . . takes one of his shoes off*) I take care of my feet. My socks are in a good state of repair. When they wear out I pass them on to someone who needs them. (*Taking off his other shoe*) Others mend their socks. I don't. I don't mind wearing mended clothes. My underwear is mended. So are my shirts, but not my socks. (*With both feet on the floor*) I have always wanted to give my feet maximum comfort. It is they who support the whole body yet they are fragile. Feet are small and fragile for the load they carry. . . . If I treat my feet with respect, my brain functions with respect.[21]

Another director might find analogies between Juster's references to his socks and his attitude toward his adulterous wife (in the next scene, he will pass her on to someone else: "Others mend their socks. I don't.") or use the discourse of psychological realism to discuss particular stages and manifestations of a nervous breakdown. For several days Fornes has in fact referred to Juster's "demented" state at certain points in the play. Now she says simply, "You take care of your feet. That's how you begin to take care of your life."

After the scene is rehearsed twice, Fornes enters the playing area where the actor is seated on a chair. She stands behind him, with her hands on his shoulders, occasionally moving her hands along his upper arms as she speaks: "Now hold your body carefully. If you let your body go, it will be poisoned. Here, in your brain [touching his head], it's like a generator . . . making electricity at a tremendous speed. It's good, in a sense, because it's keeping you alive. You walk fine, you can climb the stairs, you can wash your hands. Somehow the energy is so intense that, although you can see, you're not able to focus so much on what's going on. You see Michael when you come in but he's a little fuzzy. You can speak to him, to others; it may sound a little mechanical but to you it sounds normal.

"You are even able to notice it is a little somber in the room when you enter. You are talking to them but once you enter this room [Juster first speaks to his wife and son from offstage as he washes his hands before dinner], it's too much of a shock if you actually talk to another person one-to-one. If you do, you may fall apart. You can even tend to your own mechanism so you can take your shoes off. It feels good. But don't relax too much because you might fall apart." All during these comments, Fornes has kept her hands on the actor's shoulders and arms, as she remains standing behind his chair.

The scene is repeated once more. The actor looks very different and talks differently: There is an alien quality about him that was not present before. His pace is faster, his speech rhythms are slightly peculiar. Fornes interrupts the scene: "Don't face them [Marion and Michael] directly. They can shock you, shatter you. They have an energy that could really shatter you." The actor playing Michael, watching and listening to the transformed actor, compliments him. The actors begin the scene again. When John Seitz enters now, everything about him seems slightly askew. He does not look directly at the other two actors. His vocal rhythms are consistently a little odd; the voice itself is a little higher, thinned out. He is, in fact, spooky. His uncanniness seems to come from his own sense of what is necessary "for . . . the scene to work." He has redefined the situation of a man coming home to dinner after a difficult day of work.

The actor cannot, of course, maintain this acting style throughout his monologue on his first attempt, as he himself indicates: "It's in and out, but I'm getting it, I'm getting it." Nonetheless, John Seitz's transformation of the speech is galvanizing and retains this effect later in his finely modulated performance. Fornes congratulates him in rehearsal, adding, "The more rigid it is, the more devastating and moving it is." [22] The actor responds, referring to her earlier directorial comments, "Those are good images. That helps." Fornes's rehearsals seem to illustrate Jerzy Grotowski's remark, "The director's purpose is to create a condition which leads another [the actor] to a new experience; a thousand times it won't work, but once it will, and that once is essential." [23]

Fornes is literally revising, and often eliminating, words in the play text as she directs *Abingdon Square*.[24] She frequently discusses with the actors the history and nature, if not the genesis, of the revisions she has made and is making. The actors, rehearsing the outtakes, as it were, as well as the final form of the play script, are intimately involved in acts of authorial revision that they replicate in their rehearsal explorations of different versions of the text.

In contrast to her characteristic steadily focused concentration on the actors in rehearsals of *Uncle Vanya*, Fornes's eye is occasionally as much on the text as on the performers during rehearsal of her own play. At one point she looks down at the script in a large pink binder in her lap; she looks up over it at the actors, then back at the script. I see her making changes in the text which in a few minutes she reads aloud to the actors, adding, "The more words we take out, the more immediate it becomes." (Cf. her earlier remark to actor John Seitz, "I feel the spareness is inevitable, but I think it *is* what would have happened.") Once, when an actor suggests a revision in phrasing to Fornes, her reaction is immediate and unqualified: "No. That makes it more like grammar." But at other moments she consults with individual actors in making alterations in the phrasing of their lines, sometimes confirming her ear-sense of the line with the actor who will deliver it.[25]

It is striking that while she makes carefully considered changes in the prose rhythm and syntax of individual lines throughout rehearsal, Fornes never attempts to give line readings to the actors. The closest she comes to demonstrating vocal intonation is in a discussion of Juster's question to Marion in Scene 28: "What are you doing?" Explaining that she never knows what to stress but can hear a wrong stress, she suggests to the actor that each of the four words in the line needs to be made distinct. As she reads the line aloud, she gives the initial word, "What," a slight emphasis. Later, perhaps involuntarily, the actor uses this emphasis when he first repeats the line in rehearsal.

Fornes insists that her primary concern in directing is "for the clarity of what is happening [in the play text] . . . as manifest in the words." She trusts most not a set of principles but what she calls "a painter's eye" (she was a painter before she became a playwright) and experience: "If I have a feeling that this actor needs to get up and walk over there, then I don't know if it's right until the actor gets up and does it. . . . [What] guides me on how to block scenes and [in the] composition of scenes . . . has to do with energies that happen between shapes and persons. Something happens inside the person when the distance between objects and persons changes." Later she adds: "An unpleasant composition [on the stage] is as much of an irritant as somebody making an unnecessary movement."

Donald Eastman's simultaneous scene setting for *Uncle Vanya*—in which Vanya's study, the sitting room, the dining room, and the garden are present and visible throughout the play—is used by Fornes to allow characters possibilities of spatial definition beyond those indicated by the stage directions in the text. For instance, in the first act, which Chekhov sets entirely in a garden outside the house, Fornes has Vanya's mother seated at one point reading in the dining room and stages the final scene between Vanya and Yelena in the sitting room rather than—as the stage directions indicate—during a walk to the terrace. Early in the rehearsal of this suddenly revealing scene, in which Vanya impetuously declares his love for the professor's young wife, the director interrupts the dialogue between Vanya and Yelena to discuss the intricacies of the actress's blocking: where she rises, crosses, stands, moves, sits. Alma Cuervo verbalizes all her moves, recapitulating her previous blocking, then says: "That doesn't matter. We have a new pattern. . . . What do you want now?"

Fornes is at first silent. There is a slight misunderstanding to be cleared up about just where changes have occurred in the blocking. Now Yelena sits, then stands and moves toward Vanya, who crosses to a chair far downstage so that he is not in direct physical alignment with Yelena. The blocking—as it is being explored—clarifies, without realistically illustrating, the relationship of the two characters in the scene: It is a visual-kinetic composition of jerky, discontinuous points of contact. Yelena says to Vanya, "Do you know, Ivan, the reason you and I are such friends? I think it is because we are both lonely and unfortunate," and he replies, "You are my joy, my life, and my youth. . . . Only let me look at you, listen to your voice—."[26] As he delivers this speech, Vanya is seated in a chair, downstage right, his back to what would be the center section of the audience, his upper body inclining diagonally left upstage while Yelena stands directly behind him upstage, facing the center section of the audience. (The performance space at the Classic Stage Company is designed so that three-quarters of the stage is surrounded by the audience.)[27] Vanya's face is turned not toward Yelena but toward the couch where she had been sitting earlier in the scene.

Fornes interrupts Vanya's declaration of love to discuss the speech with the actor. The actor now experiments with delivering Vanya's lines while gazing directly at Yelena's face. Fornes stops the scene and enters the playing area. She takes the actor's hands and tentatively explores first how Vanya might seize Yelena's hands and then how Yelena might pull back, enacting what she describes as the actress watches. The actress and director exchange positions; Fornes now stands in the playing area watching closely. As Vanya reaches upward for Yelena's hands, the director interrupts the scene again to suggest that Vanya take Yelena's hands precisely at a particular moment in the speech. Finally, Fornes moves Yelena closer to Vanya and places his right arm around her waist.

During a break, Fornes points out that the obvious form of resistance if someone seizes your hands is simply to step or pull back. The placement of the actor's arm around the actress's waist helps to secure her in a position that is both physically difficult to maintain and devoid of behavioral verisimilitude. The director wants the actress to remain close by, yet arching back from, the seated actor, who reaches upward to grasp her hands "as if he is a penitent rising from the flames below." She demonstrates for me, grimacing, her head thrust upward, as she raises clenched hands. Fornes's painterly staging of this scene is a close reading in visual form of the delicately woven fabric of the play text.[28] "When you're trying to pull yourself up, if you are holding on to somebody, you are also pulling . . . [that person] down."

Fornes's staging of the penitent in torment clearly emerges when the scene is rehearsed again in the run-through after the break. Vanya's arms are upraised throughout the dialogue. Yelena, close to him, her two hands held tightly by one of his, her eyes looking upward in torment, delivers the closing line in the act: "This is torture."[29] But in performance on December 19, 1987, the scene is subtly changed. During intermission Fornes tells me that the actors found the earlier version too artificial. When I ask if she redirected the scene, she replies, "No, *it* changed." The scene as performed is an abbreviated and somewhat more naturalistic staging. What emerges in performance is an allusion to an earlier rendering in rehearsal. Only near the very end of the dialogue do Vanya's arms reach up and, oddly, from my vantage point in the theater, Yelena seems to clasp his hands near her breast as she delivers her last line, looking upward. Fornes, having watched this performance from the auditorium, confirms that the scene as it now appears does not have the effect she intended and that she prefers the earlier staging. Such is the intricate fragility of moments shaped for beholding in rehearsal.

Fornes experiences, and articulates, a sense of rehearsal "going backwards." In the third week of rehearsal of *Vanya,* I overhear the director say to production stage manager Nancy Harrington: "Two days ago I thought this was going to be extraordinary, and yesterday I thought it wasn't working. And when we come to tech rehearsals, I always think we're going backwards, that some beautiful things are disappearing." In addition, there are moments that are discussed, explored, probed, enacted, and then dropped without a trace. One is the attempt to find an opportunity for Marina, an old nurse, to exit and reenter during Act 1 so that she can bring the professor his tea. Fornes spends perhaps a quarter of an hour trying to find an appropriate staging of what might be thought a simple exit and entrance (there is no such thing), suggested by Margaret Barker, the actress playing the nurse. What is most revealing about this ultimately abortive attempt is Fornes's response when the actress first suggests the need for an unscripted exit for tea-serving: "The reason I didn't think about that is because Chekhov hasn't thought about it . . . but let's try it."[30]

In the rehearsal of her own play Fornes confronts a more serious version of the problem of what the playwright has or has not thought about. At two different points in the rehearsal of *Abingdon Square* actors raise the question of the importance and physical presence of Thomas, Marion's child. (Juster believes himself to be the biological parent of Marion's child; Thomas's real biological father is a stranger, a glazier who came once to the house to repair a window.)

John Seitz first raises the issue while rehearsing a monologue in which there is a brief reference to Thomas: "Four years later Marion had a child. I was overwhelmed with joy, but Marion was not. She became more taciturn than ever."[31] The actor begins by musing that Thomas does not figure much in the scene and in the play: "It's almost as if he's a nonpresence." When Fornes comments, "That may be the writer's problem," the actor asks, with a smile, "Can you get the writer to do something about that?" Fornes's response is disarming as she speaks in the role of playwright, "That may be my fault, I've never had a child and I think I do forget the presence of the child in the play."[32] Anna Levine, the actress playing Mary, cautions that *Abingdon Square* should not turn into a play about a child when the child really is not in the play.

The question of to what extent and exactly how the child "is in the play" is later raised more urgently by Madeleine Potter during rehearsal of Scene 28, a highly emotional encounter between Marion and Juster. Discussing the nature of Marion's uninvited return to the house from which she has been banished as an adulterous wife, the actress suddenly interjects: "I have to understand this. How much is Thomas, my child, in this scene?" The playwright's response is forthright: "Thomas isn't here [i.e., not in the house; not emotionally present in the scene]. . . . *If Thomas were the issue, this scene wouldn't take place*" (emphasis added).

In the immediately preceding scene with her Great-Aunt Minnie, Marion has delivered these lines: "I need my child. I need my child, Minnie. I need that child in my arms and I don't see a way I could ever have him again [Juster has kept Thomas hidden, threatening that a court would award him sole custody of the child if there were a divorce, on the grounds of Marion's adultery]. . . . I watch the house. I imagine the child inside playing in his room. . . . I know he's not there, but that's how I can feel him near me. Looking at the house."[33]

Now, in the discussion of Scene 28, the actress, following her own sense of through-line, argues passionately for the importance of Marion's attachment to Thomas. Fornes speaks instead of Marion's attachment to the house itself, of which Marion has said before her marriage to Juster: "In this house light comes through the windows as if it delights in entering. I feel the same. I delight in entering here. I delight in walking through these rooms and I'm sad when I leave. I cannot wait for the day when my eyes open from a night's sleep and I find myself inside these walls. Being here I feel as if I'm blessed."[34]

The distinction between writer and director becomes blurred as Fornes says to the actress: "I feel you want the house from him, and you want Thomas from him, but you want Thomas from *him* more than you want Thomas. You come to rape him [Juster], in a sense." The actress persists, involuntarily quoting a line from the play: "But this child is a baby. 'Where is it?'"

In the final speech of Scene 28, Marion says:

I had forgotten how I loved this house. I love this house. . . . I'll tell you a riddle.
    See if you can solve it:
If a person owns an object, where is it?
It's under his arm.
If a person loves an object, where is it?
It's in his arms.
If a mother's baby is not in her arms, where is it?
(*Pause*) Where is it? Where is Thomas? Where have you taken him? . . . How
    can you do this? How can you put me through this? What do you gain?[35]

As if feeling the force of the actress's investment in Marion's unanswered question, "Where is it?" but, like her script, unable to answer in literalistic terms, Fornes responds, "You're right. I may forget the child but you don't."

Actors and audiences often need to ask questions whose terms may preclude an answer by the playwright. A familiar example might be: Where are Lady Macbeth's children?[36] In Fornes's rehearsal of her own play, author and director are allied in resisting a certain way of understanding a scene between an estranged couple whose child is being kept by the husband.

Earlier in rehearsal, John Seitz describes *Abingdon Square:* "This play constantly defeats our expectancies." This defeating of our expectations—what I call Fornes's uncanny realism—is partly related to the director's recognition of the "enormous possibilities" of any acting moment in the play, despite the discomfort this may cause for an actor who understandably needs finally to reduce the possibilities. Implicit in Fornes's stress on "enormous possibilities" is a sense of the enormous range within each possibility. Her works for the stage, in rehearsal and performance, change the actor's and audience's sense of what is possible; in this way, Fornes as playwright and director alters our conventional expectations of what is meant by "realism" in the theater.

At the beginning of *Abingdon Square,* a fifteen-year-old boy and a fifteen-year-old girl wrestle for a piece of candy. We expect this to develop into a sexual relationship; it doesn't. Instead, the fifteen-year-old girl marries a man old enough to be her father. We expect this to be a Freudian situation; somehow it isn't. A young man and his father play chess. The son thinks he has checked his father's king but loses his bishop instead. We expect the play to dramatize son-father rivalry; it doesn't. Finally, a husband and wife are estranged; the husband keeps the baby. We expect (and so do some of the actors) the custody of the child to be a major issue in the play: It isn't. In each instance Fornes asks us to reconsider a situation and redefine its essence. She wishes, in her directing as well as in her writing, to "eliminate everything superfluous. . . . I don't even like to mimic the gestures and tones of voice of social behavior, which may be 'accurate,' but which are really just a mask concealing a deeper reality."[37]

This "deeper reality" is not always accessible even to the playwright, however. In a disclaimer characteristic of many writers of fiction, Fornes says to an actor during rehearsal of *Abingdon Square:* "The characters know what they're doing but I don't." As director of her own play, Fornes seems at times to discover possibilities in the text unknown to the playwright. Later that day she uncharacteristically interrupts the same actor near the beginning of a scene to explain why Juster offers money to his estranged wife: "Juster is being reasonable."[38] During rehearsal of a crucial scene between Marion and Juster, Fornes says to the actors: "I never saw this before but. . . ." Speaking as director refusing interpretative closure, she offers two unscripted options to the actor playing Juster: "It's not in the play but I think Juster does take on lovers from the street. I'm not sure whether he is actually doing these things or is having nightmares about them, but in any event he is confronting his own sexuality." The "I" here is indeterminate. Fornes speaks also as symbolist poet/playwright for whom nightmarish dreams are as indicative of reality as literal experience.

Finally, the context for directorial "knowing" in rehearsal may at times be indistinguishable from that of the actor. During rehearsal of a scene that is to be followed by Juster's abortive attempt to shoot his estranged wife, Fornes silently enters the playing area and walks to the table representing the desk at which Juster sits.[39] She stands there, rustling through loose pages of the script on this "desk," trying to decide whether Juster has his gun there, among his papers. For a moment I observe the director and playwright using the same means as the actor to map unknown terrain. Analytic energy is interchanged with tactile exploratory energies; exploration becomes, for actor and director alike, a way of knowing in rehearsal. As Fornes says to Madeleine Potter early in rehearsal of *Abingdon Square:* "Every scene has to be mapped. We all know that. But the only way to map it is to work it. Then after it's mapped, we keep working it . . . and map it again."

"THE REALM OF THE UNANSWERED"

Actors on Fornes

THE PLAYS of Maria Irene Fornes at once illuminate and conceal a vision of acting that her own directorial efforts over the past thirty years have made abundantly, brilliantly clear. Her plays have perhaps inevitably overshadowed her considerable achievements as a teacher and director of actors—primarily in her own work, but also in plays by Chekhov and Ibsen, as well as by such contemporary playwrights as Ana Maria Simo and Caridad Svich.

The following interviews, conducted in January and February and again in May and June 1997, comprise a kind of portrait of Fornes as stage collaborator—at once formalist and improvisational, demanding and permissive, fiercely insistent on the truths of her own vision, yet attuned to the contributions of others. Among other things, as Crystal Field notes, Fornes is "a master of ambivalent feeling."

Rebecca Schull created the role of Fefu in Fefu and Her Friends. *She won a 1977 Obie Award for her performance. She was interviewed by phone at her home in Los Angeles.*

COE: Is it possible to speak of a particular style of acting in response to Fornes's texts?

156

SCHULL: Irene has very, *very* particular ideas about the way she wants an actor to do something—right down to the way you might drag your finger along a wall. She'll choreograph every moment: If somebody has to tiptoe across the room, she'll tell them very specifically how to do it. She doesn't always work this way, and she does it more with some actors than others, but she usually wants complete control over the way things are done. A lot of the actors are put off by it, but it never bothered *me* because I felt it was her work and she was entitled to ask for it to be the way she sees it. It may be what happens naturally when a writer has the power to supervise. Always her imagination is visual—her concentration on the way she sees a room and costumes and lighting is probably more cinematic than it is on the [traditional] stage.

COE: That kind of cinematic visualization has to do with more than blocking, scenery, and costumes—it's gestural and expressive, too, isn't it?

SCHULL: In the movies you have a close-up, so you see the smallest movement in a big frame, and she directs that way—as if you will be aware of the smallest movement on the stage. It's how she manages to focus the audience's attention—she wants the audience to see those tiny movements. I also remember her once in rehearsal for *Fefu* saying, "Well, this scene is like a fight between Joan Crawford and Bette Davis." You knew immediately what she had in mind: that kind of catty, bitchy thing that sometimes goes on between women. I also remember a long monologue that she went over and over and over with an actor, I don't know how many times, giving directions on each line and each gesture—how to crouch behind the couch on one particular word, then to pop up on another particular word, to turn on one word, then to turn back on another particular word—and finally it was quite marvelous. It didn't mean that the actor wasn't creative or was a dolt in any sense, it was just that Irene wanted it to be a certain way. For some actors, working this way is a problem; for others, it's not.

COE: It seems to me that Irene has a special interest in stillness, in the absence of superfluous gesture. Did she stress this in rehearsals?

SCHULL: I think that she probably casts in such a way that that's going to be the natural tendency, you know? She's not going to cast people who happen to be fussy and do a lot of stuff. I do agree she's somebody who's not afraid of stillness. Or of silence. I remember doing a play at the Brooklyn Academy of

Music in which I played a woman who was hard of hearing, and Irene came to see it and afterwards told me, "Well of course you were the most interesting thing on stage, because you were just *sitting* there."

COE: How do you go about building the internal life of a character in a Fornes play? Do you consciously think about a character's internal progression or growth?

SCHULL: There's a scene in *Fefu* in the garden where they're all playing croquet, and it starts out very lighthearted, with almost a kind of idyllic feeling, and then suddenly Fefu says something about how agonizingly miserable she is. How her life isn't worth anything. It's terrible. And I remember that Irene said, "You know, there doesn't have to be any great preparation for this. It's just—all of a sudden, there it is. And it changes." I think that's the way people really behave.

COE: It's almost Chekhovian, isn't it? And it also relates to the idea of "transformation," which was a big buzzword at The Open Theater in the 1960s—a way to pull the plug on the overpsychologizing that dominated stage acting in those days.

SCHULL: I remember Irene said at one point during rehearsals of *Fefu* that the reason she set the play in the 1930s was because she wanted it to predate the time in this country when people were full of Freud and all that psychological stuff—before it had filtered down to the masses. She wanted her characters to be just "behaving," and not analyzing their behavior. Sometimes actors will turn handsprings to get from one mood to a different mood, but that's not the way people really behave in life. I can give you the example of a friend whose marriage has broken up recently, and one minute she'll be talking about something and laughing, and the next minute she'll be plunged into despair again. It happens that quickly. I think it's one of the foibles of acting to think that every change of emotion has to be prepared for and grounded, when in fact it doesn't. We can just go from one thing to another.

COE: All the same, didn't you feel in *Fefu* that there is a "journey" that your character took?

SCHULL: I doubt that I thought of it that way at the time. I think it was much more moment-to-moment, with different things coming up. It was much more about simply letting those people *be* there. Although people were generally beside themselves about *Fefu,* women were more responsive to it than men. I mean the men who responded to it were far more the "sensitive types." The middle-class men were a little bewildered, I think. Irene's writing is so evocative—women especially were so moved by the temper of the relationships among the women, and also, I would guess, by the very simple, natural behavior [of the production], nothing stagy. I remember seeing a college production of *Fefu* once that was absolutely awful—so *busy.* Making it *big* can be a problem, too, you know? You need to be very cautious about reaching for climaxes and great eruptions of emotion and all of that, because that's not what Irene's work is about.

COE: Did you "see" the character of Fefu and begin working toward that vision, or was it more a process of discovery during rehearsals?

SCHULL: I didn't have to go very far from myself to play that part. I think it was just something I felt and *did,* you know? I remember I did do some outside work in acting class on it, just to sort of fill in some things for myself about her relationship with her husband, which was only glanced at in the play.

COE: You felt a need to expand on what was in the text?

SCHULL: Even though I wasn't called upon to expose any great emotional thing in an overt way, when I said my lines about being unhappy with my husband I still felt a need to flesh it out for myself—to construct a very specific scene or two—a mood that I could actually go through in a scene, so that when those moments came in the play (even though they were glanced at) there would be a correlative for me—something that I had experienced that I could go back to and hit for a moment, so that a certain image or feeling would come. This is the kind of thing actors do all the time.

COE: How "playable" do you find Fornes's writing? Did it come easily for you?

SCHULL: For me it came very easily—almost without having to think about it. That's the other thing with Irene: When we started *Fefu* she didn't have the whole play written. The garden scene was something she wrote well into rehearsal. I think at that point she already knew who her actors were and what they could do, so I think a part of the writing was for them. The only other time she directed me was in *Exiles*, a play by a student of hers, Ana Maria Simo. Irene directed it with the same kind of meticulous attention that she brings to her own work.

COE: Irene can obviously be a very demanding director. How would you characterize the role of trust when you work with a director so obsessively tuned to detail?

SCHULL: I think that on the one hand the actor has to trust that Irene knows best, because it's her work, and if she says it's the way it's meant to be, you accept it. But I think it also works the other way—that Irene feels she has to trust that somehow there is a quality in the *actors* that expresses what she wants to express. In *Exiles*, as in *Fefu*, she started out with an actress who was absolutely wrong for the role, and let her go. Sometimes she can make casting errors. But I will say that I think Irene is a true genius of the theater. She's the only person I know that I would say that about. She just seems to have some kind of sixth sense about it. And whenever you hear her talk about other plays, she just homes in on what's wrong with it, where the flaw is. She knows more about drama and theater than anyone I know.

Sheila Dabney, whose career includes a long history with the Living Theatre, has performed in numerous works by Fornes, including Sarita, The Trial of Joan of Arc in a Matter of Faith *(creating the title roles in both),* Lovers and Keepers *(Clara and Toña), and* The Conduct of Life *(Nena). She refers to the characters she plays in Fornes's works as "the ones who put on the spangled gowns." She was interviewed in her Bronx apartment.*

COE: There seems to be a tension in Irene's stagings between a very intense directorial scrutiny of every action and word, and a tremendous freedom to play, discover, experiment, take risks.

DABNEY: Let me tell you a story about *Joan of Arc*—which was totally, totally, *totally* outrageous. Irene comes in on opening night and goes, "*Shei*-la. I have some new . . . some new . . ."

COE: *(Laughing.)* Rewrites?

DABNEY: Not rewrites. "Some new pages," she says. Opening night, in the dressing room, right? I'm putting on my makeup—for Joan I wasn't really going to wear that much—and she's standing behind me in the mirror, going, "No, you're in distress. You have to be paler." And I go, "All right. I'll put something on." Then I say, "Irene, how many new pages do you want me to *do?*" And she goes, "There's just twenty-two . . ." And I say, "You—you—you want me to learn *twenty-two* new pages? Irene, I have a thirty-minute call!" And she says, "Well, it's up to you." So I say, "Okay. We'll *do* it! No problem." So we sit in the dressing room and we read through it. But then I see that the rewrites aren't sequential—they jump. So I go, "I'm not going to remember this! But okay. Look, I can do it, but we have to carry our scripts." *(Pause.)* The most brilliant performance we ever gave! *(Hearty laughter.)* And every time we came to a new page, we'd throw the old one in the air! Which meant the whole stage was filled!

COE: She rewrote a significant chunk of the play on opening night?

DABNEY: That's right! We'd do our pages and we'd throw them, like *that!* *(Gestures expansively.)* And it was absolutely *marvelous* because we were so *committed*—it was like walking a thin line, a tight highwire—it was *blazing!*

COE: So everything is kind of up in the air.

DABNEY: I think that Irene was interested in me and *is* interested in me because I will *do,* I will absolutely *do.* If she says fall out of this chair onto the floor, I will do it.

COE: You'll find a way to make it work for you.

DABNEY: I've got the *guts* to fall out of the chair, you know what I mean?

COE: Do you think her work is particularly suited to that kind of fearlessness in actors?

DABNEY: No, no, not at all. But I *do* think her work inspires that burst of spirit that will go, like, "Come through the *door!*" *(She flings her arms wide.)* And her direction is not always congruent with what you've read [in the play]: You think you've read one thing, and it becomes something quite different onstage.

COE: Does she work extremely specifically with you in creating a performance?

DABNEY: Irene knows that if she says to me, "I want you to fall out of the chair on blah-blah-blah," then I will find a way to do that. But she doesn't direct the whole play that way. When we were doing *Sarita*, for instance, I remember sitting in an overstuffed chair, and she said, "*Shei*-la, do it upside down." So I have to find my way there. (*Turning upside down in her chair, she continues the interview.*) I'm sitting this way talking to my mom, saying, "I was thinking yesterday about blah-blah-blah." And I can trust Irene to tell me if this is working or not. (*Sitting upright again.*) Some things she says are very specific, and at other times she allows our instincts to move us. It's like a piece of clay that's molded as we go along. When we did *Conduct of Life,* I swear to you, for three hours once we did an improvisation. For three hours! One scene! Playing with the language, playing with movements, dancing, working away from the text. Until finally Irene goes, "Okay! That's it!" It was an incredible experience, because when you go through something that many times, and you're not repeating the same thing that you did before—she didn't require that—you start to *discover* things. She allows you to do that.

COE: Do you think it takes some actors longer to realize that they have this kind of freedom?

DABNEY: I think that my relationship to her directing is special, because I am fascinated by the way she directs. Most directors don't think that actors have any intelligence, for the most part. You're hired because of the way you look, or your training, or your schooling. But Irene is very much on the other side of the rainbow of *that*. The actors in Irene's plays are all inspired by her willingness to go with it, you know? There is never any "D&G"—no Doom and Gloom. It is always challenging, always provocative—like doing a scene upside down in a chair. You go, "Hmm . . . now I have one-and-a-half minutes to take my shoes off while we talk about your mother's funeral."

COE: Does she ever talk in more conventional directorial terms—for instance, about something like "pace"?

DABNEY: I don't know about other people who've worked with her, but she's never told me to go faster or slower. And I have done some real "still" things with Irene. She's much more interested in the moment being portrayed than in how her own imagination had perceived it.

COE: That's a beautiful way of describing what any director ought to be doing.

DABNEY: The beauty of Irene as she directs is that she allows you to take enormous chances. Those chances inspire you, and make your imagination work in a different way. Irene can be very loving and very brutal. You know she'll kick your ass if you mess around—she'll go right in there and go, *"Eee!"* You'll be doing something, and she'll go— (*Giving the interviewer a glowering stare, wagging a finger firmly, once.*) *"No!"* But the fun of it is you can always try something else. You can just go— (*Shifting in her seat, striking a pose.*) Or you can go— (*Moving again.*) Or you can go— (*Hitting another pose.*) And always you feel like you're *together*, you know? Because there's no fourth wall with Irene! She's sitting out there, but you don't feel separate from her! Even though she's not onstage—she doesn't sit close, and you can't see her— you feel like you're in this together! You don't know how beautiful that is! Because you function differently when you're free to explore, and not just trying to please this person.

COE: How do performances become set? How does repetition occur?

DABNEY: They do become set.

COE: It just happens?

DABNEY: No. We rehearse, we set it.

COE: When everyone's comfortable with it? (*Laughter.*) Or maybe not!

DABNEY: Maybe not! Maybe she'll bring in another *thirty*-two new pages! At some point the fourth wall goes up. And when we get to that audience situation, Irene will come and give us notes [after performances], like any director would, but in *our* relationship I will ask for notes on *closing night,* too. To the very end and beyond, I want my *notes!* Notes! Yes! Because *that* is the spirit of how we work!

COE: Uncensored expression, constant communication—

DABNEY: Yes! We're continuing to make ourselves better, okay? And there's a great deal of joy and release in that! So your question about repetition doesn't actually apply, because yes, we do acquire our sense of repetition—but when Irene directs there's a different sparkle in your eye. It's not like you're always trying to do *more*—it's just that you have more air in your lungs. It's Brechtian, in a way—only about emotions!

COE: What do you mean by that? That you're outside the work, in some way, observing?

DABNEY: It's that you're inside the work, saying, "Okay, Irene, I'm gonna *get* you *this* time. You don't love me? I'm gonna *make* you love me. Just you watch. You don't *think* you love me, but you will."

COE: But earlier you claimed that one of the rewards of working with Irene was that you weren't there to please her.

DABNEY: You're not. It's just that she is a master at perceiving each person's personality, and therefore she knows how to get what she needs from whomever she's working with. The only other director I've worked with who was like that was Peter Sellars, when we did *Ajax* in Europe. He was also a person who would give you your head, and just say—*Go!* I'm not sure how every actor might deal with Irene; some may be intimidated by her kind of freedom. Even when Irene wants very specific things, she never makes you feel like a prop. You can embrace what she requires. In her writing, it's the same—you never feel like exposition. In many plays women are used as exposition or props or something else to move the story along. They're not consequential. But in Irene's plays, everybody's consequential.

COE: Say more about that.

DABNEY: It means that when you're playing with another actor, you have a much different relationship to that actor when you know you're not just making the play go along. It's quite extraordinary, because [when everyone is consequential] it changes the whole atmosphere, the whole kinetic connection in the room—the whole chemistry of the cast! When you get up there, no matter what part you're playing, you're not playing around! We could be doing a comedy but, you *know* I'm gonna *get* you! (*Robust laughter.*) Which is extraordinary! You don't see it coming. All of a sudden—*whoosh*—where did *that* come from? She just wows you! *And* she has a whip! (*Deep laughter.*) She is totally delicious. I'm humbled that I've been able to work with her. (*Beginning to choke up.*) And I feel badly now that I can't really put into words or express the effect . . . where she takes me. And what I'm willing to give. I'm not willing to give that to everybody. (*Beginning to cry.*) The way she opens my *breast*-plate. I wouldn't do that for everybody. But somehow, she makes me feel comfortable to be exposed like that. In front of people I can't even see! There, in the dark . . . I don't know who they are. (*She breaks into sobs, tears streaming down both cheeks.*) Then she makes me show these parts of myself I wouldn't show anybody! And she makes me show it to a hundred and fifty *people!* (*Whispering, sobbing.*) I find that—extraordinary.

COE: That is extraordinary.

DABNEY: (*Composing herself a little.*) And of course it only gets better. With repetition. Although it *is* the American theater, which means we have only three weeks to rehearse, so that by the time we close we're ready to open. That's our economics. But I do think that even if our economics weren't such as they are, there would still be that *light.* There would still be that magic. There's always magic! (*Whispering.*) There's always space for it. She always gives you space for that magic. Always. It's really incredible.

John Seitz was in Winnipeg, Manitoba, performing in Death of a Salesman *with Judd Hirsch, and hoping he was on his way to Broadway. In 1987, Seitz received an Obie for his performance as Juster in Fornes's acclaimed production of* Abingdon Square *at the American Place Theatre in New York.*

COE: I wanted to ask you—

SEITZ: Before we begin you should know that Irene and I are estranged now. Which happens with everybody and Irene at some point or another.

COE: How did that happen between you?

SEITZ: I was working on a play, *Going to New England* by Ana Maria Simo, who was one of her students, which Irene was directing at INTAR, and I left after a week. Like they say on Page Six of the *Post:* "artistic differences."

COE: Can you be more specific?

SEITZ: She rearranged the play! She took the penultimate scene and put it in the middle, and it was no longer the play I wanted to do. I had 100 percent commitment to that work, but Irene—you know, she likes to break up with people. But I still love her—in fact I think she is one of the most formidable presences in theater in the world. And I also think that the work I did in *Abingdon Square* was certainly among the best work I've ever accomplished in my life as an actor.

COE: Why do you think that was so?

SEITZ: I think it was partly the way she approached her material, which gave me a wonderful range to play. And also because as a director she was always totally intuitive. A good example is when we were working on *Going to New England*. At one point she gave me a gesture—she said, "When you say this, take your hand and wipe the table clean." The scene wasn't related to cleaning—this was a guy who worked in a bank as a security guard—but as I did this gesture, the language and the emotion behind the language suddenly came to life in a completely unexpected way. If you're sensitive to that—if her images translate for you *into* something—some emotional correlative—it just opens up the *world* for you as an actor.

COE: Tell me about creating your character in *Abingdon Square*.

SEITZ: A lot of times you can look at a script—the way it's structured—and there are enough clues to give you a sense of what the journey of the character is. And then there are those miraculous times, like with *Abingdon Square*, when all you have to do is stay out of the way and let the character talk, let him move through you, and let him do things. That's happened to me maybe four or five times in my life, out of the three hundred plays I've done—when you don't feel it's you, when you're literally serving the voice of the character and the voice of the playwright. I've talked to other actors who've attempted *Abingdon Square,* and they were lost—but for me it was always very, *very* clear. A lot of it was a matter of keeping faith with Irene. When she recognized what was going on with me, it gave her the opportunity to flesh out a lot of stuff that she'd been thinking about, and also allowed her direction to become super-specific.

A good example would be this one scene in which I'm sitting in a bar talking to my son, and each of us has a glass of beer in front of us, and I'm obsessing about my wife and talking about how I'm following her around. I have maybe two gestures: I lift a glass of beer, then reach into my pocket and show a gun. It was so "formal." A kind of enhanced realism. I would say to myself, "I do this, then I do this, then I do this, now I turn." It was just *delicious*—it was this *world,* you know? [The lighting designer] Anne Militello was a major contributing factor, too. I always had the feeling onstage that the lights were extremely important, so when we closed on a Sunday matinee, I went up to the booth to talk to the people who were running the lights, and as a gift they ran all the cues for me, so I could imagine what it must have looked like. Irene had also designed [with Donald Eastman] a little teeny door I had to go through, after my character had a stroke; everything was slightly warped, in terms of perspective.

COE: Over the course of your career you've worked with Richard Foreman and Robert Wilson—two directors more associated with the kind of formalist theater you're describing in Fornes.

SEITZ: Yes, and Irene in her way was as formidable as either of them. Wilson is the equivalent of grand opera. [Seitz played Ulfhejm in Wilson's production of *When We Dead Awaken* in São Paolo.] You're doing arias and you're doing it by counts: seventeen counts to get your hand up above your head, and it's all enormous and stylized. With Foreman, I did Molière's *Don Juan* at the Guthrie, and later for Joe Papp in Central Park . . .

COE: I saw that production. Your sideways crab walk . . .

SEITZ: My knees are still killing me from that. One day he told me, "Why don't you try a funny walk?" And that's how that whole thing evolved. Foreman has no vocabulary to speak to actors. You're part of a mise-en-scène with people running across the stage with doll hands and feet stuck in their mouths and they're all growling, or else you're riding these plaster-of-paris poodles with their tails like crucifixes, and you have no idea *what* it is—it's a very private, poetic, supertheatrical kind of approach. But with Irene, it's more like her saying, "No no no, he *wants* to do this—he wants to wipe his face four times."

COE: "He" being the character.

SEITZ: Right. And so you just do it, because you know there is somebody on this planet who would do something just like that. Irene has a phenomenal sense of what human behavior is and what it's grounded in, and so she shares her palette—all of her living experiences, all of her observations of everyone she's ever known in Cuba and the United States—and just zeros in on the one behavioral aspect that releases a character. Critics can talk about it as metaphor, but eventually you'll see somebody actually doing it—you'll see someone sitting in a little Italian restaurant somewhere unconsciously smoothing a tablecloth. When you first try to inhabit it, you may find it alien, but after a while it becomes quite comfortable. When you're working with Bob Wilson, it's all just a dance—you're dancing in rehearsal. He'll leap up and say, "The *line,* the *line,* the *line,* the *line,* the *line* is *everything,*" incredibly full of himself, and you'll just watch. Your task will be to execute. Wilson's not particularly interested in how you feel. But with Irene, it's all familiar—you always recognize it as behaviorally correct, as human. You're dealing with this kind of selective realism, and it becomes very communicative. It takes you to a very specific place that you might not have arrived at on your own. With Irene I could talk about what it is to be a human being. Wilson and Foreman don't really care about that. They're very cold in the way I think genius sometimes can be.

Madeleine Potter played Marion opposite John Seitz in Abingdon Square. *At the time of this interview, she was appearing as Lady Chiltern in* The Ideal Husband *on Broadway.*

COE: It occurs to me to ask what it was like to audition for Irene Fornes.

POTTER: It's odd, I was just trying to think about that, too, actually. I don't really have a very clear memory of it, except that she was very nice. I think she only had me read once and then she gave me an idea or two, and it was pretty clear almost immediately that she wanted to use me.

COE: Irene seems to have a reputation as a fairly decisive director.

POTTER: I've worked with other playwrights who also direct their own work, and [compared to them] I found Irene to be extraordinarily open-minded, even though she does have very strong ideas. She has an incredible capacity to create an atmosphere. She's also extremely observant, obviously bright, and never obvious in her suggestions.

COE: Do you have any concrete examples of this?

POTTER: I remember one very long speech near the beginning of *Abingdon Square*. It was in a scene between me and my brother, very rambunctious, and we're sort of running around chasing each other. I was doing just fine with it in the rehearsal hall. I got to a place where I liked doing it, and I knew what it was about, and it just happened. Then we got into the theater, and I suddenly became struck with terror and couldn't do it. I just sat down at the dress rehearsal. She came over to me, sitting at the edge of the stage, and said, "What's wrong with you?" I kept saying, "I can't do it. I can't. I can't do it." She said, "You should just imagine that you're walking through the Alhambra." Now I'd never been to the Alhambra, in Spain, but I'd seen pictures of it, and I knew exactly what she was talking about. I thought of it as a space that was incredibly huge, lofty, and eternal. And also the notion of privacy: I thought of being alone. Then I said, "Oh. Okay." From that moment on I was absolutely fine. I never had anything else on my mind in that scene except the Alhambra. There was immense, massive freedom in that image for me. A lot of directors would have said, "Don't be frightened, just go through it a few times and you'll be fine." But she addressed the root of my fear—the fact that I was holding on to something—and helped me let it go. I think that she has a rare capacity to look at an individual and speak particularly to them, which is an amazing instinct—almost unheard of, in my experience in theater.

COE: All of the actors I've interviewed speak of Fornes's use of a physical gesture to key a moment.

POTTER: I remember one scene in which my character was getting married, and Irene was very specific about where she wanted our hands to be, and very specific about the significance of that. I guess that didn't strike me as unusual because it seemed in keeping with her writing, which is also very imagistic. I myself am quite bossy and full of ideas, but I love it when a director has a strong physical idea that's rooted in the truth of the moment—a truth that is logical in the real world, and also has a spiritual sense.

COE: What do you mean by a spiritual sense?

POTTER: A spiritual dimension might be a better of way of putting it. I suppose one of the definitions of a good artist is that when he or she creates an image it's both accessible and endless—it resonates in your imagination, the way a great line of poetry does. Irene's work can be earthy and simple, but she also creates a dimension of spirit. I don't quite know how to put this into words, because it's essentially intuitive, and communicates on a subliminal level that speaks to the spirit as well as to the mind. For instance, there's a section in *Abingdon Square* where my character sleeps with a workman. Now why does she do that? It's never entirely explained, and yet it felt true, and right. Irene deals with the unconscious in her writing and her direction in a deep way, which is why her writing is so special and perceptive. Irene writes about the entire value of life, in a way that's very human, and yet not obvious. I can still remember what it felt like to stand by this door at the beginning of the play with John, listening to this song, and putting my hand on this window—which was probably her idea, come to think of it. It's unusual for somebody who writes a play to be that acute a director—with the capacity to be subjective and objective at the same time. And open. Just open, you know? She taught me a lot.

Crystal Field has appeared in numerous plays and productions by Irene Fornes over the past thirty years, beginning with Promenade *at the Judson Church in 1965 (in which she played Miss O), and continuing with* Molly's Dream *(Alberta),* The Conduct of Life *(Leticia), and many others. She has also produced several of Fornes's works as Artistic Director of Theater for the New City in New York. Field was interviewed during a lunch break from a grant-writing session at TNC.*

COE: Irene's direction seems to combine very detailed physical work with a kind of deep visual and verbal poetry—things that coexist in the work of few stage artists these days. Do you think this is a fair description?

FIELD: Yes. It was always the case, but in the beginning—not the first time we worked together, at Judson Church, but later on—actors would sometimes ask her a question that she couldn't answer facilely enough, and so sometimes she pulled back a little from her original ideas. But she quickly learned that this was ridiculous, and realized that the ambiguousness and amorphous feelings in human beings are of major importance, and to give a black-and-white answer to an actor's question is often to lose the gist of what she wanted to do in the first place. So after a while she wouldn't even try to explain. My greatest respect for her is for that, because that's a true poet's understanding. A lot of directors don't have that kind of understanding, and a lot of actors' work is ruined as a result. One of the reasons I started this theater was because good or almost good writing was constantly having the guts knocked out of it by people who tried very linear understandings of work and just couldn't get near it. My father was a poet, among other things, and so I understood from the time I was a child about poetry. I understood things poetically—which is the beginning of an understanding of reality, which isn't linear, either. Sometimes you can have interesting actors in a play, but they don't really understand the style, so you have to explain it to them and demand that they execute it. Irene has made herself a master of ambivalent feeling, and if you can't act that, or if you choose not to act it, then she's got to explain it to you. She's got to hold her own with her writing. In her early days, she had more trouble doing that.

COE: What do you mean, a master of ambivalent feeling?

FIELD: One of her famous songs [from *Promenade*] is "You were there when I was not, I was there when you were not, don't love me, sweetheart, or I might stop loving you." Now you've got to be able to *act* that—

COE: (*Laughing.*) How do you act that?

FIELD: (*Laughing, too.*) I can't tell you. I can *act* it for you. If you want to take a year's acting lessons with me, I can *show* it to you. But that's the best I can say. . . . When you first study acting you need to begin by being very clear about your objectives, in the old Stanislavski style, but at some moment you have to let go of that, dispense with your own ego, and put yourself into the service of the force that drives us all. That's really what an actor has to do. That whole Stanislavski technique prepares you to act, but then you have to let go and go on your own intuition. It's like a violinist who's very skilled and has worked out the difficult part of the sonata, but then he's got to *play* it. He can't be thinking too much about the fingering. And *playing's* the thing I'm talking about that can't be explained—not in a sentence. Acting needs to be a study of human nature that comes from an actor's intuitive understanding, which you've supposedly developed over the years, along with your technique. You can't be continually asking questions that have no answers. At some point you have to get to the realm of the unanswered. And if what you're looking for is too linear or logical, you'll never be able to get there. Irene understands this deeply as a human being.

COE: So it's her texts that demand a more complex acting style—one that doesn't necessarily follow a linear route or a specific motivation.

FIELD: Or follows a very complicated motivation—one that most actors can't deal with, or won't. They don't know how to deal with it, because when you get to complicated motivations you also get to vulnerability. I've noticed in my years in the theater that actors aren't often able to become vulnerable enough. They need justification, they don't want to show the dark side, or anything that's strange about themselves. They all want to be heroes. And of course that's not what we're really looking for in art—certainly not in Irene's plays.

COE: I think we *can* look for heroes in art, and do, although I would agree this shouldn't be the extent of our search.

FIELD: It depends on what you mean by a hero. I don't know one hero in one play who was a real hero. Characters are either fighting their own egos or trying in some way to battle their own foibles. That's the way it is in this world. That's what makes us human beings!

COE: And places special demands on actors!

FIELD: Yes, absolutely.

COE: You mentioned that Irene's direction has become less compromising and explanatory over the years. In what other ways has her direction changed or grown?

FIELD: I don't think it has changed, basically. I think she's become surer of herself, but I don't think it has changed. She had all of it to begin with. You can separate her work from her direction, and you can have another director do her work, and it will be interesting. But Irene is a *brilliant* director. A lot of writers try to be directors and aren't, but she is. She understands where actors are coming from and how to motivate them. She certainly has a total understanding of the literary part of a play, and also a wonderful sense of costume and stage design. And she is a wonderful stager—her sense of space, her use of space, and the way she moves actors are all excellent. She doesn't really work any differently than any other good director—it's just that because she's usually also the writer, she can give herself more freedom than most writers would allow. And she can do it anyplace, anytime, anywhere, and get somewhere. Now that's a major craftsman, and a major artist. And most important, she knows what makes us human beings, not animals, which is our ability to deal with our darker sides in some conscious way. That's there in Irene's plays—*incredibly* there.

SCOTT CUMMINGS

"THE POETRY OF SPACE IN A BOX"

Scenography in the Work of Maria Irene Fornes

IN HER BEST work, Maria Irene Fornes creates a dramatic world as large as life itself within a small, spare, and often confining theatrical space. At the heart of that miniature universe she places a sentient creature or creatures in the throes of an emergent and unbearable feeling. Then, with a remarkable economy of means, both material and esthetic, she evokes that condition of being in images and actions, both verbal and visual, which resonate with beauty, humor, and comforting truthfulness. One of the keys to Fornes's success is her seamless integration of dramaturgy, directing, and design, an artistic unity that stems from her role as director of her own plays and from her continuing collaboration with a team of designers. My specific concern here is to examine how Fornes defines and uses theatrical space, scenographically, dramatically, and thematically.

THE DOUBLE INSIDE: RECIPROCAL INTERIORITY

In Fornes's drama, psyche is spatial. A cartographer of the human spirit, Fornes creates character as an emotional and cognitive territory and charts that "space of being" over the course of the play. This means that setting and design function in strategic and tactical ways in her work as both the visual frame *around* character and an extension *of* character. The plays are marked by what I would call a reciprocal interiority. That is, they take place indoors, in rooms that are cut off from the outside world, and they depict the interior experience (mental, emotional, and spiritual) of one or more quietly heroic figures. This reciprocal interiority accounts for a paradoxical quality of the scenic environments created for the plays: They are abstract and realistic at the same time, or, as Fornes's Dr. Kheal would say, "abysmal and concrete."

Since 1977, most of Fornes's plays have taken place in essentially the same place: a home. These homes include such familiar Fornes settings as Fefu's New England country home (*Fefu and Her Friends*, 1977), Mae and Lloyd's ramshackle hut on an earthen promontory (*Mud*, 1983), and Juster's townhouse on Tenth Street in Manhattan (*Abingdon Square*, 1987). Lesser known Fornes works reflect the same socioeconomic range of domestic environments In *A Visit* (1981), a young woman named Rachel on her way to college visits the well-to-do Tyrell family in their Lansing, Michigan home and finds herself the object of desire of several members of the household. In *Enter THE NIGHT* (1993), a nurse named Tressa and her friends gather in her warehouse loft in Chinatown to support and care for each other in the face of a world marked by sickness and disease.

The types of buildings that Fornes's characters call home vary widely, as do their geographical location and specificity. Sarita and her mother live in the South Bronx (*Sarita*, 1984); Orlando and Leticia live in an undesignated Latin American country (*The Conduct of Life*, 1985). In *Nadine*, the first play of *What of the Night?* (1989), Nadine has set up her home outdoors in an empty lot, complete with dining table, sideboard, rocking chair, baby's bassinet, a mattress, and a tree. *Hunger*, the fourth and final play of *What of the Night?*, takes place in a shelter for the homeless.

Regardless of their architectural identity or geographical location, the scenic representation of these various homes makes them feel isolated and disconnected from the surrounding environment. A Fornes set generally depicts an unadorned domestic interior plainly furnished with simple furniture; without lamps, lighting fixtures, telephones, or most other basic appliances; with tall, undecorated but heavily textured walls; with doorways, archways, or hallways that lead to other barely discernible interior spaces. Windows are rare. In fact, the design makes no effort to suggest realistically what lies outside, next door, or on the horizon. To the contrary, these settings, many of which were originally designed by Fornes's long-time collaborator, Donald Eastman, have a hermetic, self-enclosed quality. They face in on the characters who dwell there, rather than out on any specific narrative context.

The characters who live in these rooms come and go with the behavioral logic of realism. While onstage, they engage in a variety of naturalistic activities, writing a letter or reading a book, changing clothes or eating a meal, performing any number of household tasks. However, when a play's action reaches certain nodal points, the minimal realism of the room subtly drains away and it becomes more abstract. Through lighting, blocking, acting, and the occasional use of music, the space becomes more confined or confining yet more and more filled with feeling, as if it were something of an emotional echo chamber. The set's formal characteristics, particularly its lines and shapes and to a lesser degree its often monochromatic color, frame and inform the action in a way that seems to amplify and at moments even to express a character's feeling. As the play progresses and the feeling intensifies, the room seems to grow cavernous, as if it were the external projection of the existential condition that is engulfing and overwhelming the character from within.

Take, for example, Marion in *Abingdon Square*. At the beginning of the play, Marion, a fifteen-year-old orphan, feels humbled and awed about becoming the child-bride of Juster, a fifty-year-old patrician widower. In the second scene, she explains,

> I hope to be worthy of the honor of being asked to be one of this household which is blessed—with a noble and pure spirit. I'm honored to be invited to share this with you and I hope that I succeed in being as noble in spirit as those who invite me to share it with them. I know that I sound very formal, and that my words seem studied. But there is no other way I can express what I feel. In this house light comes through the windows as if it delights in entering here. I feel the same. I delight in entering here.[1]

This passage makes clear Marion's reverence for Juster's house as a domestic sanctuary and associates her directly with light itself, making her both a humble votary and, metaphorically, a source of illumination within it. She feels a strong inner compulsion to define herself, to achieve an identity. As she says, "I feel sometimes that I am drowning in vagueness—that I have no character. I feel I don't know who I am."[2] Marion's effort to achieve the same nobility of spirit that characterizes her new home runs up against her burgeoning female sexuality. Over the course of the first act, a schoolgirl fantasy about a clandestine

Fig. 1. Donald Eastman's set for the Studio Arena Theatre production of *Abingdon Square,* directed by the author (1988). Photograph by Jim Bush.

lover gradually and mysteriously comes true. Her initial yearning for character yields to a psychic tug-of-war between love and duty that drives her out of the house and to the brink of madness.

In performance, this interior struggle is played out through acting, of course, but also through scenography and mise-en-scène. The setting is unusually exact for a Fornes play: a house on Tenth Street in Greenwich Village circa 1908. Nevertheless, as directed by Fornes and designed by Donald Eastman for productions by Women's Project and Productions in New York and Studio Arena Theatre in Buffalo, the set eschewed period detail and decoration in favor of an uncluttered, austere, flat design that featured a towering upstage wall, heavily textured, and a broad and shallow plank floor (fig. 1). The play calls for two large French doors upstage center that face onto a garden. Light enters through these doors, and so does Frank, Marion's secret lover, making them a volatile, highly charged threshold, a border zone between love and duty in and around which several telling sequences are staged.

One memorable moment takes place at the beginning of Act 2. In a word-

Fig. 2. Marion (Susan Gibney) at the window in the Studio Arena Theatre production of *Abingdon Square*. Photograph by Donald Eastman.

less, motionless scene, Marion stands in low light at the door looking out with longing, warm light coming in on her face, her raised arm bent slightly at the elbow, her hand resting against the frame, as an adagio plays for a minute or more (fig. 2). At this point, the audience does not exactly know that her lover has been gone for more than two years, but the music, the still, isolated figure set against the windowpanes, the vast flat wall surrounding it, and the play of light and shadow make this a tableau of yearning so evocative, so excruciatingly lyrical, that it seems she has not moved from this spot since he left. As in so many Edward Hopper paintings, figure and ground meld symbiotically to express a complex loneliness.

THE BOX IN THE BOX: THE INNER SANCTUM

In the self-enclosed interior settings of Fornes's plays, there is almost always another space that is interior to it, a subset of the set which presents an area that is both beyond and inside the main playing area. As a discovery space that can be curtained or walled off and then opened to reveal a hidden within, this area is akin to the "inner below" of a Shakespearean stage. More often than not though, it is a feature of the set and not the theater itself. It constitutes figuratively, and sometimes literally, an inner sanctum, a small, private place of refuge for the play's protagonist, often female. This inner sanctum takes on different shapes, sizes, and functions from one play to the next, but it is such a consistent feature of the plays, as written and designed, that it represents a major scenographic trope in Fornes's work and, by extension, an indicator of her basic dramaturgical and thematic concerns.

Several plays from the 1980s place this inner sanctum upstage on an elevated platform unit that may be masked by the tall wall towering over the main playing area or perpetually in view at a distance. In either case, it amounts to a small stage-within-a-stage. When independently lighted, with the downstage main playing area in darkness, it takes on the character of a living diorama. In *Sarita* at INTAR in 1984, directed by Fornes and designed by Eastman, this upper stage represents the kitchen of Sarita's tiny tenement apartment; the larger downstage area is her mother's living room (fig. 3). In the play's fifth scene, Sarita abandons her newborn baby to her mother's care in order to be with Julio, whom she loves desperately. He, in turn, abandons her periodically only to return when he craves sex. The little room on the upper stage is where she and Julio have sex and where, in his absence, she sits alone, writing letters to Julio cursing herself for loving him. The third letter reveals itself as a suicide note, in which she writes, "I'm not doing this because I love you because this is not love.—It's like a sickness that lives in my heart and I have tried to tear it out but I can't. I am sick with it and I want to die."[3] Although her suicide is averted, Sarita's kitchen sanctum remains the locus of her torturously passionate struggle to vanquish her "sickness" until the end of the play.

In *The Conduct of Life* at Theater for the New City in 1985, directed by Fornes and designed by T. Owen Baumgartner, the upper stage represents the warehouse where Orlando, an army lieutenant, imprisons Nena, the teenage orphan he has kidnapped off the street so that he may satisfy his voracious sexual appetite whenever necessary. The downstage playing areas represent the living room, dining room, and hallway of the house where Orlando lives with his wife, Leticia. After several violent sexual encounters with Nena in the warehouse, Orlando eventually sneaks her into his home and installs her in the basement (a second inner sanctum), where he continues to rape and beat her until the end of the play.

Fig. 3. Donald Eastman's set for the INTAR production of *Sarita,* directed by the author (1984). Photograph by Carol Halebian.

In *Abingdon Square* at Studio Arena Theatre in 1988, the upper stage represents the apartment in Abingdon Square that Marion rents as a secret trysting place for herself and the lover she has imagined into existence. When Juster finds a rent receipt for the place, he throws Marion out of his house and Abingdon Square becomes her home. As originally staged by Fornes in New York City for the Women's Project, the play included several scenes at the Abingdon Square location in which Marion lounged in bohemian decadence with her lover Frank. Months later, when the play was mounted at Studio Arena, these scenes were cut, but the apartment was still the setting for angst-ridden scenes between Marion and the other female characters in the play, her friend Mary and her aunt Minnie.

In each of these three cases, the inner sanctum on the upper stage is a private, secret, sexual asylum, but a faulty or ambivalent asylum at best. For Sarita, Nena, and Marion, the sexual activity rooted there leads to more pain than pleasure. To be sure, Marion genuinely loves Frank and, against her better judgment, Sarita even loves Julio, but these relationships jeopardize the nobility of spirit to which almost all of Fornes's heroines aspire. Even Nena, the innocent victim of Orlando's brutal sex crimes, insists that she is "dirty" and "that's why he beats me. The dirt won't go away from inside me." Nena's "dirtiness" is comparable to Sarita's "sickness" and Marion's "vagueness." Each woman seeks to redress an intense, debilitating weakness or sense of insufficiency that is linked to a place of illicit sex, consensual or otherwise.

In this regard, the inner sanctum can also be the site of purification. Early in *Abingdon Square,* before she is even conscious of any erotic inclinations, Marion subjects herself to a rigorous discipline. As she explains to her aunt, "I come to this room to study. I stand on my toes with my arms extended and I memorize the words till I collapse. I do this to strengthen my mind and my body. I am trying to conquer this vagueness I have inside of me. This lack of character. The numbness. This weakness—I have inside of me."[4] The room, the attic of Juster's house, is rendered as a small wooden cubicle with a small door and situated on the upper stage right where the Abingdon Square apartment will be in Act 2. In the first part of this scene, the audience sees Marion in camisole and underskirt, standing on tiptoe, hanging from a rope overhead, reciting her catechism with such desperate haste that it amounts to a spiritual scourging. The words, from Dante's *Purgatorio,* describe the blinding approach of the light of an angel. Her speaking is passionate to the point of being vaguely erotic in a religious sense, even though the impulse behind it is chastening.

A similar quasi-erotic spiritual passion informs *The Trial of Joan of Arc in a Matter of Faith,* Fornes's staging of transcripts from the interrogation of Joan of Arc by the bishop of Beauvais. As designed by Eastman for the 1986 Theater for the New City production, the set consisted of a small, raw, gray, abstract cubicle that represents the cell where Joan is being held during her trial (fig. 4). In this instance, the entire set has the feel of an inner sanctum; nevertheless, it was subdivided so that it still had its own interior spaces. Inspired in part by the tiny rooms seen in Giotto paintings, the cell featured a pillar, a narrow passageway, and a number of niches, ledges, and recesses, including a boxlike window well wide enough and deep enough for Joan to climb into and thereby achieve a limited asylum within her own cell. Here again is a Fornes work centered on the ordeal of a young adolescent woman who spends time confined or confining herself in an inner sanctum associated with sexual freedom or oppression and nobility of spirit.

The prevalence and importance of the inner sanctum in Fornes's theater becomes all the more persuasive when the device is found in her staging of plays

Fig. 4. *The Trial of Joan of Arc in a Matter of Faith,* directed by the author, scene design by Donald Eastman, at Theater for the New City (1986). *Left to right:* Bennes Mardenn (Inquisitor A), George Bartenieff (Inquisitor B), Sheila Dabney (Joan). Photograph by Carol Halebian.

by other authors. Perhaps the most radical manifestation of the inner sanctum occurred in Fornes's production of *Hedda Gabler* for the Milwaukee Repertory Theater in 1987. As designed by Eastman and presented on the thrust stage of the Todd Wehr Theater in Milwaukee's Center for the Performing Arts, the elaborate white set was built around an odd-shaped polygonal chamber prominently positioned upstage center where the thrust meets the theater's rear wall (fig. 5). This vault had a small door set into it a foot off the ground and a tiny pass-through window that remained closed throughout most of the play. Despite its central location, this conspicuous hut was virtually unused and seemingly unnoticed by the characters onstage until the end of the play, when Hedda carries through on her threat to burn Lovborg's precious manuscript. At this point, she opens the door of the vault, steps up and into its blinding white interior, closes the door, and opens the tiny peephole window which allows the audience to see her seated inside tearing up the manuscript page by page. As the light glows orange inside and smoke begins to rise from under the door, the

Fig. 5. Donald Eastman's set for the Milwaukee Repertory Theater production of *Hedda Gabler*, directed by Maria Irene Fornes (1987). *Left to right:* Kenneth Albers (Brack), James Pickering (Tesman), Marie Mathay (Hedda), Rose Pickering (Mrs. Elvsted). The stove is upstage center. Photograph by Mark Avery.

audience realizes that this entire little room is the stove Ibsen's text calls for, and that Fornes has had Hedda go inside it, literally and figuratively, to commit her most destructive act. The image itself was stunning. And the spiritual self-immolation that it suggested made her eventual suicide with her father's dueling pistols seem like a heroic formality, as if it were the merciful coup de grâce in a death that was by now a foregone conclusion.

The recurring presence of the inner sanctum in Fornes's work can be traced as far back as her first produced play, *Tango Palace*, a theatrical pas de deux between "an androgynous clown" named Isidore and "an earnest youth" named Leopold. The set represents Isidore's padlocked lair from which Leopold is desperately trying to escape. A recess in the room's rear wall serves as a shrine and when the play begins, Isidore sits there Buddha-like and resplendent in his androgyny, surrounded by a string of flower-shaped light bulbs and a miscellany of theatrical props, all of which will eventually come into play.

As a composite space in Fornes's oeuvre, the inner sanctum, whatever its size, shape, or particular identity, operates as a crucible of the spirit, site and symbol of a character's most private psychological action. It is the domain of the inner self, where spirituality and sexuality converge either in harmony or, more often, in some type of soul-wrenching discord. This makes it the place of passion in both a religious and an erotic sense. It is a cell—a place of confinement, contemplation, and, occasionally, confrontation. And most of all, it is an overwhelmingly female space, a room of one's own as womb of the self, a psychic zone deep within, rendered architecturally as an isolated interior space, the scenographic image of a woman's desire and struggle to give birth to herself, to bring herself into being.

THE POETRY OF SPACE IN A BOX

In 1968, Fornes wrote *Dr. Kheal,* a monodrama that takes the form of a profusely illustrated lecture given by a maniacal and bombastic pedant to an unspecified group of students. Dr. Kheal expounds on a variety of topics—Poetry, Balance, Ambition, Energy, Speech, Truth, Beauty and Love, Cooking—a list of themes and principles of such abiding concern to Fornes that it makes Dr. Kheal's lecture a virtual prolegomenon for her entire body of work. Here is what Dr. Kheal has to say on the subject of poetry:

> Now, poetry is for the most part a waste of time, and so is politics . . . and history . . . and philosophy. . . . Nothing concrete. Nothing like a well-made box. Which is concrete and beautiful and you can put things in it. But what can you do with poems? Tell me. And with politics, and with history, and with philosophy?—You can wrap them up, shove them up your ass, and what do you have? (*He moves his hands as if he were doing a magic trick which ends with the middle finger up.*) . . . Nothing . . . . Ha ha ha ha ha ha. (*Invaded by an immense poetic feeling.*) But if you can make a box, think, have you not made a lyrical thing? (*He thinks he hears someone speak. He squints, and looks over his glasses, then ignores the possible speaker.*) Poetry, on the other hand, is just a few words put together. Just a few. Just words. There is poetry. . . . And then they say there are poets . . . poets of this sort, poets of that sort, and poets of the other sort. . . . But who, tell me, understands the poetry of space in a box? I do. . . . Abysmal and concrete at the same time. Four walls, a top, and a bottom . . . and yet a void. . . . Who understands that? I, Professor Kheal, I understand it clearly and expound it well.[5]

Fornes, too, understands the poetry of space in a box, particularly the architectural box known as a theater. Although she rarely uses a conventional naturalistic box set, the stage space often takes the shape of a concrete and realistic interior, whether it has three walls, or one, or none. But as a box, it is also a lyrical thing, even when unoccupied and unlighted. Realistic elements such as doorways, steps, columns, corners, blank walls, and furniture pieces are arranged in a way that makes the set an abstract composition of lines and shapes. Depending on the theatrical venue, the visual field tends to be composed either two-dimensionally (wide, shallow, and open) or three-dimensionally (narrow, deep, and closed). In either case the set features architectural detailing that catches light, casts shadows, and isolates characters. In the flatter, more horizontal sets, these elements include flooring, pilasters, molding, and other decorative trim. In the deeper, more vertical sets, they are arches, railings, pedestals, niches, and other types of nooks and crannies.

As characters enter and exit, move about or remain still, and as levels, angles, and areas of light come into play, the scenic space seems to expand and contract—to breathe. The physical presence of a character onstage takes on a rhythm as Fornes varies figure-ground relations with precisely composed stage pictures. At one moment, the set and the blocking will isolate and set off a character, seeming to release and project a character's inner being like an image on a screen. At other moments, Fornes will position actors in places that partially obscure them from view or truncate them arrestingly—outside a window, behind a chair, under a bed, down a hallway. Rather than being set off by the set, they are absorbed into it, incorporated into the domestic environment in a manner similar to the creatures who peer out from behind the reeds in the jungle landscapes of Henri Rousseau.

This spatial rhythm is augmented by movement into and out of the inner sanctum, a box within the box which intensifies and sometimes recapitulates in miniature the dynamic of the surrounding space. As the action shifts around, as characters come and go, as lights change, the rhythms of the space vary and proliferate until what is by design a simple room becomes a seemingly organic membrane attuned to the psychic pulse of its chief inhabitant, hence the notion of reciprocal interiority. Fornes's poetry of space in a box combines the force and clarity of a geometric solid with the troubling emptiness of a void. Within that void dwells a character in extremis, filling but not erasing it with her struggle to be.

SELECTED PERFORMANCE REVIEWS

THE PROMENADE
Michael Smith

Irony has invaded the church. The newest production of the Judson Poets Theatre is, I think, among its best. At face value both plays exemplify the kinds of work that have been done at Judson before—Kenneth Brown's play deals with ideas about life, love, and politics, and Maria Irene Fornes's musical is compounded of bouncy, paradoxically cheerful non sequiturs which, given the composing-directing team of Al Carmines and Lawrence Kornfeld, are noticeably reminiscent of last season's *Home Movies*.* But the attitude undermining the surface simplicity of both works—and giving them their resonance—is irony, and this is new in Judson theater.

It is not the same thing as sarcasm, which was a pervasive tone of *Home Movies*, nor satire, which has turned up repeatedly, nor loving parody, which is

Originally published as part of a review of two plays, *Devices* (by Kenneth Brown) and *The Promenade*, in *The Village Voice,* April 15, 1965. The section about *Devices* has been deleted.
*Home Movies (1964) is by Rosalyn Drexler, with music by Al Carmines. *The String Game* (1965), mentioned below, is by Rochelle Owens. *(Ed.)*

the impulse behind the priest in *The String Game,* for example. It is subtler, and I think, more insidious: Although it is used to remarkable effect in the present instance, its tendency is to destroy the values it plays against and thus make its own impact impossible. . . .

The surface of *The Promenade* is entirely frivolous.* The plot describes a pair of prisoners in a penitentiary tunneling their way out and into an elegant party in the warden's house, where they become involved with the maid. Later they are in a faraway land, maybe Cathay, where the jailer has a lot of trouble identifying them and a number of whimsical things happen and they are back at the party where the warden is desperate to be entertained and they are reunited with their mother who lost them when they were babies and eventually they are back in prison. Something like that. The plot is inconsequential and exists to provide opportunities for set pieces of entertainment; at the same time the entire play is a set piece of entertainment, achieving unity through coherence of texture rather than form. The style is similar to old-time movie musicals, say, *The Big Broadcast of 1938,* and the production is an excellent example of high, as distinguished from homosexual, camp.

Irony enters in the written words. Within this preposterous setting, the talk shines with sophistication and intelligence and is more often than not concerned with actual feelings. The ideas that are used for comic effect are by no means trivial, and the glassy glibness of their expression is devastating. The dominant emotion is romantic melancholia but the tone is vapid frivolity, and the delicate tension this creates gives the event its distinction. Only occasionally do we come upon the bitter rejection implied by cynicism; more often we confront ironic acceptance, which penetrates the target's defenses by denying the need for them.

All this is gravy. The core experience of *The Promenade* is its exquisite and delicious humor. Great stretches of it are marvelously funny, and most of the time it is funny on the broadest and the subtlest levels at the same time. Miss Fornes's words are unfailingly witty; no less admirable is the manner in which musical numbers are conceived. One is continually involved in puns and multiple references. The opening song, "Dig, Dig, Dig," is straightforwardly about two men digging their way out of prison; simultaneously one senses the digging of Con Edison and others, continually undermining the external structure of one's life, and the hip connotation of the words. A paean to "Unrequited Love"

* The article in the work's title was dropped after this first production. *(Ed.)*

states the romantic paradox succinctly while parodying two or three kinds of song. Gretel Cummings's lordly "The Moment Has Passed" and Crystal Field's "Ah That's Life" have all the world-weariness of classic Brecht–Weill with an utterly modern and hilarious point of view added. "Four Naked Ladies" and the "Laughing Song" are straightforward and irresistibly entertaining.

Al Carmines has written music that interacts with Miss Fornes's words on every level. Lawrence Kornfeld's direction is perceptive and endlessly inventive. The cast is delightful: George Bartenieff and David Vaughan as the prisoners, Michael Elias as the jailer, Florence Tarlow as the girl in the cake, Frank Emerson as a Chinaman, Miss Cummings and Miss Field as guests at the party, William Pardue as the warden, Jerri Banks as the mother. The sets by Malcolm Spooner and the costumes by Ellen Levene and Miss Fornes are beautiful and comparably witty. The event is joyous and exhilarating, transforming ideas into game values to permit them entry into this realm of delight. If this implies a loss of direct feeling, at least the nostalgia over the loss remains real.

"YOU TAKE A YES & A NO"
(*The Red Burning Light* and Other Plays)
Robert Pasolli

Irene Fornes has never that I know of been called a poet, nor do I think she has written any poems. But she writes for the theater as a poet writes for the theater; she writes with a sense of the something that nothing contains. That is, what seems to you like nothing—or very, very little—is seen by Miss Fornes to be something indeed. She looks at the little things, the pots and pans, the everyday exchanges between people, the rapport people feel with trees, and food, and murder—and sees not their size but their significance. As her plays are infused by this special knack for espying the lot in the little, they make it visible to us.

This is the tradition established in modern times by another lady poet who wrote no poems, or next to none, but did write plays, Gertrude Stein. According to this tradition one renders human experience by reference to simple and small things alone. It is perhaps a womanly impulse; it makes me think of Emily Dickinson. But there are differences; for example, Miss Fornes does not go Miss Stein's stylistic route, creating by accumulation and repetition. She does the

Originally published in *The Village Voice*, April 17, 1969.

opposite, creating by subtraction. That is one artistic response to a world-too-much-with-us. Select, subtract, pare it down, look at the small things, find the essentials. Others mirror the multiplicity of the world; Miss Fornes minimalizes it. Some other contemporary theater poets have worked in this old and resurging tradition: Ruth Krauss, Kenneth Koch, Frank O'Hara. But they have also written poems, and two of them are men. Irene Fornes and Gertrude Stein are in those ways unique.

Miss Fornes's minimal art says certainly not all, but something and something with implications for more. This is why her theatrical moments are delightful. Delight in her plays is simply the sensation of surprise that what seemed like nothing does, in fact, amount to something, sometimes to a great deal. Take the Finger Song in *Promenade*, the musical that Miss Fornes wrote with Al Carmines:

Whenever my fingers went like this,
I said: Hell, my fingers went like this.
I said, Hell, my fingers always go like that.
Until one day somebody said to me:
How original it is that your fingers go like that.

Since then, every time
Since then, every time my fingers go like this,
I say: Look.
I say: Look at my fingers go like that.
How original it is that my fingers go like this.
One of these days I'll sell them.

The delight and surprise of which I speak is not in the joke of the last line. It is in the psychology of the first three lines of the second stanza, a revelation erupting from something very tame. That is an example of delight in Miss Fornes's work.

The last line is something else, which Miss Fornes does wickedly well. It is the revelation of an attitude, a specialty of her characters: an off-hand, flip attitude that is based on an outrageous and entirely natural ignorance of "the facts." One of the things that Miss Fornes knows about people is that reality is what's in their heads, not what's outside. Fantasy and imagination, the mental embrace of what is impossible according to the laws of physics, is as real as what is every day counted, codified, or used to hold up tall buildings. Miss Fornes's characters behave according to fantasy as much as logic, mixing yes and no, compounding love and mathematics. Dr. Kheal, in her play by that name, lectures on the arithmetic of love: "Ha! You think that is contradictory? Love and mathematics. Don't you know that you can take a yes and a no and push them together, squeeze them together, compress them so they are one? That in fact that is what reality is? Opposites, contradictions, compressed so that you don't know where one stops and the other begins?" Dr. Kheal is a lunatic, but he says many true things. Also many false.

Not caring that they are ignorant is what makes Miss Forness's characters human. If ignorance is a condition of life, a human being must accept ignorance. Three of her characters, the population of *The Successful Life of 3,* actually pursue ignorance; in a song at the finale they ask to be wrong and not to know it. Here's a snatch of another song from *Promenade:*

> I know everything.
> Half of it I really know.
> The rest I make up.
> The rest I make up.
> Some things I'm sure of.
> Of other things I'm too sure.
> And of others I'm not sure at all.

This attitude is an outrageous one in a world addicted to the ethics of good and evil. But that world is outside Miss Forness's plays. Within the plays, the characters just go about their business: They move in with each other, move out, steal things, then throw them away, screw any hole they find, stop screwing, eat a sandwich, pick their teeth, yawn, go to sleep, or to the movies. Experience is random and everything seems arbitrary. This is a phenomenological approach to character, the most advanced that I know of. It functions because the characters lack feelings. Lacking feelings, they don't choose, and what they do, based on nearly imperceptible whim, seems to happen by itself. When *The Successful Life of 3* was first produced (by The Open Theater in 1965; later it was redone at the Judson), people rightly called it a comic-strip play. That was the time of pop art, and we were looking for analogues. By comic strip, people meant that the characters were two-dimensional, feelings being the third dimension; Michael Smith called them monsters.

But these characters, and those in *Promenade* too, have a good time of life. They are perpetually positive and full of energy. In *The Successful Life* they live a life of vaudeville; in *Promenade* of song and dance. Their insouciance, blithely matched by Al Carmines's music for *Promenade,* is infectious. The bright amorality of their lives makes them recognizable as our reflections. Let's be honest: The rumble and run of our lives is a source of pleasure before it's a source of pain.

The humor of Miss Fornes's work is frequently the humor of foolishness and silliness, like when the jailer in *Promenade* is out chasing 105 and 106, two prisoners who have escaped, and comes upon an accident victim lying on the ground. 105 and 106 have swapped clothes with him; he is wearing both their jackets. On his front is 105, on his back 106. Seeing the 105, the jailer says, "That's one of them! Get up 105." He kicks at the man turning him over, and sees the 106. "There's the other," he says. "Get up 106. That's them all right. Get up." But beyond foolishness is a deeper humor—the cool, ironical humor of the stoic who knows that you squeeze yes and no together to get reality. "The Moment Has Passed" is a song in *Promenade* about the death of love. Here is half of it:

You have, perhaps, made me feel something,
But the moment has passed.
And what is done cannot be undone.
Once a moment passes, it never comes again.

I once had a man who loved me well.
His mouth was smaller than his eye.
But I loved him just the same.
Yes, I loved him just the same.

He said he would kill for me.
And I said, "like, for instance, whom?"
And he said, "like, for instance, you,
Like for instance you."

Sometimes it hurts more than others.
Sometimes it hurts less.
Sometimes it's just the same.
Sometimes it's really just the same.

Don't ask Miss Fornes for more than that, but don't ask her for less.

The Successful Life, Promenade, and *Dr. Kheal* are the best known because the most produced of Miss Fornes's plays. *The Office* was prepared for Broadway production but withdrawn before the opening. *Tango Palace* is an early play that has been produced only in workshops in New York. (There were full productions in San Francisco and Minneapolis.) *Molly's Dream* is a new play that has been done at New Dramatists and will soon, I hope, be reproduced. Another new play, currently at La MaMa, is called *The Red Burning Light of the American Way of Life.**

As *The Successful Life* is a vaudeville play, so *The Red Burning Light* is a burlesque play. The play's relationship to those genres is the same: Vaudeville and burlesque are used as lifestyles rather than performance styles. It is not so much that the actors use the styles as that the characters do.

Red Burning Light is a play about eroticism, fusing a string of burlesque entertainments with a ramble through some military and political adventures. Each character is two people in one: The burlesque m.c. is the general; a pratfall comedian is a private; an Irish tenor is another private; a stripper is a transvestite soldier; a house tough-titty is a lady general. There are also two butterfly girls whom I take to be camp-followers. The scenes of out-and-out burlesque are great fun: an introduction with mockingly bad dirty jokes by the m.c., a parody of *Madame Butterfly* in a bumps and grinds dance, and a climactic strip by the transvestite soldier. The scenes of military-political romping, also rampantly sexual since these are burlesque characters, are less focused, but the point emerges, although far more subtly than it does from *Che!* that American imperialism is an incidental form of runaway and largely impotent sexuality; the proverbial red light burns at the heart of our national experience. (I don't mean to come down like an elephant's foot on Miss Fornes's spider web. What I have called "the point" is no such thing as you experience the show. But it is the presiding notion, and if I'm to tell what it is I must tell what it is.)

The evening is, as the French say, a divertissement, and many, many moments are delightfully pure Fornes: the fooling, the irony, the much in little, the amorality, the insouciance, the sense of surprise. A search for Biafra on the map, for example, is the merest pretext for a big production number—a be-bop song called "Bi-a, Bi-a, Bi-a." Some members of the cast do wonders. Ellen Schindler is the perfect dumb stripper in great trouble masquerading as a soldier. (Her boyfriend, the Irish tenor, is passing her off as a petite guy in order to take her with him on the military campaign.) Miss Schindler is a modest performer, despite the fact that she ultimately strips, so she can play the dumb broad with-

---

* The title was changed to *The Red Burning Light Or: Mission XQ3* for publication in the first edition of *Promenade and Other Plays* (New York: Winter House, 1971). *(Ed.)*

out overdoing it. Her strip, an all-American number, is extremely nervy, and, thanks to her young and attractive body, which most strippers lack, she makes of it a good show. Ron Faber is also nervy as the sexually driven general and burlesque hall m.c. He uses a husky voice like the ratchet instrument that is part of the band, and projects a real and creditable raunchiness. I also liked Ralph Lee as the frantic private and pratfall comedian, and Dorothy Lyman and Jayne Haynes as the blonde and matching butterfly girls. Miss Lyman has a special knack for quick transition between goofy frenzy and serene calm; she does some instantaneous breakaways, arms and legs flying, that knocked me out.

But the pleasure of these superlative and well-performed moments does not suffice. There are gaping holes in *The Red Burning Light* that the accomplishments slip through in spite of the extrovert intentions of the audience, which was determined, according to the new spirit at the new La MaMa, to like what it saw and have a good time. Considered overall, the production is a disaster, the composite work of five people, including Miss Fornes and Remy Charlip, who has often collaborated with her. This work has not realized the play by creating a whole of its parts. There is a tone to the affair that is extremely unsteady—as if the actors, and consequently the characters, find themselves onstage together without quite knowing why. Or perhaps it is the characters, and consequently the actors, who so find. The play has a loose construction, which may be a big contributor to the unsteadiness.

It is, in other words, hard to know why *The Red Burning Light* doesn't work. Perhaps the writing and/or the production is at fault; perhaps it just happened. One of Dr. Kheal's lessons is that the possibilities are all we can know. "Tell me," he says, "does anyone here know the answer? Does the thing happen, or does one do it? Of course sometimes it happens and other times one does it. . . . Either you do it, or else it does itself, life that is. What other way is there? None." And he leaves it at that. And so do I.

THE TRAGIC MUSTACHE (*Aurora*)
Michael Feingold

Maria Irene Fornes's *Aurora*, which is the last production in the New York Theatre Strategy's summer season of very high-quality new plays, is a witty woman's eccentricity, an attempt to catch her dramatic world off-guard by

Originally published in *The Village Voice*, September 19, 1974.

coming at it from unexpected angles. To put it another way (*Aurora* being an extremely difficult event to pin down in words), it's as if Fornes had taken an old book of nineteenth-century illustrations and comically defaced the figures with penciled-in mustaches and suchlike distortions. At first one thinks it's all a joke, then voilà! The mustaches are shown to be concealing tragic weaknesses in the faces—a different and rather wittier joke, and one with some substance to it. Just as the play, and the author's staging of it, get funnier as they go along, I suspect that it makes more sense on second viewing, so this week's observations may be contradicted if I get a chance to go back next week. In the meantime, there are enough immediate pleasures in the piece for me to recommend it; the ride is slightly bumpy but engagingly worth taking.

The characters in *Aurora* seem to be medieval, Victorian, and modern all at once. The chief actor is an impulsive young troublemaker named William, who wears a black doublet and constantly talks to an inner self or good angel named Bill, who is visible to us and him, but not to the other characters, and wears a white shirt and ribbons in his hair, like a Hungarian bridegroom. Then there is a chatty circle of aristocrats (recalling the rich crowd in Miss Fornes's *Promenade*) gathered around a boisterous count named Dezno, on whose birthday the play takes place. William appears inexplicably at Dezno's party, falls in love with the Principessa Alicia, and commits, like a child coming into the adult world for the first time, a series of social breaches serious enough to warrant Dezno's challenging him to a duel. At the duel, in which Dezno is fatally wounded, two more mysterious characters appear: a self-proclaimed miracle worker named Galindo, whose attempts to stop the fight by will power and other forms of white magic are all failures, and an Angel, visible to Bill but not to William, who has come to collect the dying man's soul and, peculiarly, convert the world to communism. (According to her version of the Crucifixion, Christ didn't say, "This day thou shalt be with me," but "Proletarians, unite!")

The remainder of the play, shifting its focus from William to Dezno, concentrates on attitudes and intrigues around the count's deathbed, climaxing in a grand spoof of those revenge-tragedy free-for-alls in which everybody gets done in by some ingenious means, and survives just long enough to do in somebody else. It might be wise for me not to reveal just who does and who doesn't stay in the land of the living at play's end. Obviously, as usual with Miss Fornes's work, we are not going to get very far by saying, "Hmm, yes, well, just what does all this mean?" The play doesn't carry a series of ideas but more a series of disconcertments of ideas. Just as you expect it to be about something (like identity and the maturation process) it turns a meaning-corner, usually to great comic effect, and pretends to be about something else for a while, until it sees the hated pigeonholes moving in to categorize it again, and scuttles off in a new direction. It might be a comment on the way society corrupts the goodness of the individual (the tragedy of Dezno) or the battle of science and religion (the conflict between Galindo and Dezno's friend Lajos, a secret alchemist), or the problem of loving and surviving in an impossibly contradictory world (the communist angel).

Whatever it is, I enjoyed it. It's full of Fornes's appealingly daft tricks with words, plus some very good moments of physical comedy, including a few notable ones in her Buster Keatonish vein of deadpan slapstick. And the tenderness of the whole thing is appealing too, though I suspect it puts a haze over the work that might be cleared off in spots to the advantage of clarity. Fornes is at her best when her rue for humanity is clinically presented, and not sweetened.

The production pretty much sums up the contradictions that can arise when a writer stages his or her own work. The best things in it, like the marvelous choreographed blocking in the duel scene, and the accelerating hilarity of the last two scenes, could never have been thought of by any other director. The worst things in it—fortunately all very minor—are mistakes no undergraduate would make, like the casting of the very bad actor who plays William. The rest of the company, happily, ranges from bearable to really excellent; I most liked Camille Tibaldeo's petulant comrade angel, Gayle Swymer as an elegant lady betrayed in love, and Lee Kissman as the closet alchemist, skulking about in a tunic that makes him look charmingly like an illustration from Waite's Tarot deck come to life. Aileen Passloff has provided a few pleasant dances, including what might be described as a galliard-cum-softshoe, and John FitzGibbon some listenable, though not assertively memorable, music. Some neat lighting effects by Susan Gregg, and some fancy capes and similar costume accoutrements that I attribute to Willa Kim's assistance, are also of great help.

THE FEAR OF THE OTTOMANS (*Eyes on the Harem*)
Richard Eder

In a way, it is female subjugation and male fear that Maria Irene Fornes is getting at in her comical-explosive vaudeville about the degenerate low points in the six-hundred-year dynasty of the Turkish Ottomans. Only in a way: her way, in

Originally published, in slightly longer form, in the *New York Times*, April 25, 1979.

fact. To draw a straightforward feminist lesson from such extreme examples as the infant Sultan Murad, who shot ten passersby each day with his little arquebus; or Ibrahim, who drowned his entire harem because one of its inhabitants might have been unfaithful; or Abdul Hamid, who believed his clothes were poisoned—this would be ponderous as well as farfetched. Miss Fornes's *Eyes on the Harem,* which opened yesterday at the INTAR Theater, is often farfetched, but it is hardly ever ponderous. Miss Fornes, one of the more interesting playwrights around, proceeds by glints and flashes.

Taking outrageous liberties with these quakey Ottoman potentates, she seems to be as interested in the images they raise as in the ideas they may or may not suggest. Take care of the fables, she is saying—hers are disassembled and lunatic—and the morals will take care of themselves. In *Eyes on the Harem,* a bumpy but occasionally quite wonderful patchwork, Miss Fornes is often as not at cross-purposes with herself, and the better for it.

With six appealing performers, Miss Fornes, who is the director as well as the author, conducts an absurd tour back and forth through the domestic history of the Ottomans. There is a deliberate fragmentation of chronology and tone. For a start, the set does the fragmenting. A most workable design by Larry Brodsky, it is divided into two parts. There is a kind of gallery, up beneath the flies, that is an elaborate red and gilt frieze of Turkish history and mythology. The players appear there from time to time, robed and sometimes fezzed, to read out chronicles about the Ottomans, or to sing, or for other mock-grandiloquent purposes. The main stage below is Balkan modern. It is an anonymous room, functional and painted green; the kind of room where a 1910 traveler might wait for a police permit to visit the Sanjak of Novi Pazar.

The first of the play's sketches is set in 1909, and we see Cliff Seidman as a starved-looking, straggly bearded Sultan Abdul Hamid. It is the terminal stage of the dynasty. Mr. Seidman's Sultan hides inside a ridiculous frockcoat. He is terrified of everything: of visitors who might kill him (he keeps his hand on a gun in his pocket so that he can shoot them first, and once he shot a daughter by mistake), of poisoned clothes, and, above all, of women. Occasionally a black-clad woman passes through the room, sending him into hysterics. Passages of history are read out. Michael Kemmering steps out of one of his roles, as a court attendant, and delivers a lecture on Turkish syntax. As his explanation becomes increasingly garbled, he takes on an increasingly glowing assurance.

Some of the sketches are very funny. Incongruity is their cornerstone; some build on it for a complex mixture of comedy and seriousness, others never really take off. There is a delightful, ironic fashion show. One performer poses seductively in a green sari; she is followed by others in increasingly cumbersome and grotesque outfits, and their efforts at striking the same winsome poses are devastating. The finest sequence is a series of conversations among three heavily veiled women, sitting on a square of cloth. They talk, half-wistful, half-unbelieving, about a future where they will be allowed to eat in public, go unveiled, and wear—a delicate irony—outrageous clothes.

The conversation is comic, and so is the seemingly ludicrous chorus of "Meet Me in St. Louis" which they periodically break into. ("We will do the hootchie-kootchie; I will be your tootsie-wootsie.") Imperceptibly the conversation grows in pain. Their talk of freedom takes on fear; one reads Byron out loud, and suddenly another weeps. The song repeats, each time slower and more sadly. It is a hallucinatory moment; an extraordinary progression from comedy to seriousness, an audacious and successful theatrical rendering of a complex vision of feminine history.

A great deal of *Eyes on the Harem* is nowhere up to this. Some of the playfulness is private and tedious; we are being played at, not with. The reading out of Ottoman histories is not always effective; a prayer sequence, performed more or less straight, seems to accomplish little; and ludicrousness is often exercised for its own sake. Also, I wonder whether some of the comical outrageousness might be more troublesome to those for whom Turkish history is personal history.

At its weakest, *Eyes on the Harem* is childish. At its strongest, the childishness grows into something that is funny, provocative and sometimes magical. . . .

LET US NOW PRAISE FAMOUS WOMEN *(Evelyn Brown)*
Erika Munk

Maria Irene Fornes, talking about emotional life before Freud, once said, "People accepted each other at face value. They were not constantly interpreting each other or themselves . . . if a person said, 'I love so-and-so,' the person listening would believe the statement. Today . . . it's implied that there's always some kind of self-deception about an emotion." Much later in the same interview she says that tenderness toward her characters is at the core of her work. I suppose Evelyn Brown is one of her characters by adoption, for the words

Originally published in *The Village Voice*, April 21, 1980.

in *Evelyn Brown (A Diary)* are from a real diary; but the first powerful feeling that comes from this piece is tenderness, a tenderness completely without sentimentality, without deception, and not for interpretation.

The diary itself is from one year, 1909, midway in the eighty-year life of a household worker in a New Hampshire village. It is not clear from the program whether this was the only volume that survived, or whether Fornes picked it from many; after a while, I began to think that Evelyn Brown, ignorant and unreflective though she may have been, could no longer face recording her days. Each entry, spare and noncommittal as an old bone, relates the weather, the chores done, tiredness, an employer or neighbor ill or dead; walks, letters, and visits are of chilling rareness. Each day is painfully the same as the last. At one point she states that she "sowed sweetpeas and painted andirons," and the imagery seemed wildly colorful. No village gossip, no festivities, no sex, no events from the outside world are reported. She characterizes no one, including herself. She *is* only dishes done, food cooked, floors washed.

And all of this, which by now must sound unutterably dreary, is absolutely beautiful. The set is plain pine, smelling good, set with many narrow white doors. Each object (pitcher, bowl, chair, bucket, broom) has perfect grace and purity—Vermeer stripped of color, the possessions of a dream-world New England grandmother. And Evelyn Brown's gestures have the self-contained, satisfying elegance of the skilled cook and homemaker. Except, of course, for those moments when the clean loveliness of the scene and the dry words of the narration come apart to reveal the impulses that such a life leaves out or hides: fragments of humor, dance, music, eroticism; moments of terrible fear.

Evelyn Brown is played by two women, Margaret Harrington and Aileen Passloff. Harrington's face has that peculiarly Irish quality in which the skull is all too clear beneath the skin—eyes deeply socketed, large almost eyebrowless forehead, a masked but disturbing inexpressiveness. Passloff—darker, rounder, more mobile—would be earthy if she were a cliché, but avoids it. Now and then the two do a little dance, more formal than joyous, to sweet dulcimer music— a moment's hedonistic respite. And once they make bread together, mixing, thumping, pressing, all the while reciting from some hilariously Beetonesque receipt and ending up all floury and irritable around an uprising lump of dough. Most of the time, however, they are simply both there, not there together. The feeling is of overwhelming solitude; the work implies children, families, shopkeepers, a community, but extraordinary loneliness triumphs. The fact that Evelyn Brown is working in other people's homes and not her own strips domesticity of any cozy aura, and any personalism.

As the piece continues there are more and more moments in which a slight change of sound reveals the irritation of sweeping a floor or placing yet one more dish on one more table; at one point Harrington's whole body shakes from constricted rage, or sensuality, or fatigue; at others, the two Evelyns collapse on a table in a posture ambiguously poised between exhaustion and eroticism.

Fornes's recent plays seem more and more constricted if they're taken literally; but as she has said (again in the interview quoted at the beginning of this piece), "A plotless play doesn't deal with the mechanics of the practical management of life but deals with the mechanics of the mind, some form of spiritual survival, a process of thought." Now, when the many-roomed environment of *Fefu* (which still had the great complexity of friendships among different lives) and the cloistered world of *Eyes on the Harem* (which still had the occasional man, the occasional picnic) have been compressed to the severity of one life, and to what looks like the mere mechanics of life, there is a great concern with processes of thought—not only Evelyn Brown's, but our own.

The doors open out, but only to other doors; the light is radiant, but the days are the same. Not a breath of distaste or contempt is shown for this life; the sadness is hard to bear precisely because Evelyn Brown's dignity is upheld with a great tenderness, and the tenderness expressed with the most exacting art.

FORNESCATIONS (*A Visit*)
Michael Feingold

Maria Irene Fornes's *A Visit* is a pixilated little entertainment which, as usual with Fornes, reveals enough new facets of her artistic persona to seem an almost total surprise. Like *Eyes on the Harem* and a few of her earlier pieces, *A Visit* takes up and toys with chunks of found text—in this case dreamy-eyed paragraphs from two Victorian hack novels for adolescent girls, one English and one Spanish, which are glued with Fornes's own writing into a scenario that is one of the standard pornographic fantasies, about the proper young miss who pays a one-day visit to some friends of the family and finds herself copulating with every member of the household.

You might expect this to be approached in the standard rowdy-bawdy fucking-is-good-for-you style of the Ridiculous and other Off-Off enclaves; or with the dry, parodistic malice of Edward Gorey's *The Curious Sofa*; or as a critique

Originally published in *The Village Voice*, December 30, 1982.

of the role-typing brought on by repression, in the slightly heavy and earnest manner of *Cloud 9*. Not by Fornes. Despite the fact that her male characters walk around with ceramic penises protruding from their flies, and her females strip off their shirtwaists to reveal delicate ceramic breasts like inverted tea-cups, she has treated the subject of sex chiefly for its emotional and moral possibilities, from a point of view that can only be called Romantic: Fornication is treated as only one among many erotic pleasures, the others including not only the various possible recombinations of organs but idealizing, fidelity, promiscuity, jealousy, and longing. Repression, in Fornes's system, is not an unhealthy obstacle to sexuality, but a sensual pleasure like all the rest, sweet if you have a taste for it. Even rejection has its charms.

Decades past the Sexual Revolution, Fornes's vision is what one might describe as The Higher Carnality. Everyone in her play loves sex, all encounters are eroticized, but there are no guilts or frustrations because the nonphysical alternatives are taken to be aspects of sex like all the others. Every relation contains its opposite, an idea summed up perfectly in the scene in which the boy mounts the girl from behind, and, reaching orgasm, gasps, "How lovely your face is!"

Not every aspect of this idea is developed so lucidly. Fornes is an artist, not an ideologue, and sometimes her gnomic, playful approach gives the piece a scattershot quality. Some promising trails are left dangling: There is no exploration, for instance, of the consequences of the heroine's vowing fidelity to several people in succession. Though the images are all masterly, as is now usual in Fornes's directing, there are silent passages that scream for verbal heightening, like the deadpan dance of the four men, which desperately needs a song, in the pretty palm-court zarzuela vein that George Quincy's music exploits so well.

Some of Fornes's lovely lyrics, too, get lost in a cast not overpacked with good singers. But these are defects to be repaired or passed over, counting for very little in the unexpected and thought-provoking charm of *A Visit* as a whole. Leave it to Fornes to invent a whole new genre—humane pornography. Among her helpers, Donald Eastman's set (mostly red) and Gabriel Berry's costumes (mostly white) deserve praise; Mary Beth Lerner, the best singer in the cast, makes a fetchingly ravishable innocent of the heroine; and Florence Tarlow is hilarious as the orgy's permanent nonparticipant, a Mexican servant who is a veritable monument of disapproval.

ENTER THE NIGHT
Sheila Rabillard

Enter THE NIGHT, written and directed by Maria Irene Fornes, received its world premiere April 16, 1993, at Seattle's New City Theater. Commissioned by the resident company, Theater Zero, the drama, originally entitled *Dreams,* began as a series of monologues that came to Fornes between sleep and waking. As she assembled these fragments, the shape of *Enter* THE NIGHT began to appear: a delicate triangle involving three friends — Tressa, a nurse who tends the dying; Jack, a gay man mourning the death of his lover from AIDS; and Paula, a woman threatened by bankruptcy and a potentially fatal heart disease. Still a rough draft when Fornes began to work with the three-member cast, the play developed in keeping with what Fornes, once a painter, has called her collage technique: incorporating material from her subconscious; from the culture's collective memories of Hollywood, Shakespeare, and Christianity; and from chance discoveries. (Among these were a nurse's diary found at an auction; a newspaper account of an eighteenth-century Chinese scholar; and the sight of a light-man on a ladder, which prompted Fornes to include a brief sample of the balcony scene from *Romeo and Juliet.*) While the final structure remains dreamlike and open-ended, a succession of haunting moments rather than a progressive march, it possesses a considerable cumulative power. When, near the end of the play, Paula cries "into the night," her outburst is provoked by Jack's self-punishing plunge into a dark world where he may be beaten to death or fatally infected, but it also sums up and impels the audience's contemplation of pain and affection shadowed forth by the play.

As in *The Conduct of Life* and *Fefu and Her Friends,* Fornes explores not simply the facts of suffering and mortality but the effort to comprehend these facts through action and imagination. Here again she creates what Susan Sontag has called her "theater of heartbreak," but in a way that combines the playfulness of her earlier drama with the passion of her more recent work. Though the characters are granted moments in which they enter one another's experience in dream or play, the dominant note of the drama is desire: the unappeased longing of these three friends to ease one another's pain, or perhaps even to conceive it fully.

Fornes's playfulness and her exploration of the longing (by turns selfless and

Originally published in *Theatre Journal* 46, no. 2 (1994).

egotistical) stirred by suffering were most vivid in Act 2. The first act established the three characters, the pace rather gentle and the mood expository. It was not until the second act that the play gripped me as Tressa, Jack, and Paula began to enact snippets from a repertoire of familiar cultural texts, among them Capra's *Lost Horizon* and Griffith's *Broken Blossoms*. At this point, the setting took on its full significance: a bare loft space in a geographically unspecified Chinatown, with a stairwell in the middle leading to the invisible ground floor. The principal acting space seemed to hover above the level of ordinary existence as a sort of temporary refuge. Quotations from the two films, popular Western fantasies of the Asiatic Other, emphasized the exotic setting and allowed Fornes to evoke more overtly the ways in which we imaginatively confront human mortality. At one extreme we deny it altogether, at the same time undoing our denial, by creating an unreachable Shangri-La; and this is the gently ironic note on which the play ends, with a reading from *Lost Horizon*.

But the most powerful scene of the play was the reenactment by Jack and Tressa of the central gestures from Griffith's silent film. There was not a hint of laughter in the house as Jack, in the Lillian Gish role, was rescued by Tressa as Huang, the gentle Chinese scholar who tries to bring teachings of peace to the West but fails to save even the frail young girl from a brutal death. As Huang, barred by race from his broken blossom, Tressa's austere yet erotically charged pantomime played out a yearning passion unexpressed in her sober diary record of her patient's decline; and Jack, as Gish, is released from rage and grateful for succor, a beautiful victim rather than a guilty survivor. When Paula happens on their scene-playing, she learns that this is a customary game of theirs, and her pleasure in this discovery adds to the scene's curious note of joy in the strength and subtlety of the allegiances binding the three.

It is interesting to speculate how much of the power of this production was due to Fornes's direction. Certainly, a great deal would be missing without the stylized choreography of the mimed scenes from *Broken Blossoms* and, given the spareness of the dialogue, the direction of the play's allusive visual language seems crucial. Fornes elicited rich performances from Mary Ewald as Tressa and Patricia Mattick as Paula; Mattick in particular brought small touches of gaiety to her role that seemed completely in tune with the play's complex tone. Brian Faker, playing Jack, was less moving, perhaps because the role was emotionally more extreme and less nuanced: The character's feelings of guilt at surviving his partner, and his consequent need to believe he too had AIDS, at one point found a visual equivalent in obvious evocations of the suffering Christ. But in the Lillian Gish role from *Broken Blossoms,* Jack was genuinely compelling; the performance confirmed that Fornes writes and directs with a special insight into the roles of women.

In fact it might be appropriate to look at this play, in part, as a response to AIDS from a woman's point of view. From this perspective, the disease joins a continuum of suffering that women traditionally have tried to assuage. Thus, Fornes pairs the specter of Jack's possible infection with the certainty of Paula's failing heart and makes both afflictions of equal concern. It is notable that when Paula questions Tressa about the ways in which she eases the last hours of dying patients, Tressa remarks that this is what *we* do—the plural drawing attention to the function of all nurses, most of them women. To be sure, Tressa is also the masculine Huang; but that, perhaps, is the point: The role of the nurse, the one who attempts to comprehend another's pain, is always that of the unworthy Other, filled with longing and distanced from what can never be touched: the feminized position of the disfavored.

PART III

FORNES

ON FORNES

A PREFACE TO *TANGO PALACE*
& *THE SUCCESSFUL LIFE OF 3*

TO SAY THAT a work of art is meaningful is to imply that the work is endowed with intelligence. That it is illuminating. But if we must inquire what the meaning of a work of art is, it becomes evident that the work has failed us; that we have not been inspired by it; that the work has not succeeded in breathing its life for us.

To approach a work of art with the wish to decipher its symbolism, and to extract the author's intentions from it, is to imply that the work can be something other than what it demonstrates, that the work can be treated as a code system which, when deciphered, reveals the true content of the work. A work of art should not be other than what it demonstrates. It should not be an intellectual puzzle, or at least not primarily. A true work of art is a magic thing. To comprehend magic we must be in a state of innocence, of credulity. If there is wisdom in the work it will come to us. But if we go after it, we become wary, watchful. We lose our ability to taste.

A work of art must have its function, like a car, a window, or a bridge. We

Originally published as "Playwright's Preface" in *Playwrights for Tomorrow: A Collection of Plays*, vol. 2, ed. Arthur H. Ballet (Minneapolis: University of Minnesota Press, 1966).

all know how a car, or a window, or a bridge must function. We know whether the designer or engineer has succeeded. However, we are not too sure how art must function. Art must inspire us. That is its function.

If art is to inspire us, we must not be too eager to understand. If we understand too readily, our understanding will, most likely, be meaningless. It will have no consequences. We must be patient with ourselves.

We have learned to think of inspiration as the property of artists. It is not. Inspiration belongs to all of us. What the artist does with his inspiration is quite clear. He creates his work of art. The product of his inspiration becomes public. The inspiration of the layman generates itself in his personal life. It enriches it, and ennobles it. Inspiration is a precious gift that we have relinquished without any struggle. We do not believe that it belongs to us.

Art is created by the artist for the layman. The layman must take possession of it. He must become familiar with it. He must make himself worthy of being its judge. He must love it.

ORDER

I LOVE ORDER. Don't think I don't. Without it, what would we be? Just think of it for a moment. All would be ugliness. We would hate each other and ourselves. The thought of the plains, a meadow, the ocean, would be our only respite. Our position of repose would be looking at the sky. The indoors would still be a shelter against rain and cold. But it would lose its tender touch. The winter would indeed be the worst time of the year. Order is peace, serenity, and beauty. But order doesn't come easily. That is, it doesn't come at all. It has to be made . . . constantly. We spend half our lives making it. And the other half making things for which order has to be made.

I have nothing against offices. I know they have to exist. How else could order be maintained? How else would it be possible to keep track of things when they go from hand to hand? In fact offices frequently save all the time, labor, and damage that go into moving things from hand to hand. They can change hands from manufacturer to jobber, intermediary, distributor, wholesaler, without ever leaving their depot. They can stay put.

Written for the *New York Herald Tribune* in April 1966, but never published. The essay's appearance was intended to coincide with the Broadway opening of Fornes's *The Office,* a comedy set in a Lower Manhattan business and based, in part, on Fornes's own experiences. *The Office* closed during previews.

The fact that sometimes strange things happen, like a product can be sold and resold and sold again, each time becoming a little more expensive, without ever existing, is really irrelevant. One finds crooks in all walks of life.

I remember once hearing that this country bought large quantities of meat from Argentina so that Argentina would have enough currency to buy American meat. I don't know if this is true. I don't remember who told me. But at the time I thought: "Is it possible that the two freighters loaded with meat met in mid-ocean?" And then I thought: "If when they meet each one would turn around and go back to its port of departure, would anyone notice the difference?" Probably yes. Because of the papers. And this is how papers are really the thing. You can't be sure, if things are what they are, or where they are, but for the papers. And it is offices that straighten all that out. It is offices that implant order.

A pencil factory manufactures pencils, and offices manufacture order. Now, order is a strange commodity. You cannot touch it or see it. And it is a disquieting feeling to manufacture something invisible. So the office worker must for his own health of mind ignore the fact that he is manufacturing the order of the world and work under the illusion that he is simply making order in the office, the same way a housewife would make order in her home.

The first principle of order is putting things away. The second is not just putting them away anywhere but putting them away where they can be found when they are needed. Whether things are really needed or not, and whether they are needed enough to make it worthwhile keeping, falls in another category, a sort of religious detachment that we are not interested in at the moment. The first principle is easy to follow, it only requires dedication. The second one is more complex, it requires thought. And that is the one I have trouble with.

I have my own complex filing system. My notes, for instance, I file under "Current Notes." Those are the notes I haven't sorted out yet. Then I have "Social," "Personal," and "Diagrams." Under "Social" I might find something like: "The other day riding uptown on a Madison Avenue bus, I suddenly looked up and I saw the backside of St. Patrick's Cathedral. I blushed and looked away." "Social" are the things I find looking out into the world. Under "Personal" I might find something like: "The saddest moment when I am alone is when I tie a package and no one puts his finger on the knot while I tie the bow." That is "Personal" because it has to do with my feelings. "Diagrams" are thoughts that need illustration.

Then there is "La Folie," where I put away writings that are not quite ideas yet, they are some sort of stream of consciousness—dreams that I dream when

I'm awake. The label is in French in an attempt to give it charm, to make it more inviting, otherwise I would never go near it.

Then I have a folder labeled simply "Notes," and I'm not sure what's in it.

I am satisfied with my classifications. That doesn't bother me. The problem is that the nature of notes is much more evanescent than invoices, for instance. Notes frequently fall under several categories at the same time. What I have to find now is the way to remember what notes I have written and under what category I have filed them. Because there isn't much point to having written them or having filed them in the right place, if I don't know they are there.

I am not trying to say that people should only keep track of what they can remember. Not at all. If this were so, things would be much too simple. And then only those with good memories would get ahead in life. In any case, my system is not a total failure. It is an incentive for me to keep order in my house.

The filing system in offices is much more effective. But that is just because of the nature of the things that are filed away. Invoices have numbers, you can file them in numerical order. They can be filed in alphabetical order under the name of the customer. They have a date, and they can be filed under that. Frequently the copies come in different colors, and you can file them under color. In the future they might come in different flavors too, to make our lives more tasty. (We already have mint-flavored envelope glue.) Only, I suppose it would be the IBM machine that gets to have all the fun.

Anyway, I love order, but, as it often happens with things you love, order for me is hard labor. It is not so with most people. For the usual office worker order is second nature. And here is where something interesting happens. When people are idle, or involved with each other primarily socially, they are conscious of themselves. That is, they are self-conscious. When people together concentrate on something other than themselves, making something, investigating something, they become considerably less self-conscious, and that is quite a beautiful thing to watch. In the years I have spent working at a job, I was able to observe that the relationships among people who work together are quite different from relationships in other circumstances. An undercurrent of deep feeling flows from person to person. The feelings are very true, very deep, but they are toned down, somewhat like in a dream. The feelings have no sense of urgency, it is not imperative for them to come forth. They are permitted to exist without any demand to become resolved and formulated. Infatuations are usually platonic. Friendships seldom go beyond the four walls of the office. I often found that when I met an office friend for dinner or a movie we had nothing to talk about. However, within those four walls feelings have a subtle but definite passionate and irrational nature. Feelings have time to be. There is no need to precipitate them. The person you love will be there the next day. The person you hate will also be there. Because of the involvement with the work, people seldom confront each other face to face, and when they do it is with a piece of paper between them.

My play, *The Office,* is about these feelings. In the play, because a play must be dramatic, the feelings do come forth.

As I watch rehearsals of *The Office* I am fascinated to see how similar the forming of a play onstage is to what I have described. As the actors become more familiar with their lines, with their movements, with their routine, as one might say it all becomes second nature, feelings are then allowed to exist more deeply, more truly. The actor is not preoccupied with them. They do not have to be manifested. They take their own course.

I have also observed, with a demonic smile, how the nature of rehearsal plays a delicious joke on my friend order.

Since rehearsing demands that a scene be played over and over without thought of continuity, a few minutes of the play are rehearsed, then the scene must start again. But before it can start again the stagehands must put things back where they were at the beginning of the scene. A paper that was filed must be taken out of the file and put back in its envelope or filing basket. Every paper in the wastepaper basket must go out again, and every written letter must become blank paper. The ultimate purpose of order was never accomplished. But that was just rehearsal.

I WRITE THESE
MESSAGES THAT COME

THOUGHTS COME to my mind at any point, anywhere—I could be on the subway—and if I am alert enough and I have a pencil and paper, I write these *messages* that come. It might be just a thought, like a statement about something, an insight, or it could be a line of dialogue. It could be something that someone says in my head.

I have a box filled with these scribbles. Some of them are on paper napkins or the backs of envelopes. These things are often the beginning of a play. Most of the lyrics of the songs that I write are based on these notes—as opposed to a play, which, once it starts, *I* make. I usually gather a number of those things that have some relation—again, I do not even know why I consider that they are related—and I put them together. I compose something around those messages using a number of lines that have come into my head.

Now sometimes I am trying to get myself organized, and I am sharpening pencils and doing all those things. So I go to that pile of notes—it's a mess because it is scribblings. Sometimes I cannot read what I wrote because often I

Originally published, in slightly longer form, in *The Drama Review*, vol. 21 (December 1977). From an interview conducted and edited by Robb Creese.

make notes in dark theaters when I am sitting through a play. (A lot of thoughts come into my mind when I am watching a play, especially a play that I am not at all absorbed by.) I start typing through some of these things and very often I find things I cannot imagine why in the world I thought they were anything special. They are the most mundane thoughts or phrases. Sometimes I think, "There is some value here that I do not recognize now, but at *some* point I thought, 'This is a message.' It must be that it is, but I have lost the thought." When that happens I often type it out and leave it, even though it is without any faith at all. I leave it because at some point I did have this faith.

The feeling I have about these messages is very different from what I have about what I am writing when it is *I* writing. I might write something that I like, and it feels good. But the feeling I have about those other things is really as if it is a message that comes in an indivisible unit. I feel if a word is changed, then it is lost. A thought comes—sometimes I do not have a pencil with me—I try to repeat it in my head until I get to a pencil. I know I must remember the exact construction of the sentence. I might be wrong, you see. It could be that it does not matter more or less how it is said. But still I feel that it is a block and that is how it should look, whether it is a page of dialogue that comes in the message or three pages or one line.

That dialogue then could become a play. When I am to write a work, I never start from a blank page. I only start from one of these things that I do, that I receive. Sometimes I start a play from one line of dialogue. It has to be something that has the makings of a play.

The only play that I started from an idea—and it was an idea that was very clear in my head—and that I sat down and wrote was *Tango Palace*. I think it is quite clear that that is how it is written because the play has a very strong, central idea. None of my other plays does. They are not Idea Plays. My plays do not present a thesis, or at least, let us say, they do not present a formulated thesis. One can make a thesis about anything (I could or anyone could formulate one), but I do not present ideas except in *Tango Palace*. I lost interest in that way of working.

The play writes itself. The first draft writes itself anyway. Then I look at it and I find out what is in it. I find out where I have overextended it and what things need to be cut. I see where I have not found the scene. I see what I have to do for the character to exist fully. Then I rewrite. And of course in the rewrite there is a great deal of thought and sober analysis.

One day I was talking to Rochelle Owens, and I was telling her how when I start working on a play the words are just on paper. Perhaps I will see some things or I hear something. I feel the presence of a character or person. But then there is a point when the characters become crystallized. When that happens, I have an image in full color, technicolor. And that *happens!* I do not remember it happening, but I get it like *click!* At some point I see a picture of the set with the characters in it—let us say a picture *related* to the set, not necessarily the exact set.

The colors for me are very, very important. And the colors of the clothes the people wear. When it finally happens, the play exists; it has taken its own life. And then I just listen to it. I move along with it. I let it write itself. I have reached that point in plays at times. I have put scripts away then and picked them up three years later, and, reading them, suddenly I see that same picture with the same colors. The color never goes away. It could be ten years later. The play exists even if I have not finished writing it. Even if it is only fifteen pages. It is like an embryo that is already alive and it is there waiting.

I am always amazed how an audience knows when a play is finished. That is something that I have always found very beautiful. Sometimes when I go to the theater when it is not written in the program that there is going to be an intermission, and when it is quite clear that something has ended, people say, "Is it over?" But they say it with surprise. The actors have left the stage, but it does not look over. People know. And then when it is really over, there is that immediate knowledge that it has ended, and people applaud. In that same way, I know when a script has completed itself. I sense the last note of the play.

One play of mine has about three endings. It looks like it has ended, but then there is another ending, and then there is another ending. These are *almost-endings,* and they do not have that total satisfaction of a real ending. It could have been that I could have left it. But probably people would have been asking, "Is it over?" "Oh, it's over."

The characters: They talk. And when it talks, a character starts developing itself. I never try to reproduce a real character. I did, in fact, try to reproduce real people that I knew in one play, *The Office.* I got into trouble because the characters in the situation were from real life, and I changed a lot of things in the play. I felt that I lacked the objectivity to make the play really sharp and for me to be sure exactly what I was doing. Since I started with a reality of what happened, it was the event that was important. And that event would not work for the play.

I know a lot of people write either about a real person or else they put a familiar character into an invented situation. I find that it just confuses me, that I do not see that as useful for me in any way.

In that same conversation with Rochelle Owens, I told her about my colors.

She found it very interesting. And I said, "You mean you don't see color when you write? I thought everybody saw color!" But she does not. I asked what happens to her, and she said she hears voices. She hears the sound of what the play is saying. Sometimes she is writing and she knows that a sentence should be bah-bah-bah-bah, but the words do not come immediately. Rather than stopping, she goes on and she leaves that blank space. She goes on because the other words are coming. She knows how it has to sound, and she goes back to it. It comes in exactly that form. That is very different from my own work.

Everything that I have written has had a different start. *Successful Life of 3* started when I heard two men speaking to each other. One of them was an actor I knew. That conversation was actually in my head. Not that I wanted to write the play for that actor, it is just that he was there and this other guy was there, and he did not have a very definite face. That caught my imagination completely. I wrote the play in two weeks.

At the same time, I was writing *Promenade,* which I wrote as an exercise I gave myself. I wrote down the characters on one set of index cards. On another set of cards, I wrote different places. I shuffled them together. I picked a card that said, "The Aristocrats." And I picked the card that said, "The Prison." So the play started in prison for that reason. But I found it very difficult to write a scene with aristocrats in prison, so the first thing that happened was that they were digging a hole to escape. I wanted to get them out of there.

For some reason it worked for me that the prisoners remained prisoners. And in the next scene, they were at a banquet where there were aristocrats. After that, I found using the cards for the characters was not helping me at all. But I kept using the place cards. That is why the play has six different locations. I would write a scene and when I was finished writing that scene I would turn to the next card. That was the order the scenes came in.

By the way, I find doing exercises very valuable. It is good for me not to do things too deliberately: to have half my mind on something else and *let* something start happening. I am really very analytical. I like analyzing things, but it is better for me not to think very much. Only after I have started creating can I put all my analytical mind into it. Most of my plays start with a kind of a fantasy game—just to see what happens. *Fefu and Her Friends* started that way. There was this woman I fantasized who was talking to some friends. She took her rifle and shot her husband. . . .

A playwright has a different distance from each script. Some are two feet away, and some are two hundred feet away. *Fefu* was not even two inches away.

It is right where I am. That is difficult to do when one feels close. A different kind of delicacy enters into the writing. Each day I had to put myself into the mood to write the play. I wrote it in a very short period of time, in a very intense period of writing, where I did nothing but write, write, write. Every day I would start the day by reading my old folder (a different folder from the one where I keep my "messages"), where I have all my sufferings, personal sufferings: the times when I was in love and not, the times I did badly, all those anguishes which were really very profound. There were times that I just had to sit down and write about it because I felt anguish about it. It was not writing for the sake of writing; it was writing for the sake of exorcism. A lot of those things had been in this folder for many years. I had never looked at them. That was where the cockroaches were, so to speak.

I would start the day by reading something from that folder. Actually, there were even a couple times when I used things I found there, but most of it is garbage, really garbage, a collection of dirt: the whining, the complaining. But it would put me into that very, very personal, intimate mood to write.

I never before set up any kind of environment to write a play! This was the first time that I did that because the play was different. I had to reinforce the intimacy of the play.

Then I would put on the records of a Cuban singer, Olga Guillot. She is very passionate and sensuous. She is shameless in her passion. And I wrote the whole play listening to Olga Guillot. (My neighbors must have thought I was out of my mind.) There was one record, *Añorando el Caribe,* that particularly seemed to make my juices run. I just left it on the turntable and let it go on and on and on. The play had nothing to do with Olga Guillot. Her spirit is very different. She is very dramatic. And *Fefu* is very subtle and very delicate. But her voice kept me oiled.

I started the final writing of *Fefu* in February 1977. At that time I had about a third of the play written. It opened May 5, 1977. In those three months, I finished writing, I cast it, and I rehearsed it. I finished the play four days before it opened. I do not mean the very last scene. There were scenes in the middle I had to do. I made no revisions during rehearsals. I have to do some rewriting of the play now. I believe I must approach the rewrite in the same way as before: with the pile of writing and Olga Guillot.

Space affected *Fefu and Her Friends.* In late February, I decided to look for a place to perform the work. I had finished the first scene, and I had loose separate scenes that belonged somewhere in the second part of the play. I did not like the space I found because it had large columns. But then I was taken backstage to the rooms the audience could not see. I saw the dressing room, and I thought, "How nice. This could be a room in Fefu's house." Then I was taken to the greenroom. I thought that this also could be a room in Fefu's house. Then we went to the business office to discuss terms. That office was the study of Fefu's house. (For the performance we took some of the stuff out, but we used the books, the rugs, everything that was there.) I asked if we could use all of their rooms for the performances, and they agreed.

I had written Julia's speech in the bedroom already. I had intended to put it onstage, and I had not yet arrived at how it would come about. Part of the kitchen scene was written, but I had thought it would be happening in the living room. So I had parts of it already. It was the rooms themselves that modified the scenes which originally I planned to put in the living room.

People asked me, when the play opened, if I had written those scenes to be done in different rooms and then found the space. No. They were written that way because the space was there. I had to figure out the exact coordination for the movements between one scene and the other so the timing would be right. I had rehearsed each scene separately. Now I was going to rehearse them simultaneously. Then I realized that my play, *Aurora*, had exactly the same concept. There was the similarity of two different rooms with simultaneous life. I did not consciously realize until then that it had some connection with *Aurora*.

I mention this because people put so much emphasis on the deliberateness of a work. I am delighted when something is not deliberate. I do not trust deliberateness. When something happens by accident, I trust that the play is making its own point. I feel something is happening that is very profound and very important. People go far in this thing of awareness and deliberateness; they go further and further. They go to see a play and they do not like it. So someone explains it to them, and they like it better. How can they *possibly* understand it better, like it better, or see more of it because someone has explained it?

I am very good at explaining things. And whatever I do not understand, I can even invent. There are people who do beautiful work and do not know why, and they think it is invalid. Those who are not good at explanation are at a disadvantage, but their work is as valid.

I think it is impossible to aim at an audience when writing a play. I never do. I think that is why some commercial productions fail. They are trying to create a product that is going to create a reaction, and they cannot. If they could, every play on Broadway that is done for that purpose would be a great success.

They think they know. They try and they fail. I know I do not know, but even if I did, I do not think I would write for the audience.

As a matter of fact, when the audience first comes to one of my plays, my feeling is that they are intruders. Especially when I have directed the play, I feel that I love my play so much, and I enjoy it so and feel so intimate with the actors, that when opening night arrives I ask, "What are all those people doing in my house?" Then it changes, of course, especially if they like it. I might even think I wrote it for them if they like it. I love to have an audience like a play. But during the work period, they are never present. Basically I feel that if I like something, other people will like it, too.

I think there is always a *person* I am writing for. Sometimes it is a specific person that I feel is there with me enjoying it in my mind. In my mind, that person is saying, "Oh, yes, I love it!" Or if it is not a specific person, it is a kind of person. It might be someone who does not really have a face, but it is a friend, someone who likes the same things. If we saw a play, we both would like it or we both would dislike it. So in a way I am writing for an "audience." But it is not for the public, not for the critics, not the business of theater.

I feel that the state of creativity is a very special state. And most people who write or who want to write are not very aware that it is a state of mind. Most people when they cannot write say, "I can't write. I'm blocked." And then at another point they are writing a lot and they cannot stop; it appears to be a very mysterious thing, writing. Sometimes the Muse is speaking and other times it is not. But I think it is possible to put oneself in the right state of mind in the same manner that some people do meditation. There are techniques to arrive at particular states of consciousness. But we artists do not know the techniques. I do not know, either. I learned to do it with *Fefu and Her Friends* with my notes and record. But who knows? Maybe I could have done the play anyway.

I find that when I am not writing, *starting* to write is not just difficult— it is impossible. It is just excruciating. I do not know the reason, for once I get started it is very pleasurable. I can think of nothing more pleasurable than being in the state of creativity. When I am in that state, people call me, say, to go to a party, to do things that are fun, to do the things where usually I would say, "Oh yes! Of course!" And nothing seems as pleasurable as writing.

But then I finish writing, and that state ends. It just seems that I do not want to go back to it. I feel about it the same way I feel about jumping off a bridge. And to keep from writing, I do everything. I sharpen pencils. In the past few days, it has been a constant thing of sitting at a typewriter and saying, "Oh! Let me get my silverware in order!" It seems very important because, when I might need a cup of coffee, the spoons will be all lined up. Incredible. It is incredible. So I go back to the typewriter. I say, "Oh! I need a cup of coffee." And then, "I better go get a pack of cigarettes so I'll have them here." And then there is starching my clothes. That is something I started this summer. It is a very lovely thing. I make my own starch. I have to wash my clothes. I have to let them dry, then starch them. They are hard to iron. I usually do not press my clothes. I just wear them. But now that I am writing, all my jeans are starched and pressed and all my shirts are starched and pressed. Anything is better than writing.

NOTES ON *FEFU*

Fefu and Her Friends is about women. It's a play that deals with each of these women with enormous tenderness and affection. The play is not fighting anything, not negating anything. My intention has not been to confront anything. I felt as I wrote the play that I was surrounded by friends. I felt very happy to have such good and interesting friends. Is it a feminist play? . . . Yes, it is.

The women were created in a certain way because of an affection I have for a kind of world which I feel is closer to the 1930s than any other period. Simply because it is pre-Freud, in the way that people manifested themselves with each other there was something more wholesome and trusting, in a sense. People accepted each other at face value. They were not constantly interpreting each other or themselves. Before Freud became popular and infiltrated our social and emotional lives, if a person said, "I love so-and-so," the person listening would believe the statement. Today, there is an automatic disbelieving of every-

Originally published, in slightly longer form, in the *SoHo Weekly News,* January 12, 1978. The article draws from an interview with Fornes conducted by Bonnie Marranca for the American Place Theatre newsletter, 1977–78 season. The last section was originally published in *Centerpoint* 3, no. 11 (1980), as part of a roundtable entitled "Women in the Theatre."

thing that is said, and an interpreting of it. It's implied that there's always some kind of self-deception about an emotion.

The character of Fefu took over the play. . . . She is the woman in the first scene that I wrote, the woman who shoots her husband as a game. The source of this play is a Mexican joke: There are two Mexicans in sombreros sitting at a bullfight and one says to the other, "Isn't she beautiful, the one in yellow?" and he points to a woman on the other side of the arena crowded with people. The other one says, "Which one?" and the first takes his gun and shoots her and says, "The one that falls." In the first draft of the play Fefu explains that she started playing this game with her husband because of that joke. But in rewriting the play I took out this explanation.

Fefu is complex. I find her a very unified person. However, by conventional terms she is contradictory, she is very outrageous. Fefu is very close to me so I tend to understand her, and find her not unusual at all. . . . I said that Fefu took over the play but it's not really so. Julia is a very important voice and there are times when I feel the whole play is about her. Although Fefu has more of a mind than Julia, Julia is the mind of the play—the seer, the visionary.

When I was casting it was very clear to me when an actress entered the room whether she belonged in the world of *Fefu*. In the process of auditioning there were people who read for me who were extremely talented but I thought they would shatter the play. I began to see the play almost as if it had glass walls, and I felt there were people who would break the walls. A lot has been said about the style of acting and the style of production in *Fefu* that surprised me. I told the actors that the style of acting should be film acting. That's how I saw it. Perhaps when you do film acting onstage it seems very special.

Fefu and Her Friends started in 1964. That is when I wrote some of the first scene—when Fefu takes a gun and shoots at her husband out the window. I began working on it again about five years ago, in 1972. Then I stopped working on the play—for whatever reason—I put it away and didn't think about it again until the beginning of 1977. . . .

I think what makes [the second act] special is the fact that there are four walls in each room. If the audience went inside a set which had only three walls, there would be a sense that this is not a room but a set. It would be quite different. The fact that you are enclosed inside the rooms with the actors is really the difference. You are very aware of the four walls around you. I expected that the audience would feel as if they are really visiting people in their house.

In a later discussion of Fefu and Her Friends, *Fornes elaborated on its origins.*

I started it because I had six dresses that I bought in a thrift shop, 1930s dresses, chiffon, lovely. I wanted to write a play about women so I could use these dresses. But the dresses were never used for this production; they were used for another one. . . . At that time I was working with The Open Theater. I asked a few of the women from the group to come to my house and put on the dresses. There was also a photographer there, and some pictures were taken. I still have them. Nothing much happened except we had a very good time getting dressed up, and taking pictures.

At that time I wanted a man in the play, but I thought he would play a woman. There wouldn't be then a real man in the play, but we'd still have a man on the stage. I guess I was afraid of having an all women cast. When Fefu's husband is outside, the women in the house see him, and they talk about him being out there, on the lawn. Audiences at the American Place Theatre said in post-play discussions . . . that they felt his presence very strongly although he was never on the stage. In some ways *Fefu* is about Phillip, not to my mind of course. You see the door is open, and people refer to him, and some characters move out to see him.

FROM AN INTERVIEW
WITH ALLEN FRAME

FRAME: I thought your staging, when I saw it a few years ago at the American Place Theatre, of *Fefu and Her Friends* was ingenious. . . .

FORNES: When I worked with the actresses in those [four different] spaces it was one of the most beautiful directing experiences for me because I was sitting with them right in the room. And it would be only us—whoever was in the scene and me sitting there. And it was more real to me than anything. Because when there's a set and you're on a stage, you're further away. I would be sitting at the table with them. There was a table in this kitchen. Or in the study, I would be sitting in a chair, and it was completely quiet. There was total silence. To me that silence was necessary. If I had at that point written down stage directions that would have been forever binding, I would have said, "It's important that the rooms be totally isolated so that there's no sound at all."

Now when I was trying to synchronize the scenes, the sound of the other scenes was too loud, so we started putting curtains and blankets on the

Originally entitled "Maria Irene Fornes" and published, in longer form, in *Bomb* magazine, no. 10 (Fall 1984).

windows and on the doors. My aim would have been to isolate the sound completely. Since we were not successful, there was a little bit of sound that drifted through it. It was actually the audience then that said, "What a wonderful thing that you hear the other conversations faintly. And sometimes you recognize lines, and sometimes they're lines you've heard, and sometimes they're lines you know you're going to hear." So you think, "Oh, my God! Of course!" But I didn't know that. And I think when you deal with a play that's completely a new form you know a little about it, and you say, "Yes, this is how it should be done," because from what you see it's exciting, but then you don't anticipate many, many other things.

FRAME: There's a heightened reality in your work that's almost superreal. In *Mud* the writing was so compressed, so spare, that the play achieved an intensity that seemed superreal. One critic interpreted the story as a post-apocalyptic situation. The setting actually looked like something from the Depression era, but the terms of the play were so bleak and unpromising that the situation almost appeared to be a futuristic nightmare.

FORNES: I understand seeing that, but I didn't intend it. My plays are clean. Most plays have four, five vital moments in the play and the rest of the play is just getting to it. It's just fill. I don't know why, whether it's just to create the sense that it's real or that you have to spend two hours to experience the power (you have to see not just snapshots). But I find it very boring. I go to sleep when I see plays like that, and I go to sleep writing it. I would just actually fall asleep at the typewriter and would not be able to finish a scene written like that. What's different now is that my work is much more emotional and connected to story. Because of that and the fact that the air around it is clean, it's very strange. It reminds me a little bit of Edward Hopper's paintings—where there's something very real about the situation, it's very mundane, but the air is always so clean you feel there's something wrong.

FRAME: It's different from the "magic reality" of a lot of Latin American writers whose structure is also looser.

FORNES: You mean the novelists?

FRAME: Yes.

FORNES: The Latin American artist is almost always a surrealist, whether it be painters, artists, or poets. I don't know that they ever see themselves as being surrealists. That's just how they conceive art. Art is something you don't just reproduce—what you see every day doesn't seem to be inspiring to them. But you do something with it so that it's not bound by the law of reality. My work has always had that influence. I've never felt that it was necessary at all to write realistic plays. . . . I think my theater is the way it is because I spent a few years painting.

FRAME: I thought maybe sculpture because there's such a strong sense of structure in your work.

FORNES: I have to structure it. I have to make sure that the staging is something important, in the same way that if somebody comes in in the wrong scene I would say, "No, this is not your scene, you come in in the next." When I was working in Seattle there was a scene where I wanted the actor's hand to be in a particular place on the chair, and I said, "Try it further back," and he kidded a little. And I said, "Don't laugh. Wait till I get to the fingers." Sometimes I'm not even hearing the words, what they're saying, but I always know where people are and the distance between them and the wall and the furniture. It's very important. Just yesterday I went to see a play that is directed exceptionally carefully and yet I would say it's two weeks behind where it should be for opening in terms of the experience of people in relation to things, a little further this way, a little further that way.

FRAME: You give a workshop for Hispanic playwrights through INTAR in which the participants receive a sizable stipend while they take the workshop. Do you think that Hispanic immigrants to this country have more urgency about writing because they've been displaced from their cultures?

FORNES: Well, I don't know if they have the urgency. I have, and I think everybody should feel, in general, very concerned about a whole generation of people who come to this country from Latin America and because of their lack of connection with the arts don't document their existence. They don't document how they think, how they see. There is a spirit that is very special, like the spirits of any immigrant group, but other immigrant groups, perhaps because of their background, have had a need to document their spirit, their way of doing things, their way of reacting to things.

FRAME: I find it bold of you to express your own sense of despair through a situation of poverty in Appalachia, as you did in *Mud*. My guess is your experience is nothing like the dire deprivation of those three characters. Were you criticized for this?

FORNES: No. I grew up during the Depression in poverty. But when I did a shorter version of it at the Padua Hills Playwrights Festival last year there was a critic who said I treated men like pigs. And I was shocked by that because first of all I think these three people are wonderful. I think if you're going to call the men pigs then call them all pigs because they're all quite brutal in some way and quite tender in another sense. But the men are not any more piggish than she is. They have a bigger heart than she has. She's more self-centered, more ambitious, in a way harder than they are. The three of them are trying to survive as best they can. And they're not bad people. That critic is anticipating that I'm going to write a play that has a feminist point of view, maybe because I wrote *Fefu* which is a pro-feminine play rather than a feminist play. . . .

I think *Mud* is a feminist play but for a different reason. I think it is a feminist play because the central character is a woman, and the theme is one that writers usually deal with through a male character. The subject matter is— a person who has a mind, a little mind, she's not a brilliant person, but the mind is *opening*, and she begins to feel obsessed with it, and she would do anything in the world to find the light. And some people can understand that as a subject matter only if it were a male character wanting to find that. It has nothing to do with men and women. It has to do with poverty and isolation and a mind. This mind is in the body of a female.

FRAME: How do you start a play?

FORNES: My plays usually start in manners that are very arbitrary. I try for my head not to interfere, and I try to see what's coming out. When I wrote the first scenes of *Mud* in a writing workshop I was doing at Theater for the New City, I didn't envision the characters in the country. In my mind they were in some European city. It was very general and vague. They were in some kind of basement, and they were very poor. When I arrived in California ready to start rehearsal all I had was that one scene. In fact, I was already a week late. They had already set up auditions for me. I thought, "I'll work on that scene because it wasn't even finished so I have a good scene for auditions and the actors think there is a play behind it."

The next day some people were going to a flea market near where we were, and I went with them because I often need objects or furniture to get a hold on a play. I need the props. We were at the flea market and I was looking for my set. (Also, you know, we had to put on these plays for hardly any money at all so when you find something cheap, then you write a play about that.) There were two little country chairs that were, for the two of them, only $5. They were very nice. They had been stripped down to the wood, and they were wonderful, and I said, "That's very good." Then we went a little further, and there were a hoe, an axe, and a pitchfork, also very cheap. The axe was $10. The hoe and pitchfork were 2 for $5. And I thought, "This is a sign. I think it's going to be a play in the country." Then I went a little further and there was the prettiest little wooden ironing board for $3. Those things are antiques. You know, they cost $30, $50, $70 anywhere. So I said, "That's it, that's my play. Now I know where they live, they live in the country. The play takes place in their living room or wherever they have two chairs, and I know what he does, he works the land, and I know what she does, she irons." The reason why she's ironing all the time is because that ironing board was so pretty and so cheap.

A couple of days later they asked me for the title of the play. They needed it for the program and the press releases. So I said, "I'll tell you in a couple of hours." As we worked on the speech where Mae keeps saying, "You're going to die in the *mud*," etc., I thought, "Oh," and so that was the title.

FRAME: One thing I liked about *The Danube* was the use of the frequently changing backdrops. It seemed as though you were making a reference to the passing pageantry of theater. They rolled up and they rolled down, and they were in direct contrast to the style of the play, which made them almost satirize proscenium theater with curtains and lavish backdrops. It was like an intellectual comment on . . .

FORNES: What is the comment?

FRAME: A reference to theatrical convention.

FORNES: What is the reference, though?

FRAME: Theater's use of illusion. You used the painted backdrops to express an obvious illusion while you used the foreign language tapes to break down the illusion of their speech, interrupting it between lines with the tapes.

FORNES: But the idea of illusion. Is that something that is presented as a mistake, as false?

FRAME: No, when I say satire, that's not right. It was *humorous* to see the incongruousness of an experimental play about the end of the world using these backdrops, which were a throwback to an old kind of theater. You could say you were celebrating a tradition rather than satirizing it.

FORNES: Yes, that is it. To me the quality of those language tapes has the same quality as those backdrops, which is a kind of innocence. I just loved those tapes, the little skit they make for a language lesson. And I long for that innocence. To me the loss of that innocence and oversophistication is a crime against humanity. It's like a violation of the personality or the environment with pollution.

FRAME: In your work you often juxtapose beauty and horror.

FORNES: Right. And innocence . . . A lot of people have said to me about *Mud* and *Sarita*, that they like it, they feel very much, but they feel at the very end there is a hole. "What are you saying?" they ask. "That there's no hope?" . . . I wasn't saying any such thing. Even though *Sarita* has a tragic ending—she kills her lover and then goes crazy and to a mental institution—I'm not saying any such thing! I'm showing what could *happen*. *Precisely*. I'm giving them an example of what is *possible*. There are works, though, in which you feel the writer is relishing in the despair, in the pain. And now, how can you tell the difference between one and the other? It's something you feel in your heart. You know the writer doesn't have to show the good side. It doesn't have to be there. It's in the spirit of the work and you know in the spirit of the work immediately whether the writer is just relishing in pain. Maybe it is that these people who want the uplifting message right in the characters' lives rather than in the spirit of the play—maybe it is that they can't tell the difference in those that are relishing in pain and those that are talking about goodness.

CREATIVE DANGER

THE QUESTION of theater—the question of art in general—is a question of honesty. I don't see how a dishonest person could possibly write. And I don't see how honest people could not lean in their writing to what they are, to the things they know best. If my pen is honest, I will sometimes—frequently—portray characters who, like me, are women. If my expression is honest, it is inevitable that it will often speak in a feminine way.

If I think of it, it seems natural that I would write with a woman's perspective, but I am not aware that I am doing any such thing. I don't sit down to write to make a point *about women* if the central character of my play is a woman, any more than I intend to make a point *about men* when I write a play like *The Danube,* where the central character is a young man. *The Danube* is, in fact, a play about the end of the world.

Often, there are misunderstandings about my work because it is expected that as a woman I must be putting women in traditional or untraditional roles, or roles of subservience or subjugation or dominance, to illustrate those themes. Or when one of my women characters is portrayed in a position of work or

Originally published in *American Theatre* 2, no. 5 (1985).

leisure, certain assumptions or simplifications are made about the character which might be quite the opposite of what is presented in the play. When those contradictions occur, the critics never question their initial premise. Instead, they see it as a fault in the play.

The same thing happens if you have a non-white character or actor in a play. Immediately people assume the play is dealing with racial questions. One can almost hear those people asking, "If you want to deal with a 'person,' why don't you put a 'person' onstage?"

In my play *Mud,* the character Mae works very hard. She earns the little money that comes into the house. The two men don't earn money. That is not, traditionally, a woman's position. The work that she does is ironing, which is traditionally viewed as a woman's job, although Chinese laundrymen iron as well. It was my choice for her to iron because, in her situation, what other choices are there? She could be sewing. I have often been told that in *Mud* I have written a play about women's subservience, by virtue of Mae's job. While it is true that ironing is work that women do, the play also makes it very clear that Mae is willful and strong-minded, and that the men in the play accept her as such and love her without making any attempt to undermine her strength. These people are too poor to indulge in bizarre ego games. They have a reality to deal with, which is poverty. That is the way things have worked out for them. The concepts of sex roles and role playing are a luxury, an indulgence that re-quires a degree of affluence.

The fact remains that there may very well be women whose temperaments, in a very profound way, are closer to the temperaments of men. If you reversed the sexes in *Mud,* you would see that Mae's nature is more male than female in terms of dominance, and that the men's natures are more female in terms of tenderness and acceptance. People see the character Lloyd as violent, but if a young woman were to take a gun and shoot a man who had used her emotion-ally and sexually—the way Mae has used Lloyd—they would applaud. That is because there is more compassion for women in relation to emotional abandon-ment. But the attention to sex roles, protest against sex roles, defense against the guilt that results from that protest, all these things keep us from seeing a work with a full perspective. They prevent us from seeing characters as human beings; we see them rather as party members.

To understand *Mud* as being about Mae's oppression and my more recent play *The Conduct of Life* about the subjugation of Latin American women is to limit the perception of those plays to a single-minded perspective. It is submitting your theatergoing activity to an imaginary regime or discipline that has little to do with the plays. I would like to be offered the freedom to deal with themes other than gender. But again, people think, what right does she have as a woman to be writing about military cruelty in Latin America?

I'm pleased that at this time in my writing I am finding expression for strong female characters who are able to speak of their longing for enlightenment and of their passions, or who make political or philosophical observations. If I were limited to writing plays to make points about women, I would feel that I was working under some sort of tyranny of the well-meaning. It is unavoidable that every choice I make comes exactly from who I am—including the fact that I love to iron. I think it's magic! Every single thing I have lived through in my life, everything I have witnessed, in some way gets into my work. The fact that I'm a woman is one of the most present things. Each day of my life something happens to me that is different from what would happen were I a man. Most of those things are rich and passionate, and I don't refer to them by way of complaint.

As a writer, I am in an odd position in relation to feminism: Radical feminists don't consider me a feminist, but a great many people who are sympathetic consider me a feminist and see my characterizations of men as a harsh criticism. This began in 1977 when I wrote *Fefu and Her Friends.* The idea that I was a feminist was confirmed to them when I followed *Fefu* with *Evelyn Brown,* a piece about women's work, based on a journal of a New England woman who worked as a servant and wrote down her household chores in great detail. After that came *Eyes on the Harem,* which concerned the Turkish Empire with an emphasis on the harem.

The next play I did was an erotic, turn-of-the-century piece, rather risqué and naughty about sex; the men wore these white porcelain erect phalluses decorated with a blue circle like very fancy Swedish dishware, and the women wore white porcelain breasts with the nipples similarly decorated. There were a number of women who came to this play assuming that they would see feminist art, and they were *horrified* to find a work of such frivolity where men's penises were paraded around with delight.

I feel myself as a woman in that I sense myself as a female organism, not as a woman in the way that society considers what I should do or think. If women suffer abuse because of the kind of organism they are—if they struggle in defense of this organism or this nature—I feel a great deal of excitement witnessing that struggle and I want to write about it. But if a woman suffers that abuse or confinement as a result of the world's expectations, I feel compassion but I'm not as interested in writing about it. I'm not as interested in the rules of the world. I don't like those rules and I suffer enormously from them, but the whole question is less interesting to me as a writer.

In any case, I have never set out to write in a particular manner or about a particular subject. The creative system is something so delicate and easily damaged that I would never impose anything on it. I know it has its own mind and its own will and that the system is my boss. If I think I know what I want to write about, I soon find out that I can't write at all. But if I start writing and am patient enough, I sooner or later find something which is in the lower layers of my being, and that is the thing I should be writing about. These things are passionate yearnings that activate my writing and activate me as a person. Sometimes these things are minute, sometimes they are puzzling, but if I am patient and a good observer they will always reveal themselves to me and uncover the nature of the work I am doing, like pieces of a larger mass that crumble and reveal its nature.

The possibility of being creative depends on not being shy with one's intimate self and not being fearful for one's personal standing. We must take very delicate chances—delicate because they are dangerous, and delicate because they are subtle; so subtle that while we experience a personal terror it could be that no one will notice. It is this danger which in my mind is very connected to what is truly creative.

It is precisely at a time in my life when my work is following its most mysterious and personal course that it has become more political. I think this is because, although my examination is personal, my concerns are less directed at my own person. I am very happy that I have gained enough independence in my writing that the theater around me doesn't have so much influence as to keep me from following my own course.

FROM AN INTERVIEW
WITH SCOTT CUMMINGS

CUMMINGS: What was it like the first time you heard actors read your material?

FORNES: The first time was at the Actors Studio in a director's workshop. The actress was standing and she said a few lines, looked around, and then she walked and stood behind a chair. And I said, "That is wonderful! That is wonderful!" and I stood up and walked around the way she had gone and I said, "but instead of stopping here, you can continue on . . . ." Everybody was looking at me and I thought, "I must be doing something wrong." But I couldn't figure out what it was. Then the director came to me very politely and he said, "Please, Irene, any kind of comment that you want to make I am happy to hear. You make a note of it and then, after rehearsal, we go and have a cup of coffee and talk about it."

This seemed to me like the most absurd thing in the world. It's as if you have a child, your own baby, and you take the baby to school and the baby is crying and the teacher says, "Please I'll take care of it. Make a note; at the end

Originally entitled "Seeing with Clarity: The Visions of Maria Irene Fornes" and published, in longer form, in *Theater* magazine 17, no. 1 (1985).

of the day you and I can talk about it." You'd think, "This woman is crazy. I'm not going to leave my kid here with this insane person." I felt that way but actors were in agreement with the director. And I thought when you are with insane people, you might as well just accept it. I thought, "Well, maybe this will work." Of course, it didn't. We had some very frustrating discussions in the cafeteria on Eighth Avenue near the Actors Studio.

CUMMINGS: So, in a sense, you began directing your own plays right from the very beginning.

FORNES: I never saw any difference between writing and directing. I think you have to learn that there's a difference. I don't think the difference is natural. Because I didn't know anything about theater it was like: "You cook a meal and then you sit down and eat it." Of course, they are different things, but they are sequentially and directly connected. So that to me rehearsing was just the next step. To continue working on it was natural.

I didn't direct my own play for what seemed to me like an eternity. It was 1968, five years from my first production. But it did seem like a whole life, a whole career. Like at the end of my career I started directing.

CUMMINGS: How did you learn to work with actors?

FORNES: I was a member of the Actors Studio Playwrights Unit. That meant that I could observe the acting and directing classes. I saw scenes being worked on and commented on. Strasberg didn't actually teach technique there. He taught technique at his institute. There he criticized scenes or maybe referred to certain exercises. I went to Gene Frankel's school and took a course, a beginning acting course where we did sensory exercises. Also, I took a three-month directing class, which just means you get the experience of not knowing what to say to an actor. You're going to go through that anyway, you might as well go through it at school.

I went to the Actors Studio with the interest of somebody who wants to find out what is an actor. I was very impressed with Strasberg's work as an actor's technician or a director's technician but I would completely ignore anything he would say about esthetics. My own personal taste was already quite developed. I was an artist, I lived in an artistic world, my artistic taste was already extremely sophisticated. In the theater I was green but not artistically. Two productions had this great impact on me. One was *Waiting for Godot* and the other was the adaptation of *Ulysses in Nighttown* directed by Burgess Meredith with Zero Mostel.

CUMMINGS: How did your work at the Actors Studio affect your playwriting?

FORNES: My writing changed when I first found out what the principle of Method is. My writing became organic. I stopped being so manipulative. In *Tango Palace* I felt I knew what needed to happen in a scene and that the writing was serving me. You can see the moments when a character is speaking for my benefit rather than from their own need. The first play that I wrote that was influenced by my understanding of Method was *The Successful Life of 3*. What one character says to another comes completely out of his own impulse and so does the other character's reply. The other character's reply never comes from some sort of premeditation on my part or even the part of the character. The characters have no mind. They are simply doing what Strasberg always called "moment to moment." There I was applying the Method technique for the actor to my writing and it was bringing something very interesting to my writing.

CUMMINGS: Your formal theater training was in the American Method but the Off Broadway theater that excited you at the time was not at all in that tradition. Wasn't there a conflict?

FORNES: Not at all. The question of esthetics has nothing to do with Method. A Method actor should be able to work in a play of O'Neill as well as Ionesco as well as Shakespeare. You don't need any special training to do Ionesco. What you need is to be esthetically aware, and to understand that imagination is a part of natural life, of everyday life. There were many people whose acting careers really suffered because they had the same feeling as Strasberg: that these exercises were only to do naturalistic plays.

CUMMINGS: What is the difference in the theater scene between 1985 and 1965?

FORNES: For me it's not that different. Because I work at the Theater for the New City. Which in New York is probably the place that most resembles the original Off-Off-Broadway. You have to do everything yourself. There's a lot of madness around. And wonderful people who are very unpretentious and working very hard. They're very generous. It's a kind of place where anybody looking for any order would go crazy. I love working there.

The original Off-Off-Broadway situation centered very much around the playwrights. The exciting thing was when Sam Shepard was going to do a new play, or Murray Mednick, Megan Terry, Rochelle Owens, Ronnie Tavel. Everybody got excited about the idea. That didn't last very long.

By 1968 already the directors had taken over. Most of the playwrights who were very active in the early years of the Off-Off-Broadway movement became sort of outcasts. So we started the New York Theatre Strategy which was a production organization to produce the plays of these people. I was the office, the fundraiser, the production coordinator, the bookkeeper, the secretary, the everything. I did everything. We started in 1972 and went until 1979. In 1977 I did *Fefu*. *Fefu* was such a breakthrough for me. I had the feeling I didn't want to do managerial work. I wanted to write. From then I didn't supervise the whole thing. I had other people to help me.

CUMMINGS: What kind of a breakthrough was it?

FORNES: My style of work in *Fefu* was very different from my work before. I hadn't been writing for a few years. When you start again something different is likely to happen.

The style of *Fefu* deals more with characters as real persons rather than voices that are the expression of the mind of the play. In *Fefu*, the characters became more three-dimensional. What I think happened is that my approach to the work was different. Instead of writing in a linear manner, moving forward—I don't mean linear in terms of what the feminists claim about the way the male mind works—I started doing what you might call "research," work where you just examine the characters. I would write a scene and see what came out and then I would write another as if I were practicing calligraphy. You write whatever happens. You don't say, "I'm not going to waste my time writing a scene with five characters that are not going to be in the play."

That's one thing that is wonderful about writing this way: You realize how much you learn about the characters when you put them in situations that are not going to be in the play. That's one thing we haven't learned from the rehearsing process. Can you imagine if a director asked an actor to do an improvisation and he said, "Why should I do this scene? This scene is not going to be in the play." They do it gladly. They're thrilled. They know they're going to gain an enormous depth by going to the past, to the future, to other times that are in between scenes. They do it all the time, but we writers don't do it.

It's very difficult to change your style of writing. It's the hardest thing for a writer to do and the most important thing for a writer to do. I feel like we set our style of work very early for no reason at all. It's totally arbitrary. I think that any style you write in you dry up. You get exhausted and you get bored.

CUMMINGS: Your recent plays are deceptively realistic in style. Do you think they're diminished by a straightforward, realistic approach?

FORNES: I don't know what straight realism means. Realism is just behavior. I like acting that is true, that I can see and believe something is happening to that character. I've always considered that a necessity. It's a basic thing— A . . . B . . . C—that's the A. You have to suffer that; if you don't you are in trouble. You have to be well grounded, grounded not with your intellect but with your humanity, your body, your carnality. As long as your feet are always on the ground, you can go incredible distances. To me, that is realism. But the moment you are separated from the ground and you start with conceptual things, it is completely dull and very pushy.

To a lot of people realism means mildness and plainness. Some people think that realism has to concern itself with practical matters like your job or your marriage, but even marriage from the point of view of the practical matters. They don't realize they consider that realism because that happens to be their concern. If you deal with the same marriage or the same job but not with the practical part but with something much more complex—as *realistic* as the other because it's as *abundant* as the other—they are not as concerned with it so they think it doesn't exist. They think you are fantasizing. They don't notice that it is all over, that it is right in front of their eyes.

CUMMINGS: It sounds like your plays talk to you as much as you talk to them.

FORNES: What I teach in my workshop is simply to learn how to listen to the characters, not only how to listen to the characters you have planted there but even how to have a character appear in front of you. You don't know where that person came from or what that person is doing there, but you follow that vision and follow it through.

CUMMINGS: What sort of techniques do you use to do that?

FORNES: We do half an hour of yoga. After the yoga we go to our tables and I give an exercise that comes out of meditation, visualization mostly, with eyes closed, often a memory that is very specifically visualized.

CUMMINGS: What kind of instruction do you give them to trigger the memory?

FORNES: It could be anything. I might say something like, "Transport yourself toward a moment between the ages of seven and ten, for example, and remember something in connection with water." Now water may be anything from a glass of water to a river to an ocean to being on a boat or at the beach or in the shower. Each person goes their own direction. I ask them to visualize the place. And I guide the visualization. If it's a room, I ask them to visualize the floor, whether it's wood or carpet, the walls, the windows. I go through a whole list of things. After this I ask them to make a drawing. If the place is empty, I might say, "Let somebody come into that place." It may be a familiar character you've already worked with or somebody you've never seen before. Watch the person for a while and see what they do. You're really just watching. You are completely passive. You begin to distinguish the difference between when you're manipulating and when you're not. When you start manipulating, everything gets brittle and fake.

Usually if the visualization is personal, I give them an element that takes it into the imaginary. I throw in lines of dialogue, which brings in the fictional. It intrudes upon it but at the same time it triggers something else. The line I pick from anything. A newspaper or a book. I like having to do a new exercise every day so I don't get lazy. If I'm really into it, everybody else is inspired. Then, as they start writing I become more inspired too. That's where I get my writing done. That's why I've been writing so much lately. The workshop is a discipline for writing that I don't have.

CUMMINGS: So the last thing to come is language or speech. It comes after you establish an environment, trigger a memory, and put a person in that environment.

FORNES: Yes. I wrote a play called *Dr. Kheal*. Dr. Kheal is talking about the will and he says, "In the beginning was the word—the work of the devil, son of a bitch." What he means is that the *devil* passed the word around that in the beginning was the word and that it's sinister to think that. Can you imagine? I don't know why words want to become authoritarian.

CUMMINGS: You also wrote in *Dr. Kheal:* "Words change the nature of things. A thing not named and the same thing named are two different things."

FORNES: The experience of drinking a glass of water is one thing and you say, "I just drank a glass of water" and you immediately alter that experience. Words do not have the scope that the experience of drinking a glass of water encompasses. You may be lucky and evoke practically everything that was experienced. That's what makes a writer, of course. But you're always being lucky that you're evoking. Already you're conceding that all the words can do is try to accomplish in terms of evocation rather than—I don't know what— words fail.

CUMMINGS: What is your characters' relationship to language?

FORNES: What I want language to be is an expression of the characters, but a very careful expression so that they or the words don't get carried away and become their own expression. The action of the words coming out or form- ing in the brain is a delicate one. It is as if words are dampness in a porous substance—a dampness that becomes liquid and condenses. As if there is a condensation that is really the forming of words. I want to catch the process of the forming of thought into words.

CUMMINGS: How does music and song figure in your work? How do you know when to turn from prose dialogue to song or music?

FORNES: I think that has to do with a taste for lyricism. I'm a romantic. I have a very feminine nature. I'm very tough in some ways but I have a taste for the feminine. Lyricism is romantic. I remember having what became almost an argument with a friend of mine who is very political. It was about my play *Molly's Dream.* She said it was romantic and meant it as a criticism and I said, "Yes, isn't it?" and meant it as a high compliment. I remember we were in a bar, we were drinking beer, and I said, "Have you ever been with a per- son when just being with them makes you see everything in a different light.

A glass of beer has an amber, a yellow that you've never seen before and it seems to shine in a manner that is—" and she said, "Yes!" and I said, "That is romantic! That is romance!" and she said, "Well, in that case . . ." I said, "It *is* more beautiful. It isn't that you want it to be more beautiful or that you are lying to yourself. It *is*. Your senses are sharpened."

CUMMINGS: There is a power in that feeling that can make a character do things that are not in his or her own best interest. I'm thinking of Sarita now.

FORNES: Romance is romance. It's like intelligence. Now you can say that some people are so intelligent that sometimes they become too mental and brainy and it leads to their destruction. Well, of course anything can go wrong, but you cannot criticize intelligence for that. In some cases it does happen that people want it so much that they start deceiving themselves but there is no deceit in romance. There should not be. It's only when it goes wrong that you start fooling yourself. Why blame the feeling? When the glass of beer looks like the most beautiful amber, there's no deception, because it is actually. Everything is very beautiful. We get gray and we don't see anything as being beautiful because we are gray, we are dull, nothing shines for us. To respond to the beauty that's around you, there's no deception in that. That's why I like lyricism. . . .

CUMMINGS: Do you have any desire to write anything in Spanish?

FORNES: I want to write English *and* Spanish which I have been doing. In *The Conduct of Life,* when Crystal Field was memorizing some of her speeches she found it very difficult. I said, "Why?" She said, "The language, the language!!!" In English, you have short sentences that add up to a thought. In Spanish, many sentences are linked, so you could have a whole paragraph that is one sentence, a lot of commas and one period. I was doing that in English. And that was what Crystal felt. When she started memorizing, it was hard, but once she would get going she just loved it. She said it was like taking a flight. You'd start a sentence and you knew it was going to take you around and around and around until you land. That's even more important than writing in Spanish and writing in English: what you bring from one language into the other. . . .

FROM "AGES OF THE AVANT-GARDE"

I THINK that aging has made a difference in my writing in a very important way. Young writers are usually very deeply involved with their ego and they confuse their writing with their image. They think of their writing as the thing that is going to present them as a person to the world. As you get older either you realize that writing has nothing to do with you or you simply give up on trying to enhance your personality through your writing. You realize that in fact the writing is more important than you. I don't mean in the way of sacrificing yourself, but that in order to be a happy person, successful, a person who is admired or sought after or even sexy, the best thing is for your writing to be good rather than to keep thinking of whether this is the way you want to present yourself.

I didn't realize when I started writing that that was the case, although I was not a baby. I was close to thirty. Therefore I was not that involved with the question of my image. But I see it a lot in the students I work with. I can see that the way they write is the way they want to be seen. If somebody wants to be seen as smart and sharp and worldly then the writing comes out that way, be-

From a series of essays by twenty-one writers originally published in *Performing Arts Journal* 46, vol. 16, no. 1 (1994). Fornes's comments were taped by Bonnie Marranca.

cause that's how they want to attract people. This is mostly women who want to present themselves as sensitive, and the writing comes out that way. I believe that there is a creative system inside of us. It's a system that's almost physical. I can compare it with the digestive system or the respiratory system. There are a number of parts of oneself that are involved in creativity. The only way that the system is going to function well is if you don't encumber it with the question of personality or how it will benefit you.

For me, and I don't know if it's the same for most writers, it has been very good. The older I got, the more sexual my work became, for the same reason. If a character of mine started doing the most grotesque, sexual thing, I let it do it, because the character was doing it, not me. It had nothing to do with me.

On the other hand, I don't think that I'm aging an hour. Part of it is because my mother is 102 years old, and when I'm with her I'm a baby. In comparison to my mother, I'm a kid. I have energy and I can go up and down the stairs, and I do this and I do that—it's not entirely true. I do this like any old lady, but I'm younger than she is.

I feel that my work has more energy every year that passes. There's a kind of courage—of voice, of style, and of emotion, the same thing that I said about sexuality. The sexuality just comes out of the character. It's not my sexuality. This is something that may be difficult to understand for someone who is not a writer, because our dreams are supposed to be connected with our psyche. Our creativity must be connected to our psyche, but I think in some way our creativity goes aside of it, too. It has its own independence, and if you free it, if you let it be free, it can do things that amaze you and surprise you and there's an energy in allowing it to be outside yourself, and watching it as if it's in front of you, and you are looking at it. That's what I mean by energy. The writing is not asking me for permission but it is taking force and just going. It can be an energy of imagery, not necessarily that the characters are energetic.

The more I write, I see that it has to do with experience, too, knowing that something works. But only in the sense that if this works, maybe I can do this other thing—maybe it would work as a kind of balance, almost like you think of engineering. If you understand engineering then you can modify things, knowing sometimes that you're taking a chance and you're not so sure. But when it pulls together you think you can go beyond and beyond in dealing with structure and the way you play with themes, and the way you play with surprise. It's very complex, and the more you think about it you realize it has nothing to do with personality.

I feel that in my writing every time I write I'm inventing something. And I don't think you can ever feel that you're aging when every day your work is something that is new to you. In a sense, each time you're a baby who feels nervous about stepping on strange ground. You think you've lost it. You wonder, what is the place I'm in? You feel you will never be able to find your way back. You have that fear because you are always on new ground. You're always renewed, and young, and ignorant and afraid. But you also have the energy of feeling something is happening, and that gives you enormous courage.

CHRONOLOGY

1930   Maria Irene Fornes born on May 14 in Havana, Cuba

1945   Emigrates to New York City (naturalized, 1951)

1954   Studies painting with Hans Hofmann in New York and Provincetown; moves to Paris; returns to New York in 1957 and works as a textile designer

1961   Writes *La Viuda* (*The Widow*) (produced for radio in 1978 by the University of Mexico)

1963   *There! You Died* (later entitled *Tango Palace*) produced by The Actor's Workshop (San Francisco)

Joins Playwriting Unit of the Actors Studio (New York)

1964   *Tango Palace* produced by the Actors Studio

1965   *The Successful Life of 3* (music by Al Carmines) produced by Firehouse Theater (Minnesota) and The Open Theater (New York)

Promenade (music by Al Carmines) produced by the Judson Poets Theatre

Obie award for playwriting (*Promenade* and *The Successful Life of 3*)

1966   *The Office* produced on Broadway (closed in previews)

1967   *A Vietnamese Wedding* produced for Angry Arts Week at Washington Square Methodist Church (New York)

The Annunciation (adapted from Rilke and the Gospels of John and Luke) produced by the Judson Poets Theatre

The Successful Life of 3 revived by the Judson Poets Theatre

1968   *Dr. Kheal* produced by the Village Gate (New York), New Dramatists (New York) and the Judson Poets Theatre

The Red Burning Light produced by The Open Theater in Zurich, Milan, and Copenhagen (produced by La MaMa [New York] in 1969)

Molly's Dream (music by Cosmos Savage) produced by New Dramatists (produced by New York Theatre Strategy in 1973)

1969   *Promenade* revived at Promenade Theater (New York)

1972   Cofounded New York Theatre Strategy

The Curse of the Langston House produced by Cincinnati Playhouse in the Park

1974   *Aurora* (music by John FitzGibbon) produced by New York Theatre Strategy

1975   *Cap-a-Pie* (music by Jose Raul Bernardo) produced by INTAR (New York)

What of the Night?; Charlie was retitled *Nadine*) produced by Milwaukee Repertory Theater (produced by Trinity Repertory Theater [Providence, R.I.], 1990)

1990   Directs *Going to New England* by Ana Maria Simo at INTAR

Directs *Shadow of a Man* by Cherrie Moraga at Eureka Theater/Brava (San Francisco)

1992   *Oscar and Bertha* produced by the Magic Theatre (San Francisco)

La Plaza Chica (Fornes's Spanish version of *Abingdon Square*) produced by San Diego Repertory Theatre

1993   *Enter THE NIGHT* produced by New City Theater (Seattle)

1994   Directs *It Is, It Is Not* by Manuel Pereiras Garcia at Theater for the New City

1995   Directs *Any Place But Here* by Caridad Svich at INTAR

1996   A revised, one-set version of *Fefu and Her Friends* directed by Fornes at Muhlenberg College (Allentown, Pa.)

1997   *Terra Incognita* (music by Roberto Sierra) produced by INTAR

Springtime produced by The Other Theater at Theater for the New City

Balseros (music by Robert Ashley) produced by Florida Grand Opera (Miami)

1998   *The Summer in Gossensass* produced by the Women's Project and Productions at the Judith Anderson Theater (New York)

1999   A season-long retrospective of Fornes's work produced by the Signature Theatre Company (New York)

NOTES

MARC ROBINSON, INTRODUCTION

1. Elinor Fuchs, "*Fefu and Her Friends*: The View from the Stone" (in this volume); Paul Berman, "The Conduct of Life," *The Nation*, April 6, 1985; Erika Munk, "Let Us Now Praise Famous Women" (in this volume); Allen Frame, "Maria Irene Fornes" (interview; see excerpts in this volume). Scott Cummings and Bonnie Marranca, in their essays published here, discuss the use of the frame in Fornes scenography; Marranca briefly describes how "the stage privileges the portrait [and] the still life of the tableau."

2. Norman Bryson, *Looking at the Overlooked: Four Essays on Still Life Painting* (Cambridge, Mass.: Harvard University Press, 1990), 64–65. My own discussion of still-life painting is indebted to this excellent study.

3. Maria Irene Fornes, *Abingdon Square, American Theatre* 4, no. 11 (1988): 5 (separately numbered insert).

4. Maria Irene Fornes, *Promenade*, in *Promenade and Other Plays* (New York: PAJ Publications, 1987), 18.

5. James Schuyler, "February," in *Selected Poems* (New York: Farrar Straus Giroux, 1988), 6–7.

6. Maria Irene Fornes, *Oscar and Bertha*, in *Best of the West*, ed. Murray Mednick, Bill Raden, and Cheryl Slean (Los Angeles: Padua Hills, 1991), 70.

7. Gertrude Stein, *Listen to Me*, in *Last Operas and Plays* (Baltimore: Johns Hopkins University Press, 1995), 414.

8. Gertrude Stein, "Portraits and Repetition," in *Lectures in America* (Boston: Beacon, 1985), 183.

9. Maria Irene Fornes, *Springtime, Antaeus*, no. 66 (Spring 1991): 88.

10. Maria Irene Fornes, *A Visit*. Unpublished manuscript, 1981, 6a.

11. Ibid., 13.

12. *Abingdon Square*, 4.

13. Author's conversation with Fornes, February 4, 1998.

ROSS WETZSTEON, IRENE FORNES

1. *The Anatomy of Inspiration* was never completed. (*Ed.*)

W. B. WORTHEN, *STILL PLAYING GAMES*

1. Maria Irene Fornes, *A Vietnamese Wedding*, in *Promenade and Other Plays* (New York: Winter House, 1971), 8.

2. Fornes describes *The Successful Life of 3* as arising from her association with the Actors Studio: "The first play that I wrote that was influenced by my understanding of Method was *The Successful Life of 3*. What one character says to another comes completely out of his own impulse and so does the other character's reply. The other character's reply never comes from some sort of premeditation on my part or even the part of the character. The characters have no mind. They are simply doing what Strasberg always called 'moment to moment.'" Insofar as Fornes applies acting exercises to the techniques of dramatic characterization, she seems accurately to have evaluated her relationship to Strasberg: "I was very impressed with Strasberg's work as an actor's technician or a director's technician but I would completely ignore anything he would say about aesthetics" (Scott Cummings, "Seeing with Clarity: The Visions of Maria Irene Fornes, *Theater* 17, no. 1 [1985]: 52).

3. See Clive Barnes, Review of *Promenade*, by Maria Irene Fornes, *New York Times*, June 5, 1969, 56; Stephen Holden (Review of *Promenade*, by Maria Irene Fornes, *New York Times*, October 25, 1983, C3) compares the play to Bernstein's *Candide*, Beckett, and Carroll; and Daphne Kraft (Review of *Promenade*, by Maria Irene Fornes, *Newark Evening News*, June 5, 1969, 74) describes the play as a hybrid of "Marc Blitzstein's 'The Cradle Will Rock' and Leonard Bernstein's 'Candide.'"

4. See Patrice Pavis, "On Brecht's Notion of *Gestus*," in *Languages of the Stage: Essays in the Semiology of Theatre* (New York: PAJ Publications, 1982), 44.

5. Maria Irene Fornes, "I Write These Messages That Come," *The Drama Review* 21, no. 4 (1977): 27.

6. See C. W. E. Bigsby, "The Language of Crisis in British Theatre: The Drama of Cultural Pathology," in *Contemporary English Drama*, ed. C. W. E. Bigsby (New York: Holmes & Meier, 1981), 23, and Terry Eagleton's suggestive account of the relation between text and production in *Criticism and Ideology* (London: Verso, 1978), 64–68.

7. On "identification" and ideology, see Kenneth Burke, *A Rhetoric of Motives* (Berkeley: University of California Press, 1969), 88 and *passim*.

8. Göran Therborn, *The Ideology of Power and the Power of Ideology* (London: NLB, 1980), 77–78.

9. Louis Althusser, "Ideology and Ideological State Apparatuses," in *Lenin and Philosophy and Other Essays*, trans. Ben Brewster (London: NLB, 1971), 153.

10. Cummings, "Seeing with Clarity," 52.

11. Ibid., 51.

12. *Tango Palace*, in *Promenade and Other Plays* (New York: Winter House, 1971), 131. All subsequent references will appear parenthetically in the text.

13. Martin Washburn (Review of *Tango Palace*, by Maria Irene Fornes, *The Village Voice*, January 25, 1973) suggests not only that Fornes has "absorbed the continental traditions" but that "Isidore may actually represent the toils of continental literature which the playwright wants to escape."

14. Bonnie Marranca, "The Real Life of Maria Irene Fornes," in *Theatrewritings* (New York: PAJ Publications, 1984), 70.

15. Ross Wetzsteon, "Irene Fornes: The Elements of Style," *The Village Voice*, April 29, 1986, 43.

16. It should be noted that some scenes have no taped opening, some have a tape recording of the opening lines only in Hungarian, and some scenes proceed throughout in this manner: English tape, Hungarian tape, actor's delivery.

17. *The Danube*, in *Plays* (New York: PAJ Publications, 1986), 44. All subsequent references will appear parenthetically in the text.

18. Teresa de Lauretis, *Alice Doesn't: Feminism, Semiotics, Cinema* (Bloomington: Indiana University Press, 1984), 14.

19. As, for instance, when a waiter delivers a sudden, trancelike tirade: "We are dark. Americans are bright. — You crave mobility. The car. You move from city to city so as not to grow stale. You don't stay too long in a place. . . . Our grace is weighty. Not yours. You worship the long leg and loose hip joint. How else to jump in and out of cars" (52).

20. Frank Rich, Review of *The Danube*, by Maria Irene Fornes, *New York Times*, March 13, 1984, C13.

21. *The Conduct of Life*, in *Plays* (New York: PAJ Publications, 1986), 68. All subsequent references will appear parenthetically in the text.

22. *Fefu and Her Friends*, in *Wordplays: An Anthology of New American Drama* (New York: PAJ Publications, 1980), 6. All subsequent references will appear parenthetically in the text.

23. The gun business derives from a joke, as Fornes reports in "Notes on *Fefu*" (*SoHo Weekly News*, January 12, 1978, 38): "There are two Mexicans in sombreros sitting at a bullfight and one says to the other, 'Isn't she beautiful, the one in yellow?' and he points to a woman on the other side of the arena crowded with people. The other one says, 'Which one?' and the first takes his gun and shoots her and says, 'The one that falls.' In the first draft of the play Fefu explains that she started playing this game with her husband as a joke. But in rewriting the play I took out this explanation." It's notable that the gun business dates from Fornes's original work on the play in 1964, as she suggests in "Interview," *Performing Arts Journal* 2, no. 3 (1978): 106.

24. Although he seems to have disliked leaving his seat, Walter Kerr offers a description of the procedure of the play: See his Review of *Fefu and Her Friends*, by Maria Irene Fornes, *New York Times*, January 22, 1978, D3. Kerr's painful recollections of his displacement are recalled several months later, in "New Plays Bring

Back Old Songs," *New York Times*, June 13, 1978, C1, C4. See also Pat Lamb, Review of *Fefu and Her Friends*, by Maria Irene Fornes, *Chelsea Clinton News*, January 19, 1978 ("at stake here is the quality of experience, of life itself"); and the unsigned review of *Fefu and Her Friends* in the *The Village Voice*, May 23, 1977 ("this enclosed repetitiveness sums up entire trapped lifetimes").

25. In Alan Ayckbourn's trilogy (*The Norman Conquests* [Garden City, N.Y.: Doubleday, 1975]) the same romantic comedy is replayed three times. In *Table Manners* the audience witnesses a series of misadventures transpiring over a country-house weekend and hears about a variety of offstage events; in *Living Together* these offstage events and others are dramatized while we hear about (and recall) the now-offstage events of the first play; in *Round and Round the Garden* the material from the first two plays is now offstage, and we witness a third series of scenes.

26. Fornes, *Fefu and Her Friends*, 13.

27. Fornes, "Interview," 110.

28. Stanley Kauffmann's reading of the play's filmic texture is at once shrewd and, in this sense, misapplied: "I doubt very much that Fornes thought of this four-part walk-around as a gimmick. Probably it signified for her an explanation of simultaneity (since all four scenes are done simultaneously four times for the four groups), a union of play and audience through kinetics, some adoption by the theater of cinematic flexibility and montage. But since the small content in these scenes would in no way be damaged by traditional serial construction, since this insistence on reminding us that people actually have related/unrelated conversations simultaneously in different rooms of the same house is banal, we are left with the *feeling* of gimmick" (Review of *Fefu and Her Friends*, by Maria Irene Fornes, *The New Republic*, February 28, 1978, 38).

29. As Richard Eder remarked of the bedroom scene, "Julia is lying in bed, and we sit around her. Our presence, like that of the onlookers in Rembrandt's 'Anatomy Lesson,' magnifies the horror of what is going on" (Review of *Fefu and Her Friends*, by Maria Irene Fornes, *The Village Voice*, May 23, 1977, 80). See also Michael Feingold, Review of *Fefu and Her Friends*, by Maria Irene Fornes, *The Village Voice*, January 23, 1978, 75.

30. Fornes, "Interview," 106.

31. For this phrase I am indebted to my colleague Joan Lidoff.

32. Patrocinio P. Schweickart, "Reading Ourselves: Towards a Feminist Theory of Reading," in *Gender and Reading*, ed. Elizabeth A. Flynn and Patrocinio P. Schweickart (Baltimore: Johns Hopkins University Press, 1986), 54–55.

33. Ibid., 55.

34. David Bleich, "Gender Interests in Reading and Language," in *Gender and Reading*, ed. Elizabeth A. Flynn and Patrocinio P. Schweickart (Baltimore: Johns Hopkins University Press, 1986), 239. In terms of the theatrical structure of *Fefu*

and Her Friends, it is also notable that Bleich's male students not only tended to "see" the novel from "outside" its matrix of relationships but tended to privilege the "plot" in their retellings: "The men retold the story as if the purpose was to deliver a clear, simple structure or chain of information: these are the main characters; this is the main action; this is how it turned out. . . . The women presented the narrative as if it were an atmosphere or experience. They generally felt freer to reflect on the story material with adjectival judgments, and even larger sorts of judgments, and they were more ready to draw inferences without strict regard for the literal warrant of the text, but with more regard for the affective sense of human relationships in the story" (256).

35. Cummings, "Seeing with Clarity," 53.

36. Emma's speech on acting is taken from the prologue to Emma Sheridan Fry, *Educational Dramatics* (New York: Lloyd Adams Noble, 1917). Elsewhere in the book Fry defines the "dramatic instinct" as the process that relates the subject to its environment: "It rouses us to a recognition of the Outside. It provokes those processes whereby we respond to the attack of the Outside upon us" (6).

37. As Jane Gallop describes it, "Nothing to see becomes nothing of worth. The metaphysical privileging of sight over other senses, oculocentrism, supports and unifies phallocentric sexual theory (theory—from the Greek *theoria*, from *theoros*, 'spectator,' from *thea*, 'a viewing'). *Speculum* (from *specere*, 'to look at') makes repeated reference to the oculocentrism of theory, of philosophy" ("The Father's Seduction," in *The (M)other Tongue: Essays in Feminist Psychoanalytic Interpretation*, ed. Shirley Nelson Garner, Claire Kahane, and Madelon Sprengnether [Ithaca, N.Y.: Cornell University Press, 1985], 36–37).

38. Cummings, "Seeing with Clarity," 55.

39. Bertolt Brecht, *Brecht on Theatre*, ed. and trans. John Willett (New York: Hill and Wang, 1964), 283.

HERBERT BLAU, WATER UNDER THE BRIDGE

1. Maria Irene Fornes, *Tango Palace*, in *Promenade and Other Plays* (New York: Winter House, 1971), 139.

2. Roland Barthes, *The Pleasure of the Text*, trans. Richard Miller (New York: Hill and Wang, 1975), 17.

3. Garry Kasparov, "IBM Owes Mankind a Rematch," *Time*, May 26, 1997, 66.

4. "Throwing shade" is a phrase used to describe the competitive rituals of drag-ball culture, though vogueing itself is virtually synonymous with throwing shade on the dance floor. The competitive spirit flourishes through the ability to read and expose, through personal insult, a rival's weaknesses or vulnerabilities.

5. Samuel Beckett, *Waiting for Godot* (New York: Grove, 1954), 7.

6. See Eve Kosofsky Sedgwick, *Epistemology of the Closet* (Berkeley: University of California Press, 1990).

7. Maria Irene Fornes, *Mud,* in *Plays* (New York: PAJ Publications, 1986), 19.

ELINOR FUCHS, *FEFU AND HER FRIENDS*

1. Maria Irene Fornes, *Fefu and Her Friends,* in *Wordplays* (New York: PAJ Publications, 1980), 13. All subsequent page references will appear parenthetically in the text.

2. In dictionaries of symbolism and iconography, the house is frequently associated with the body, and especially the female body. See Philip Thompson and Peter Davenport, eds., *The Dictionary of Graphic Images* (New York: St. Martin's, 1980).

3. In *Fornes: Theater in the Present Tense* (Ann Arbor: University of Michigan Press, 1996), Diane Lynn Moroff also notes a discrepancy of tones in the house, locating its source in the difference between what we hear and what we see: We may hear about suffering, but we see a network of supportive relationships.

4. Julia Kristeva, *Powers of Horror: An Essay on Abjection,* trans. Leon S. Roudiez (New York: Columbia University Press, 1982), 3–4.

5. Writing in the *SoHo Weekly News* of January 12, 1978, Fornes states her "affection . . . for a kind of world which I feel is closer to the 1930s than any other period . . . because it is pre-Freud. . . . Today there is an automatic disbelieving of everything that is said. . . . It's implied that there's always some kind of self-deception about an emotion" (38).

6. Octavio Paz, *Labyrinth of Solitude,* trans. Lysander Kemp, Yara Milos, and Rachel Phillips Belash (New York: Grove, 1985), 30. For the purposes of reading Fornes, this passage is interestingly quoted in Liza Bakewell, "Frida Kahlo: A Contemporary Feminist Reading," *Frontiers* 13, no. 3 (1993): 165–89.

7. "Voltairine de Cleyre," *American Women Writers: A Critical Reference Guide from Colonial Times to the Present,* vol. 1, ed. Lina Mainiero (New York: Frederick Ungar, 1979), 482–83.

8. Hans Biedermann, *Dictionary of Symbolism,* trans. James Hulbert (New York: Facts on File, 1992), 92–93.

9. This seemingly essential structure is abandoned in an alternate version Fornes has recently written to be performed by large theaters in which the breakup of the audience into small groups is impracticable.

10. Stacy Wolf, "Re/Presenting Gender, Re/Presenting Violence: Feminism, Form and the Plays of Maria Irene Fornes," *Theatre Studies* 37 (1992): 17–31.

11. Maria Irene Fornes, "I Write These Messages That Come," *The Drama Review* 21, no. 4 (1977): 26–40, 32–35.

12. W. B. Worthen calls this scene the "shaping vision" of the play. He sees the

spectator as standing in for the coercive male "guardians" whose gaze "constructs, enables, and thwarts the women of the stage." "*Still Playing Games:* Ideology and Performance in the Theater of Maria Irene Fornes," in *Feminine Focus: The New Women Playwrights,* ed. Enoch Brater (New York, Oxford University Press, 1989), 167–85, 177.

13. Telephone interview with the author, August 1997.

14. Fornes is not alone among contemporary women playwrights in creating a composite image of the social-cum-bodily shattering of women. The method appears in Joan Schenkar's *Signs of Life,* in Adrienne Kennedy's *Funnyhouse of a Negro,* and in Rachel Rosenthal's *Pangaean Dreams.* In the latter, Rosenthal appears in a wheelchair, crippled. The action of the piece, an archeological dig to reassemble her own shattered form, was a metaphor for the restoration of the shattered environment, the body of the earth. Barbara Ehrenreich has echoed this entanglement of personal and political, sexual and social, in her introduction to Klaus Theweleit's *Male Fantasies,* in which she writes that male power is predicated on the derogation and suppression not only of the female body but of a wide range of categories men gender "feminine."

15. Fornes, *SoHo Weekly News.*

16. Elaine Scarry, *The Body in Pain: The Making and Unmaking of the World* (New York: Oxford University Press, 1985), 38–39.

17. Kristeva herself notes a connection between apocalyptic literature and a "horror for the feminine." Kristeva, *Powers of Horror,* 205.

18. Ibid., 4, 53.

19. Fredrika Blair, *Isadora: Portrait of the Artist as a Woman* (New York: McGraw-Hill, 1986), 401–2.

20. I am indebted to Katherine Profeta, a student at the Yale School of Drama, for pointing out the similarities between the views of Julia's judges and those of the notorious Weininger, whose 1903 *Geschlecht und Charakter* (*Sex and Character,* 1906) attributed positive energy and morality to the male, and negativity and amorality to the female.

21. For a brief outline of Fry's career, see Beatrice L. Tukesbury, "Emma Sheridan Fry and Educational Dramatics," *Educational Theatre Journal* 16, no. 4 (1964); 341–48.

22. Emma Sheridan Fry, *Educational Dramatics* (New York: Moffat, Yard, 1913).

23. Ann Daly, *Done Into Dance: Isadora Duncan in America* (Bloomington: Indiana University Press, 1995), 136–37.

24. Stacy Wolf, Gayle Austin, and Assunta Kent have variously summarized the range of responses to this ending. See Wolf, "Re/Presenting Gender," 27–28. In "The Madwoman in the Spotlight: Plays of Maria Irene Fornes," in *Making a Spectacle: Feminist Essays on Contemporary Women's Theatre,* ed. Lynda Hart (Ann Arbor: Uni-

versity of Michigan Press, 1989), 76–85, Gayle Austin sees Fefu as Julia's "double," who fights, even shoots, rather than give in to "women's predicament" (80). In *Maria Irene Fornes and Her Critics* (Westport, Conn.: Greenwood, 1996), Assunta Bartolomucci Kent critiques the too easy affirmations of Fefu's rash shooting as a "necessary sacrifice" of the "woman-as-victim" (138–40).

25. Kristeva, *Powers of Horror*, 4.

26. These two quasi-formalist readings stand somewhat outside the feminist discussions of the ending. Toby Silverman Zinman claims that Fornes's concluding move is a piece of absurdist theater speaking in "the powerful shorthand of concrete images" and not subject to realist interpretation ("Hen in a Foxhouse: The Absurdist Plays of Maria Irene Fornes," in *Around the Absurd: Essays on Modern and Postmodern Drama*, ed. Enoch Brater and Ruby Cohn [Ann Arbor: University of Michigan Press, 1990], 203–20, 209). Diane Lynn Moroff (*Fornes*) sees the ending, and much of the play, as metatheatrical, in keeping with the play's "deliberate theatricalization of character" (36).

27. Fornes tells the story of the audience's response to the rabbit in the discussion sessions that took place at the American Place Theatre. At each of these, someone would always mention that Fefu made her final entrance holding the black cat in her arms. To counter the creation of this false symbol, Fornes says, she stayed up all one night sewing a new, all-white, rabbit. But at the next audience discussion, a man raised his hand and asked, "Why was the black cat white?" (Author's interview, August 1997). This persistent audience confusion may account for the changed stage direction in the single-edition version of the play (New York: PAJ Publications, 1990). Here Fefu drops the rabbit before taking up her position behind the wheelchair. The result is a somewhat less mysterious and supernatural ending.

28. In her account of Fornes's staging of *Uncle Vanya* in *Directors in Rehearsal* (New York: Routledge, 1992), Susan Letzler Cole quotes Fornes as directing the actor playing Vanya to perform a scene as if he were a "penitent rising from the flames below" (48). When questioned by Cole about this "painterly" staging, Fornes "clarifies that she does not have a particular work of art in mind but that her stage image of the penitent has some resemblance to certain Mexican paintings" (239n. 34).

MARC ROBINSON, *THE SUMMER IN GOSSENSASS*

1. Assunta Bartolomucci Kent, *Maria Irene Fornes and Her Critics* (Westport, Conn.: Greenwood, 1996), 156.

2. Several critics have discussed images of reading in Fornes: Una Chaudhuri, "Maria Irene Fornes," in *Speaking on Stage: Interviews with Contemporary American Playwrights*, ed. Philip C. Kolin and Colby H. Kullman (Tuscaloosa: University of

Alabama Press, 1996); Bonnie Marranca, "The State of Grace: Maria Irene Fornes at Sixty-Two," *Performing Arts Journal* 14, no. 2 (1992); Lurana Donnels O'Malley, "Pressing Clothes / Snapping Beans / Reading Books: Maria Irene Fornés's Women's Work," in *Studies in American Drama, 1945–Present,* vol. 4 (1989).

3. Fornes's interpretation of *Hedda Gabler* is discussed in Janice Paran, "Redressing Ibsen," *American Theatre* 4, no. 8 (1987); James Fisher, "Plays in Performance: *Hedda Gabler," Journal of Dramatic Theory and Criticism* 2, no. 1 (1987); and in an interview with Fornes published in the Milwaukee Repertory Theater program for *Hedda Gabler.* Fornes's skeptical view of Hedda's pregnancy has at least one precedent: In her Preface to her translation of *Hedda Gabler* (London: Faber and Faber, 1953), Eva Le Gallienne writes, "Some actresses, among them Mary Shaw I believe, felt that Hedda only pretended pregnancy when she mentioned it to Tesman in the last act, using it as an excuse for burning the manuscript" (13).

4. Letter to Moritz Prozor, December 4, 1890, quoted in *Henrik Ibsen: A Critical Anthology,* ed. James McFarlane (Harmondsworth, U.K.: Penguin, 1970), 127.

5. These and other details about Robins's production are from Michael Meyer, *Ibsen: A Biography* (Garden City, N.Y.: Doubleday, 1971), 664–67; and Angela V. John, *Elizabeth Robins: Staging a Life, 1862–1952* (London: Routledge, 1995), 55–63.

6. Mrs. Patrick Campbell, *My Life and Some Letters* (1922), quoted in *Elizabeth Robins,* 59. Eva Le Gallienne echoes this idea in her Preface to her translation of *Hedda Gabler:* "In order to achieve a successful performance of an Ibsen play, it is necessary that the actor be capable of such concentrated thinking, that his thoughts actually take shape; the audience must see the thought, must be made a part of it" (19). Such conditions could easily apply to a number of Fornes's own plays.

7. Maria Irene Fornes, *Fefu and Her Friends* (New York: PAJ Publications, 1992), 43.

8. Maria Irene Fornes, *The Summer in Gossensass,* unpublished script of Women's Project production, April 1998, sc. 1, p. 5, and sc. 4, p. 21. All subsequent references will appear parenthetically in the text.

9. Virginia Woolf, "How Should One Read a Book?" in *Collected Essays,* vol. 2 (New York: Harcourt, Brace and World, 1967), 8.

10. Susan Letzler Cole, *Directors in Rehearsal: A Hidden World* (New York: Routledge, 1992), 40.

11. Randall Jarrell, "The Age of Criticism," in *Poetry and the Age* (New York: Vintage, 1959), 79.

12. Wallace Stevens, "Materia Poetica," reprinted in *View: Parade of the Avant-Garde 1940–1947,* ed. Charles Henri Ford (New York: Thunder's Mouth, 1991), 7–8.

13. Elizabeth Robins, *Ibsen and the Actress* (London: Hogarth, 1928), 20–21, 27.

SUSAN LETZLER COLE, "TO BE QUIET ON THE STAGE"

1. Unless otherwise noted, all citations to *Uncle Vanya* are taken from *Plays* by Anton Tchekoff, trans. Marian Fell (New York: Charles Scribner's, 1916).

2. Charles Marowitz argues that "the act of interpretation is every bit as creative as authorship." Directors may "rejig . . . restructure . . . , and occasionally complement . . . the original play with new material." Fornes's astonishing achievement is to give a sense of newness without violating what Marowitz calls "the formal limits of the work as originally written." *Prospero's Staff* (Bloomington: Indiana University Press, 1986), 33, 36, 37.

3. Gordon Rogoff describes her production of *Uncle Vanya* as "languorous" and refers to "Fornes' infatuation with drift and pause" (*The Village Voice*, December 22, 1987, 132, 133). Mel Gussow also accuses Fornes of having "made the play languorous" and counsels her to "speed . . . up the tempo" in "a production that mistakenly communicates boredom by being boring" (*New York Times*, December 15, 1987, C21). Mimi Kramer, however, admires "the gentle, becalmed pacing. . . . What makes most productions of 'Uncle Vanya' so boring is the murky miasma of actors' personalities that you have to grope through in order to get to the play. The acting in the C.S.C. 'Vanya' is not trying to . . . impress us with how realistic it is" (*New Yorker*, January 4, 1988, 59). (Mimi Kramer is one of the rare critics to note in the course of her review significant differences between two performances of the production she is discussing: in this case, one before and the other after the appearance of a negative review in the *New York Times*.)

4. Cf. director Charles Marowitz, "Is it not possible to use theatre to reflect states of mind more accurately?" (137).

5. Chekhov's characters' names are spelled in the program as rendered by Marian Fell in her translation of the play. Thus, Vanya appears as Voitski.

6. Fell, *Plays*, 45.

7. With her characteristic scrupulousness about language, Fornes adds: I said, 'taking away' . . . [to the actress] but I meant 'taking over.'" I think, however, that she meant both taking away and taking over.

8. Cf. Stanislavski on the difficulty of sitting onstage in *An Actor Prepares*, trans. Elizabeth Reynolds Hapgood (New York: Routledge/Theatre Arts Books, 1989), 33–37. The actor Kostya describes the attempt to sit quietly on the stage: "My legs, arms, head, and torso, although they did what I directed, added something superfluous of their own. You move your arm or leg quite simply, and suddenly you are all twisted, and you look as though you were posing for a picture. Strange! . . . It was infinitely easier for me to sit affectedly than simply. I could not think what I ought to do." The director comments later: "the external immobility of a person sitting on the stage does not imply passiveness. You may sit without a motion and at the same

time be in full action. Nor is that all. Frequently physical immobility is the direct result of inner intensity, and it is these inner activities that are far more important artistically. The essence of art is not in its external forms but in its spiritual content" (34, 37).

9. Fell, *Plays*, 23.

10. All references to *Abingdon Square* are to the version published in *American Theatre* 4, no. 11 (1988): 1–10 (separately numbered insert). An earlier rehearsal version of the scripted stage direction read: "as if in a deep emotional trance."

11. The next day, rehearsing another two-person scene with different actors, Fornes characterizes Marion's cousin, Mary, whose role it is to remain silent in a scene composed entirely of Juster's long monologue, as "a generous ear." This kind of comment mediates between literary analysis of her play text and directorial suggestion to the actress.

12. What Juster reads is a description of the fertilization of flowers in language that is at once highly technical and erotic. The excerpt was originally much longer, but when the speech needed to be shortened Fornes ended up excising what had originally drawn her to the passage, a description of someone walking in a garden saying farewell to the plants.

13. The characteristic Chekhovian extended family with its retainers seems to find a representation in the company assembled for rehearsal. In the *Vanya* rehearsals, there are particular echoes: An actor whose stories seem to go nowhere plays a long-winded character; two gossipy actors play gossipy characters; the actor playing the most repressive character in the play requires that I leave the rehearsal whenever he is there. More generally, however, people who don't necessarily know, understand, or even like each other, who criticize each other's actions implicitly or explicitly with sudden intensity or sly humor, who may never really enter into each other's lives, come together in a space where whatever is going to go on between and among them is going to go on.

14. *The Collected Poems of Wallace Stevens* (New York: Alfred A. Knopf, 1969), 524.

15. In rehearsal of the scene in Act 3 in which Astroff embraces and kisses Yelena just as Vanya enters the room with a bouquet of roses, Yelena pulls away from the doctor and delivers the line, "This is awful!" (rehearsal version; also Ann Dunnigan's translation, *Chekhov: The Major Plays* [New York: New American Library, 1964], 211) to Astroff and herself, without appearing to notice Vanya. In the performance I attended on December 19, 1987, Yelena sees Vanya watching, as she seems to be about to kiss Astroff for the second time, and says, "This is awful!" (The stage directions in the text indicate that Yelena sees Vanya, leaves Astroff's embrace, goes to the window, and then says, "This is awful!").

16. Fell, *Plays*, 45.

17. Ibid., 17.

18. Interestingly, shortly after this, the actor offers his own version of this precept in what I call a "private moment" in rehearsal. He begins to discuss what he has worked out in understanding Astroff's seeming betrayal of Vanya, then stops himself: "Better to keep that a secret."

19. Fell, *Plays*, 34.

20. Ibid., 35–36.

21. *Abingdon Square*, 8.

22. In the performance of *Abingdon Square* that I saw on November 18, 1987, the rigidity Fornes had encouraged was somewhat modified but still present.

23. Quoted by Robert Benedetti, *The Director at Work* (Englewood Cliffs, N.J.: Prentice-Hall, 1985), 165.

24. The script of *Abingdon Square* is not only in revision but without a final version of the last scene during the rehearsals I watch. The actors' reactions to this vary, but nervousness prevails. On the eighth day of rehearsal I overhear an actress ask, "Irene, when will we have [copies of the final revisions of] the last scenes?" The following day one actor says, "I'm having trouble not knowing the end of the play," and a second actor responds, "That makes us like the characters." It is Fornes's usual practice to begin rehearsals of her own plays with an incomplete or unfinished script. She tells me, "There are things that only happen in rehearsal and could not happen if the script were complete. *But* there are things that don't happen because you don't have time to sit down quietly and write. You have to make quick decisions in rehearsal. But it's *exciting* to work in this way. (Private communication, December 7, 1985.)

25. Some of these in-rehearsal revisions may seem minute but all are treated with equal importance by the playwright. Revisions that are made during my observation of rehearsal include occasional addition of a few lines, frequent elimination of words, and changing some contractions to their full grammatical form. A few examples follow: Fornes changes Michael's line in the scene in which he is playing chess with his father from "No, I'm not good enough to win" to "No." In rehearsal of Scene 25, Fornes dictates a line she is adding to Juster's long monologue: "Then she said, 'This is a love letter.'" The actors and the stage manager write down the new line. In consultation with the actor playing Juster, she changes the word "uniform" to "clothes" in his long monologue in Scene 20 to avoid the unwanted implications of a *military* uniform. (All these revisions appear in the text of *Abingdon Square* published in *American Theatre*.) Finally, after listening to actor John David Cullum reading aloud Michael's line, "I'm going to school outside of the city," Fornes stops him, saying "That line doesn't sound right." When the actor responds, "I'm just fooling around," Fornes clarifies, "No, I mean the line itself doesn't sound right." In consultation with the actor, Fornes tentatively changes the line so that it reads, "I'm going to *a* school outside of the city." This line does not appear, in either version, in the text published in *American Theatre*.)

26. Fell, *Plays*, 27.

27. The visual composition of scenes in the rehearsals of *Uncle Vanya* is made particularly difficult by the fact that the performance stage is a foot wider than the rehearsal studio. Fornes is never literally able to see scenes in rehearsal from the vantage point of the audience at the Classic Stage Company theater: "I try in some way to project my eye from the side." At times during rehearsal Fornes will sit far downstage in the playing area itself in an attempt to ascertain whether an actor will in fact be visible to the audience in the theater. The *Vanya* rehearsal is an exacerbated version of the situation of every director who must rehearse somewhere other than in the performance space itself.

28. When I first ask if the scene as she directs it is like a painting in her own mind, Fornes answers affirmatively. She later clarifies that she does not literally have a particular work of art in mind but that her stage image of the penitent has some resemblance to certain Mexican paintings.

29. Fornes's rehearsal script version. Fell's translation is: "This is agony!" (I, p. 27). Fornes considers Vanya to be the penitent in this scene. As my description suggests, in rehearsal I see two penitents trying to rise "from the flames below."

30. Chekhov has not specifically indicated an exit and reentrance for the purpose of bringing tea to the professor, although it is theoretically possible for the nurse to leave and return during the tea-drinking scene in Act 1.

31. *Abingdon Square*, 8.

32. Later Fornes adds, "I prefer to tell the actors about my shortcomings and let them try to cover up for . . . [the shortcomings] rather than to try to cover up my shortcomings from the actors." The child does appear in one scene. The stage directions for Scene 19 indicate a prominent position for the objective correlative, if not the child himself: "*Center stage, there is a playpen with a teddy bear sitting in it. Marion enters from left. She carries Thomas, eight months old. She takes the teddy bear*" (*Abingdon Square*, 6). Of this scene, in rehearsal, Fornes says that if Thomas is played by a real child as she would like him to be, the child's presence in Marion's arms will be a tremendously potent image.

33. *Abingdon Square*, 10.

34. Ibid., 2.

35. Ibid., 10.

36. I understand Fornes's silence on the question of where the child is when it is not in the play in the same way that I might imagine Shakespeare's response to the question of where Lady Macbeth's children are.

37. Quoted by Ross Wetzsteon, "Irene Fornes: The Elements of Style," *The Village Voice*, April 29, 1986, 43.

38. Fornes stresses that Juster's offer of money to Marion is not an act of kindness but "more in the nature of a kind of honor, like not fighting an unarmed man."

39. In both *Uncle Vanya* and *Abingdon Square* a young woman marries a much

older man with whom she has no passionate connection. I am struck by these parallels in the two plays that Fornes is rehearsing within a period of approximately three months. (Fornes herself, however, is not.)

SCOTT CUMMINGS, "THE POETRY OF SPACE IN A BOX"

1. Maria Irene Fornes, *Abingdon Square, American Theatre* 4, no. 11 (1988), 2 (separately numbered insert).

2. Ibid., 4.

3. Maria Irene Fornes, *Sarita,* in *Plays* (New York: PAJ Publications, 1986), 108.

4. *Abingdon Square,* 4.

5. Maria Irene Fornes, *Dr. Kheal,* in *Promenade and Other Plays* (New York: Winter House, 1971), 62–63.

SELECTED BIBLIOGRAPHY

Essays, reviews, and interviews published in this anthology do not appear in the bibliography.

WORKS BY MARIA IRENE FORNES

Abingdon Square. American Theatre 4, no. 11 (1987).

Cold Air (translated and adapted from Virgilio Piñera). In *New Plays USA 3*, ed. James Leverett and M. Elizabeth Osborn. New York: Theatre Communications Group, 1986.

La Conducta de la Vida (Fornes's Spanish translation of *The Conduct of Life*). Mexico City: El Milagro, 1994.

Drowning. In *Orchards: Seven Stories by Anton Chekhov and Seven Plays They Have Inspired,* ed. Anne Cattaneo. New York: Alfred A. Knopf, 1986.

Enter THE NIGHT. In *Plays for the End of the Century,* ed. Bonnie Marranca. Baltimore: Johns Hopkins University Press, 1996.

Fefu and Her Friends. New York: PAJ Publications, 1990.

Lovers and Keepers (with Tito Puente and Fernando Rivas). In *Plays in Process* 7, no. 10. New York: Theatre Communications Group, 1987.

Oscar and Bertha. In *Best of the West,* ed. Murray Mednick, Bill Raden, and Cheryl Slean. Los Angeles: Padua Hills, 1991.

Plays (includes *Mud, The Danube, The Conduct of Life, Sarita*). New York: PAJ Publications, 1986.

Promenade and Other Plays (includes *Promenade, The Successful Life of 3, Tango Palace, Molly's Dream, A Vietnamese Wedding, Dr. Kheal*). New York: PAJ Publications, 1987.

Promenade and Other Plays (includes all of the above and *The Red Burning Light Or: Mission XQ3*). New York: Winter House, 1971.

Terra Incognita. Theater 24, no. 2 (1993).

La viuda (The Widow). In *Teatro cubano: Cuatro obras recomendadas en el Il Concurso Literario Hispanoamericano de la Casa de Las Américas.* Havana: Casa de Las Américas, 1961.

What of the Night? In *Women on the Verge: Seven Avant-Garde American Plays,* ed. Rosette C. Lamont. New York: Applause Theatre Books, 1993.

WORKS ABOUT MARIA IRENE FORNES

Books

Austin, Gayle. "The Madwoman in the Spotlight: Plays of Maria Irene Fornes." In *Making a Spectacle: Feminist Essays on Contemporary Women's Theater*, ed. Lynda Hart. Ann Arbor: University of Michigan Press, 1989.

Byers-Pevitts, Beverly. *"Fefu and Her Friends."* In *Women in American Theatre*, ed. Helen Krich Chinoy and Linda Walsh Jenkins. New York: Theatre Communications Group, 1987.

Chaudhuri, Una. "The Language of the Future" (on *The Danube*). In *Staging Place: The Geography of Modern Drama*. Ann Arbor: University of Michigan Press, 1995.

Garner, Stanton B. "(En)gendering Pain: *The Conduct of Life.*" In *Bodied Spaces: Phenomenology and Performance in Contemporary Drama*. Ithaca, N.Y.: Cornell University Press, 1994.

Geis, Deborah R. "Wordscapes of the Body: Performative Language as *Gestus* in Maria Irene Fornes's Plays." In *Postmodern Theatric(k)s: Monologue in Contemporary American Drama*. Ann Arbor: University of Michigan Press, 1993.

Gruber, William E. "The Characters of Maria Irene Fornes: Public and Private Identities." In *Missing Persons: Character and Characterization in Modern Drama*. Athens: University of Georgia Press, 1994.

Kent, Assunta Bartolomucci. *Maria Irene Fornes and Her Critics*. Westport, Conn.: Greenwood, 1996.

Moroff, Diane Lynn. *Fornes: Theater in the Present Tense*. Ann Arbor: University of Michigan Press, 1996.

Robinson, Marc. "Maria Irene Fornes." In *The Other American Drama*. New York: Cambridge University Press, 1994; Baltimore: Johns Hopkins University Press, 1997.

Schuler, Catherine A. "Gender Perspective and Violence in the Plays of Maria Irene Fornes and Sam Shepard." In *Modern American Drama: The Female Canon*, ed. June Schlueter. Rutherford, N.J.: Fairleigh Dickinson University Press, 1990.

Zinman, Toby Silverman. "Hen in a Foxhouse: The Absurdist Plays of Maria Irene Fornes." In *Around the Absurd: Essays on Modern and Postmodern Drama*, ed. Enoch Brater and Ruby Cohn. Ann Arbor: University of Michigan Press, 1990.

Periodicals

Bottoms, Stephen J. "'Language Is the Motor': Maria Irene Fornes's *Promenade* as Text and Performance." *New England Theatre Journal* 8 (1997).

Cummings, Scott. "Notes on Fornes, Fefu and the Play of Thought." *Ideas and Production* 8 (Winter 1988).

———. "Fornes's Odd Couple: *Oscar and Bertha* at the Magic Theatre." *Journal of Dramatic Theory and Criticism* 8, no. 2 (1994).

Farfan, Penny. "Feminism, Metatheatricality and *Mise-en-scène* in Maria Irene For-nes's *Fefu and Her Friends.*" *Modern Drama* 40, no. 4 (1997).

Gargano, Cara. "The Starfish and the Strange Attractor: Myth, Science, and The-atre as Laboratory in Maria Irene Fornes' *Mud.*" *New Theatre Quarterly* 13, no. 51 (1997).

Harrington, Stephanie. "Irene Fornes, Playwright: Alice and the Red Queen." *The Village Voice,* April 22, 1966.

Keyssar, Helene. "Drama and the Dialogic Imagination: *The Heidi Chronicles* and *Fefu and Her Friends.*" *Modern Drama* 34, no. 1 (1991).

Kiebuzinska, Christine. "Traces of Brecht in Maria Irene Fornes' *Mud.*" *The Brecht Yearbook* 18 (1993).

Kintz, Linda. "Permeable Boundaries, Femininity, Fascism, and Violence: Fornes' *The Conduct of Life.*" *Gestos* 6, no. 11 (1991).

Koppen, Randi. "Formalism and the Return to the Body: Stein's and Fornes's Aes-thetic of Significant Form." *New Literary History* 28, no. 4 (1997).

O'Malley, Lurana Donnels. "Pressing Clothes / Snapping Beans / Reading Books: Maria Irene Fornés's Women's Work." *Studies in American Drama, 1945–Present* 4 (1989).

Paran, Janice. "Redressing Ibsen" (Fornes's *Hedda Gabler*). *American Theatre* 4, no. 8 (1987).

Rabillard, Sheila. "Crossing Cultures and Kinds: Maria Irene Fornes and the Per-formance of a Post-Modern Sublime." *Journal of American Drama and Theatre* 9, no. 2 (1997).

Wolf, Stacy. "Re/Presenting Gender, Re/Presenting Violence: Feminism, Form, and the Plays of Maria Irene Fornes." *Theatre Studies* 37 (1992).

Interviews

Austin, Gayle. "Entering a Cold Ocean: The Playwriting Process." *Theatre Times,* March 1984.

Betsko, Kathleen, and Rachel Koening. "Maria Irene Fornes." In *Interviews with Contemporary Women Playwrights.* New York: William Morrow, 1987.

Chaudhuri, Una. "Maria Irene Fornes." In *Speaking on Stage: Interviews with Con-temporary American Playwrights,* ed. Philip C. Kolin and Colby H. Kullman. Tuscaloosa: University of Alabama Press, 1996.

Marranca, Bonnie. "Interview: Maria Irene Fornes." *Performing Arts Journal* 2, no. 3 (1978).

Savran, David. "Maria Irene Fornes." In *In Their Own Words: Contemporary American Playwrights.* New York: Theatre Communications Group, 1988.

Wooden, Rod. "Maria Irene Fornes." In *In Contact with the Gods? Directors Talk Theatre,* ed. Maria M. Delgado and Paul Heritage. Manchester, U.K.: Manchester University Press, 1996.

CONTRIBUTORS

HERBERT BLAU, Distinguished Professor of English and Comparative Literature at the University of Wisconsin–Milwaukee, has also had a long career in the theater, beginning with The Actor's Workshop of San Francisco. He was also co-director of the Repertory Theater of Lincoln Center, and later artistic director of the KRAKEN group. Among his many books are *The Audience, To All Appearances: Ideology and Performance,* and, most recently, *Nothing in Itself: Complexions of Fashion.*

ROBERT COE is an author, journalist, and playwright. His articles have appeared in the *New York Times Magazine, Vanity Fair, Rolling Stone,* and *Esquire,* among other publications. His plays have been produced in theaters around the country.

SUSAN LETZLER COLE, a professor of English and the director of the Drama Concentration at Albertus Magnus College, is the author of *The Absent One: Mourning Ritual, Tragedy, and the Performance of Ambivalence* and *Directors in Rehearsal: A Hidden World.* She is currently completing a new book, *Playwrights in Rehearsal.*

SCOTT CUMMINGS is an assistant professor of dramatic literature and playwriting at Boston College. His essays and reviews have appeared in *American Theatre, Theatre Journal, Modern Drama,* and *Theater,* among other publications.

RICHARD EDER is a book critic for the *New York Times.* He was the chief drama critic for the *New York Times* from 1977 to 1980.

MICHAEL FEINGOLD is a theater critic for *The Village Voice* and a translator of plays by Ibsen, Brecht and Weill, and Ionesco. He is also the editor of *Grove New American Theater,* among other books.

ALLEN FRAME is a photographer living in New York City.

ELINOR FUCHS is a professor (adjunct) of dramaturgy and dramatic criticism at the Yale School of Drama and also teaches at Columbia University's School of the Arts. She is the author of *The Death of Character: Perspectives on Theater after Modernism* and the editor of *Plays of the Holocaust: An International Anthology.* With Joyce Antler, she wrote the documentary play *Year One of the Empire.*

RICHARD GILMAN is the author of *Chekhov's Plays: An Opening into Eternity, The Making of Modern Drama,* and *Decadence,* among other books. He was a professor (adjunct) of dramaturgy and dramatic criticism at the Yale School of Drama until his retirement in 1997.

TONY KUSHNER is the author of *Angels in America: A Gay Fantasia on National Themes, Slavs!, A Dybbuk: Between Two Worlds,* and many other plays.

PHILLIP LOPATE is the author of *Totally, Tenderly, Tragically, Against Joie de Vivre,* and *Portrait of My Body,* among other books, and is the editor of *Writing New York* and *The Art of the Personal Essay.*

BONNIE MARRANCA is the author of *Ecologies of Theater* and *Theatrewritings* and the editor of *The Theatre of Images* and *Plays for the End of the Century,* among other books. With Gautam Dasgupta, she cofounded *Performing Arts Journal/PAJ* Publications and edited *Conversations on Art and Performance, Interculturalism and Performance,* and *Theatre of the Ridiculous.*

ERIKA MUNK is the editor of *Theater* magazine. Her essays and reviews have appeared in *The Village Voice,* the *Nation, TDR,* and other publications. She teaches at the Yale School of Drama.

ROBERT PASOLLI contributed theater criticism to *The Village Voice* and the *Nation* from 1965 to 1970. He is the author of *A Book on the Open Theatre.*

SHEILA RABILLARD is an associate professor of English at the University of Victoria (Canada). Her essays have appeared in *Modern Drama, Theater Journal,* and other publications. She is the editor of *Essays on Caryl Churchill.*

MARC ROBINSON is the author of *The Other American Drama* and editor of *Altogether Elsewhere: Writers on Exile.* He teaches at Yale College (where he is also the director of Theater Studies) and at the Yale School of Drama.

MICHAEL SMITH is the author of *Theatre Trip* and editor of *Eight Plays from Off Off Broadway,* among other books. He was a theater critic for *The Village Voice* from 1957 to 1974.

SUSAN SONTAG is the author of *The Volcano Lover, Alice in Bed,* and *AIDS and Its Metaphors,* among many other books. Her adaptation of Ibsen's *The Lady from the Sea* was directed by Robert Wilson in 1998.

ROSS WETZSTEON (1932–98) was an editor and theater critic at *The Village Voice*. He is the editor of two collections of Obie-winning plays and author of the forthcoming *Republic of Dreams: An Intellectual History of Greenwich Village*.

W. B. WORTHEN is a professor of dramatic art at the University of California–Berkeley. He is the author of *The Idea of the Actor: Drama and the Ethics of Performance, Modern Drama and the Rhetoric of Theater*, and *Shakespeare and the Authority of Performance*. He has edited the collections *Modern Drama: Plays/Criticism/Theory* and the *Harcourt Brace Anthology of Drama*.

INDEX

Credits